I0902344

IMAGES of America

IMPERIAL CALCASIEU

IMAGES
of America

IMPERIAL CALCASIEU

Robert Benoit
Southwest Louisiana Historical Association

in cooperation with

The Archives Department, McNeese State University

ARCADIA
PUBLISHING

ISBN 978-0-7385-0581-7

Published by Arcadia Publishing
Charleston, South Carolina

Printed in the United States of America

Library of Congress Catalog Card Number: 00-104662

For all general information contact Arcadia Publishing at:
Telephone 843-853-2070
Fax 843-853-0044
E-Mail sales@arcadiapublishing.com
For customer service and orders:
Toll-Free 1-888-313-2665

Visit us on the Internet at www.arcadiapublishing.com

In Memory of Early Photographers and Maude Reid

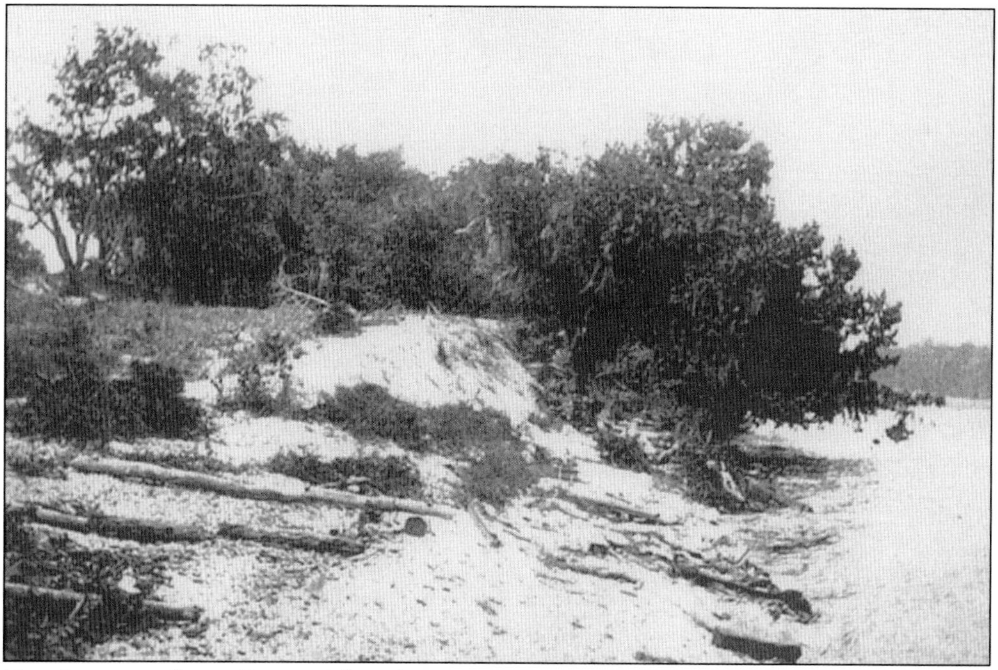

THE ORIGINAL SHELL BEACH. This photograph, taken around 1885, shows the ancient shell mound and beach that the first settlers of Southwest Louisiana found on the south shore of Lake Charles. It is believed to have been created by many generations of Native Americans of the Attakapas tribe as they took clams from the lake. Today all of the shells are gone, but the road beside the site still bears the name Shell Beach Drive.

CONTENTS

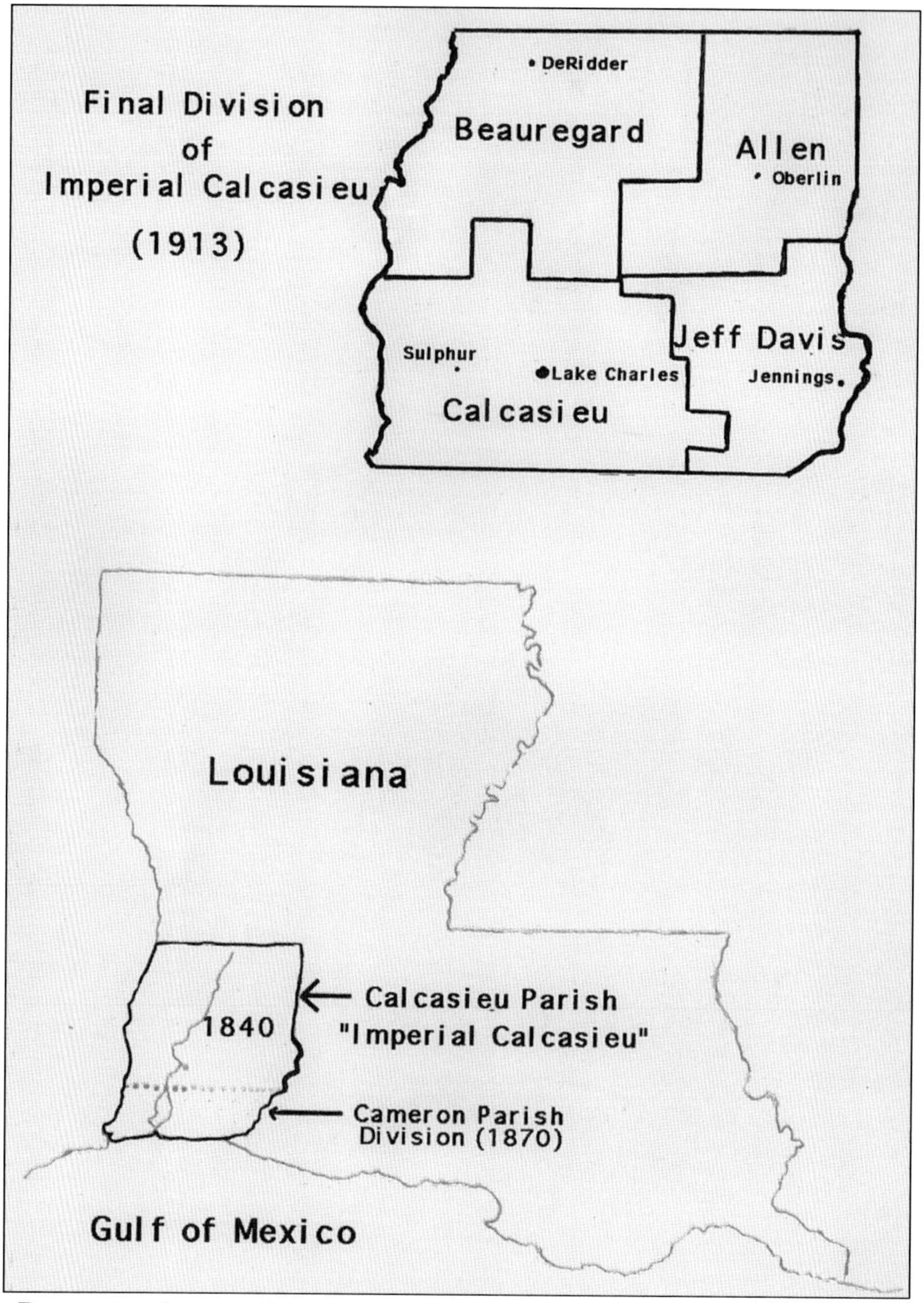

THE DIVISIONS OF IMPERIAL CALCASIEU. In 1840, the Louisiana Legislature created Calcasieu Parish (county) in the southwest corner of Louisiana, as shown in the above map. This historic area is now commonly called "Imperial Calcasieu" because of its tremendous size. In 1870, the Louisiana Legislature reduced "Imperial" Calcasieu Parish by creating Cameron Parish out of the portion bordering the Gulf of Mexico (see inset area). Effective January 1, 1913, the Louisiana Legislature established Beauregard, Allen, and Jefferson Davis Parishes out of the northern and eastern portions of the old Calcasieu, thus reducing Calcasieu Parish to its present size (see map at the top of this page).

INTRODUCTION

In the spring of 2000, *Industry Week Magazine* ranked Calcasieu Parish among the nation's "world-class manufacturing communities" for the fourth year in a row. This may sound to many people like a "modern" achievement, but Calcasieu Parish (here meaning the old, larger parish) was considered to be a world-class industrial area a century ago, when in most other ways it was still a newly conquered frontier. Granted, some things have changed over the past 100 years. Calcasieu's industrial emphasis was once on lumber, sulphur, and rice, instead of today's emphasis on oil refining, petrochemicals, and shipping. Also, Calcasieu's ranking a century ago was achieved, not in a magazine, but in the talk of people throughout the parish and the country, all of whom said "Calcasieu Parish, Louisiana, is *the* place to go if you want to invest money, farm rice, raise livestock, homestead land, or simply get a job."

The word "Calcasieu" as used in the above paragraph and in the title of this book needs a bit of explaining. Calcasieu is the name of both a large Southwest Louisiana river and the parish (county) through which that river flows. The word is believed to have originated with the Attakapas tribe, who inhabited Southwest Louisiana when the first Europeans arrived. According to tradition, Calcasieu in Attakapas meant "crying eagle," which was the name of one of their chiefs. After the early Europeans adopted the Attakapas name for their river, it was eventually given official recognition by the Louisiana Legislature when it created Calcasieu Parish in 1840.

Calcasieu Parish originally took in over 5,000 square miles of land in the southwest corner of Louisiana, stretching northward from the Gulf of Mexico for 75 miles, ending on a line drawn between the Sabine River on the west and the Mermentau River on the east. Thirty years after its creation, old (or "Imperial") Calcasieu Parish was downsized by the creation of Cameron Parish out of its southernmost part. Although reduced by this action to about 3,700 square miles, the parish was still larger than the combined areas of the states of Delaware and Rhode Island. In 1913, Imperial Calcasieu Parish was downsized a final time by the creation of Allen, Beauregard, and Jefferson Davis Parishes. This downsizing ended the period (1840–1913) fondly referred to by local historians as the era of Imperial Calcasieu. Today the phrase "Imperial Calcasieu" is often used in Southwest Louisiana. In the name "Imperial Calcasieu Museum," for example, it means "Southwest Louisiana in the days when the parish was as large as an empire." In the name "Imperial Calcasieu Regional Planning Office," Imperial Calcasieu simply means "Southwest Louisiana."

Bits of the recorded history of Southwest Louisiana date back to the early French and Spanish explorers and the first European settlers who arrived in the area when it was under Spanish control in the late 1700s. Charles Sallier, the person for whom Lake Charles was named, was one of those early settlers. When the United States bought the Louisiana Territory from France in 1803, much of the Calcasieu River region became ungoverned. This came about through confusion over the exact western boundary of the Louisiana Purchase. The government of Spain said the boundary was the Calcasieu River. The United States government, on the other hand, contended that the boundary lay much farther west, possibly at the Brazos or the Rio Grande.

In 1806, both Spain and the United States sent armed forces to the area to protect their interests. When these forces met at the Sabine River, their leaders worked out an agreement instead of going into battle. This agreement called for making the land between the Calcasieu and Sabine Rivers a neutral territory, or no-man's land. The neutral territory took in all of the western half of what would later become Calcasieu Parish and made the area a haven for outlaws and malcontents until the dispute was settled in 1819. At that time, the boundary was finalized as the Sabine River. In 1812, however, while the West Calcasieu land was still a no-man's land, the part of Southwest Louisiana lying east of the Calcasieu River became part of the United States with the statehood of Louisiana. In the organization of Louisiana government, the Calcasieu region became part of St. Landry Parish; it remained in that parish until the creation of Imperial Calcasieu Parish in 1840.

The first settlers of old Calcasieu Parish discovered that it contained three distinctly different east-west bands of terrain. Near the Gulf of Mexico lay a band of broad sea marshes lined with coastal ridges. North of the marshes lay a band of wide prairies covered with tall grass. North of the prairies lay a huge band of mostly longleaf yellow pine forest. They also found that the region's three large north-south rivers and connecting tributaries made boat travel possible between the different types of Calcasieu terrain and throughout most of the parish.

In 1855, Daniel Goos, an immigrant from Schlesweg-Holstein Island, Germany, moved to Lake Charles and opened a sawmill to exploit Calcasieu timber. Goos' sawmill was the beginning of the industrialization of Calcasieu Parish. After the Civil War, the lumber industry started by Goos grew steadily as other people opened additional sawmills and shipbuilders began producing the schooners needed to haul Calcasieu lumber to Texan and Mexican markets. In the 1880s, after the coming of the railroad, the lumber business continued to increase and rice farming began. Finally, during the first two decades of the 20th century, Calcasieu Parish achieved its first sustained period of industrialization by becoming nationally recognized in the production of lumber, rice, sulphur, and oil.

This book is the result of a cooperative effort of the Southwest Louisiana Historical Association and the Archives Department in Frazar Memorial Library at McNeese State University. The purposes of this project were to find "new" photographs of the early years of Calcasieu Parish and to publish those photographs—and others from the same period—in a book. The first phase of this project took about six months. During this time copies were made of photographs in the Imperial Calcasieu Museum, photographs in some private collections, and photographs brought by area residents to two "photo fairs." These fairs, or copying sessions for the public, were held in the Southwest Louisiana Genealogical Library in Lake Charles and in the DeQuincy Railroad Museum. Over 1,000 historic photographs, or copies of originals, were added to the McNeese Archives in this phase of the project, with all expenses being paid by the Historical Association. The completion of this work meant the time had arrived to put together a book, and I volunteered.

Putting together this book took about four months. It involved going back through the copied photos, examining hundreds of additional photos (including those collected by the late Maude Reid in her scrapbooks), selecting 223 that seemed best to cover the years 1870–1920, and writing the captions. The captions are based upon my reading and my historical files, what little information came with the photos, and the information provided by Maude Reid and the McNeese Archives.

Looking back after all of this work was completed, I must say that I found both phases of the project interesting and enjoyable. I was pleasantly surprised to view so much convincing evidence of just how optimistic, alive, and industrious the people of Imperial Calcasieu really were back during the time they were civilizing a wilderness and making it productive. My major regret concerning this book is that its photos were not perfectly preserved during their many years of life. Perhaps what they "say" will overcome some of their defects in appearance.

Finally, this last thought before you see what's in the book: if you end up liking any part of this book, please make a point of honoring the photographers who took these pictures—and the photographers who shot the old photographs that are somewhere in your attic—by taking good care of your priceless old photographs. The alternative to doing this is to donate your old photographs to the McNeese Archives.

One

People

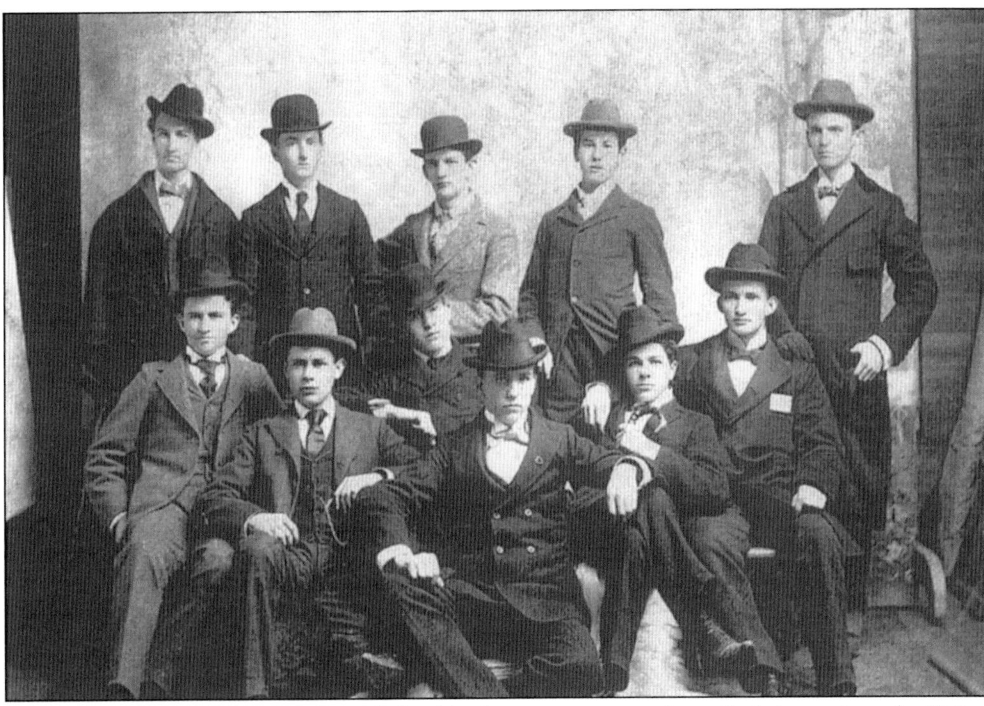

The Dirty Dozen. In 1896, these Lake Charles young men, who called themselves the "Dirty Dozen," formed an organization known as the Calcasieu Athletic Club. The name Dirty Dozen reflected their love of playing pranks. They are as follows, from left to right: (sitting) James Williams, Wesley Welsh, John Marshall, Charley Mitchell, John T. Wentz, and Columbus Pitre; (standing) Dan Gorham, Elisha Clement, Ernest Bel, Selzor Pickett, and Robert "Ted" O'Brien. Edgar Taylor and Louis Cruickshank were also members of the group. (Courtesy of McNeese Archives.)

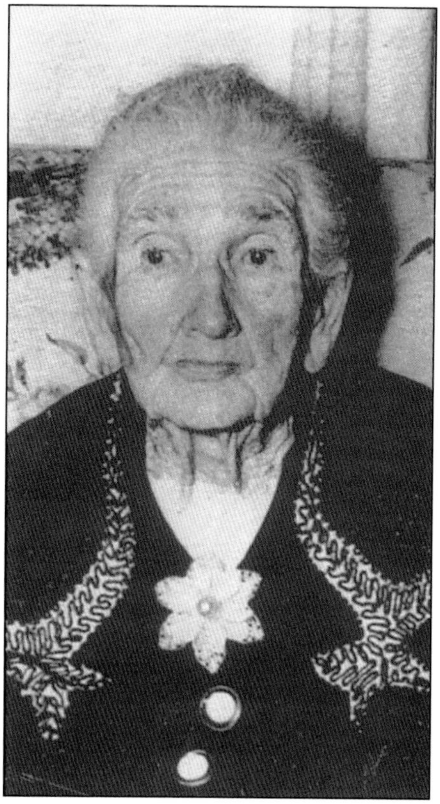

By Boat and Wagon. Alice Madison, age 90 in this photo, was eight years old when her mother, a Civil War widow, left Choctaw County, MS, with Alice's grandparents in 1867. The family traveled by cotton wagon, house boat, and ox wagon until they arrived and settled in the Big Woods area of Imperial Calcasieu Parish. When Alice grew up, she married James Madison, a Danish sawmill worker. They settled at Prien Lake near Lake Charles, where they had eight children. (Courtesy of McNeese Archives.)

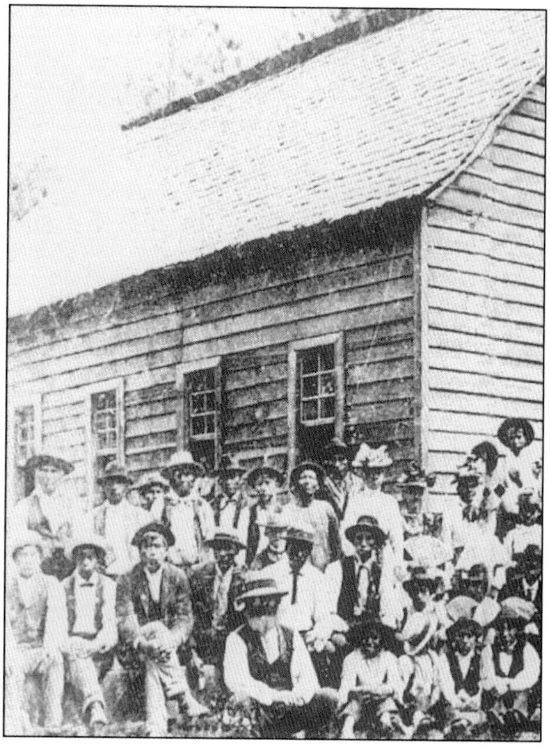

A Coushatta Gathering. Members of the only Native-American tribe now living in Southwest Louisiana gathered in the early 1920s at their school near Elton for this photograph. Their ancestors migrated to Southwest Louisiana from Alabama in the mid-1800s, and replaced the disappearing Attakapas tribe, the original residents of the area.

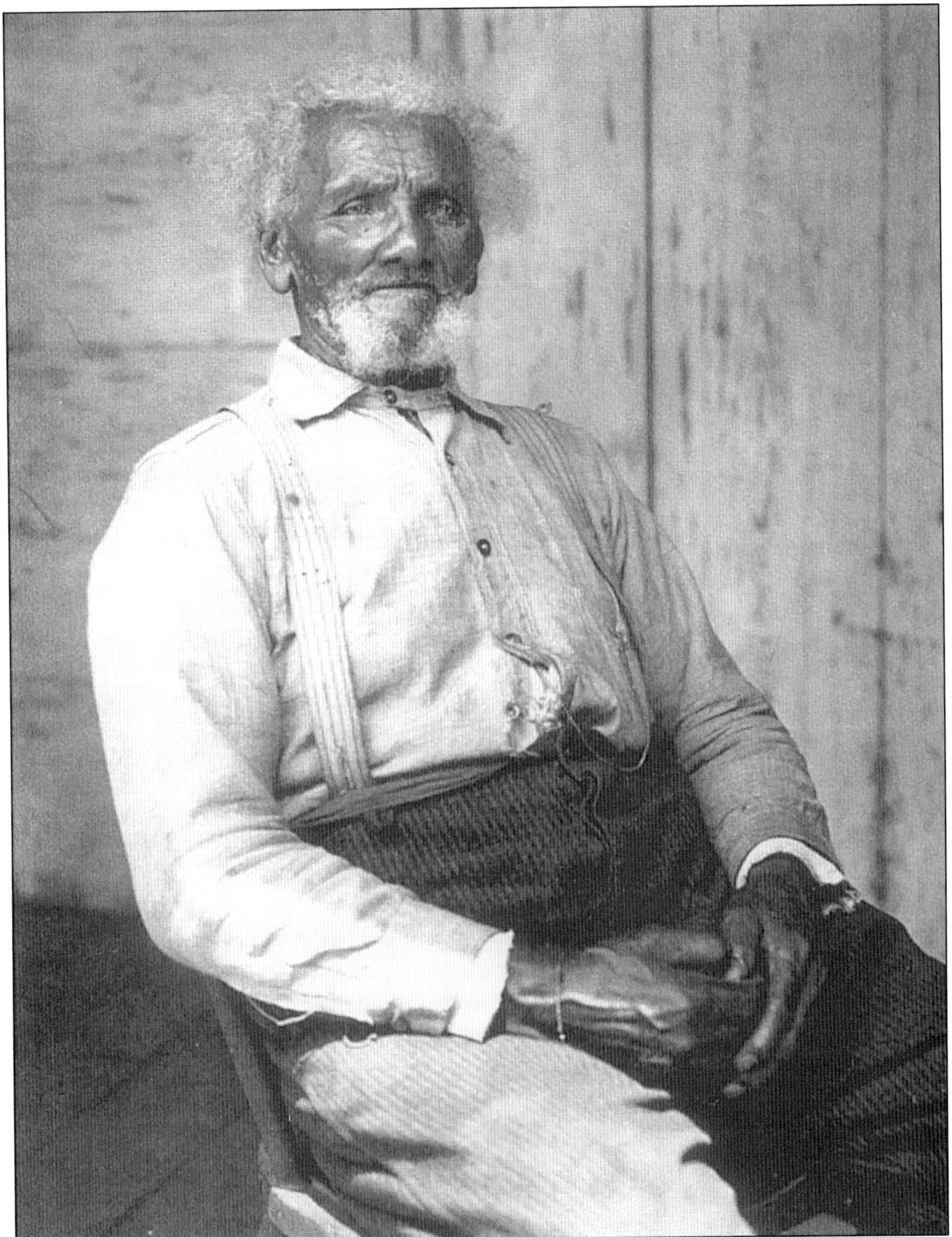

HE MOVED THE ORIGINAL COURTHOUSE. "Uncle" George Ryan, a former slave of both Jacob Ryan Sr. and Jacob Ryan Jr., was in his nineties when he sat for this photograph. According to George Ryan, when Sheriff Jacob Ryan Jr. made the decision to move the Calcasieu Parish Courthouse from Old Town (Marion) on the Calcasieu River to the east shore of Lake Charles, he put George in charge of building the raft on which to float the log building to its new site. At the time of this photograph, c. 1920, the former slave had lived for 60 years in the house he had built for himself on Kirkman Street, using lumber sawed in Jacob Ryan Jr.'s sawmill. (Courtesy of Imperial Calcasieu Museum.)

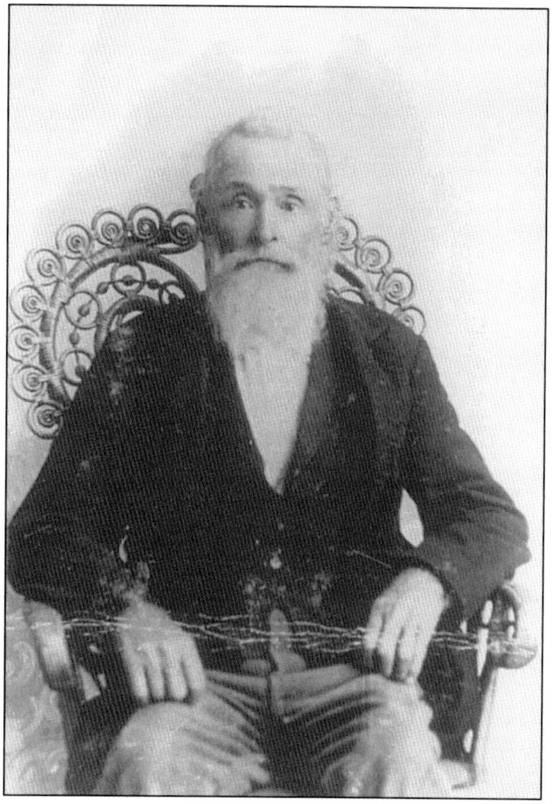

A Mill Operator. Lastie Reon was the son of Louis Reon, one of the very first settlers of Southwest Louisiana, and Artemise Ryan, sister of Jacob Ryan Jr., the "father of Lake Charles." Lastie Reon served in the Louisiana Cavalry during the Civil War and returned to farm, raise cattle, and operate a horse-powered gristmill south of Lake Charles near Contraband Bayou. His many descendants also bear other French names such as Ogea, Nelson, Piboin, LeBleu, LeBlanc, Benoit, Vincent, and Billeaud. (Courtesy of Charlsie Benoit.)

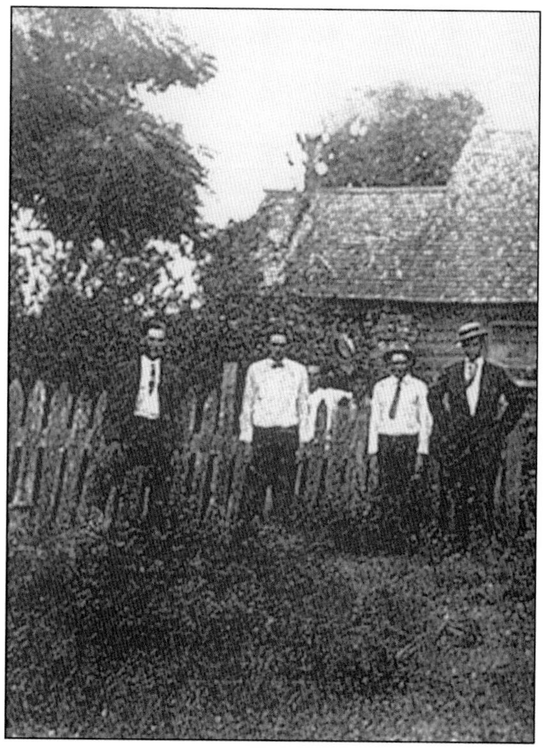

At Grandmother's House. Some of the many Cajun descendants of Lastie Reon assembled for this photograph in 1915 at the home of their step-grandmother, Leona Ogea Reon, south of Lake Charles. Their grandfather Lastie Reon, had died a year earlier. After his death, his large gristmill was sold and dismantled, and the timbers were sawed into lumber to build a house. Most of the young men in this photo turned to business and industry for their livelihoods, and some of them were called into military service during World War I. (Courtesy of Charlsie Benoit.)

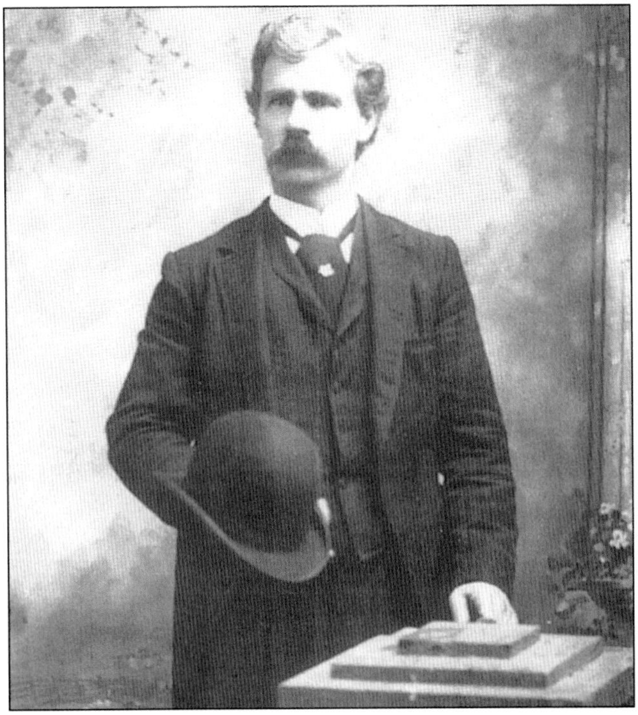

CURTAIN PAINTER. Paul Sullivan painted many signs and houses in Lake Charles in the 1890s, but he was best known as the man who painted the bright patchwork advertisements that adorned the curtain of the Williams Opera House. A boxy, four-story building on the west side of Ryan Street, the Opera House played host to many traveling shows and performers in its day. It was destroyed in the great fire of 1910. (Courtesy of McNeese Archives.)

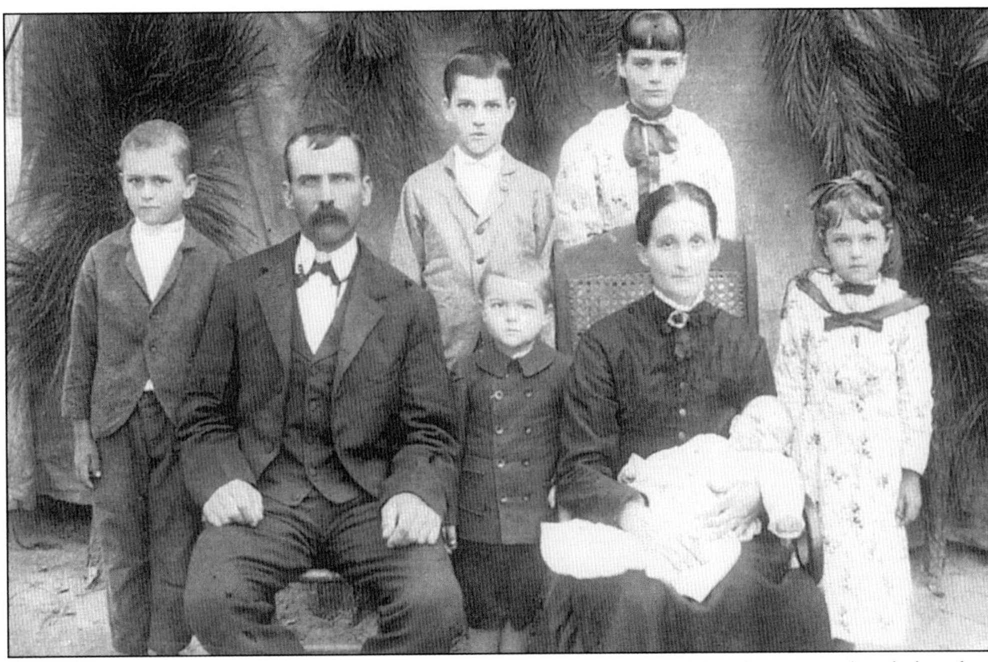

PINEY WOODS DWELLERS. In 1896, the Harvey and Amanda (Neighbors) Morrow family lived on a farm in northern Calcasieu Parish near Elizabeth. The family raised corn, cotton, vegetables, horses, and cattle and worked in the surrounding forests. Harvey was born in Arkansas while his parents were en route by wagon to Louisiana from Tennessee. Amanda was born in Alabama and came to Louisiana with her mother and stepfather when she was a child. (Courtesy of George Ann Benoit.)

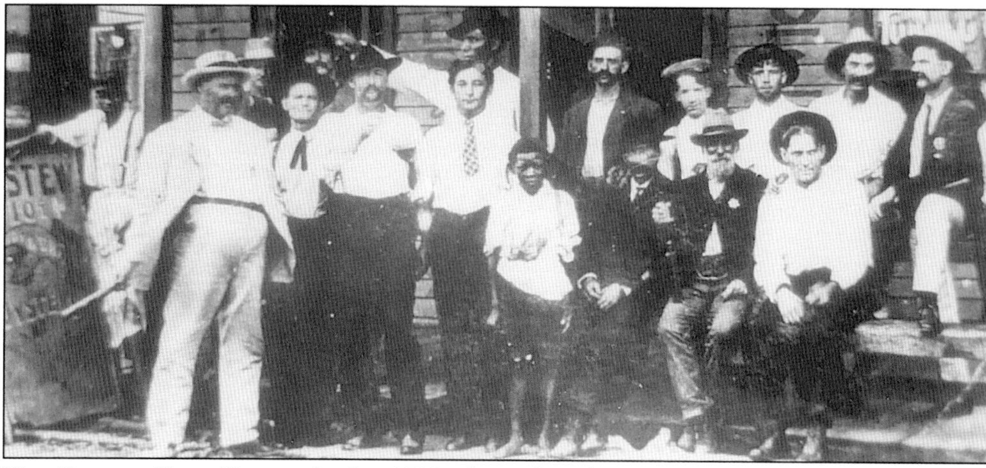

The Chicken Thief Bunch. In this 1890s photo these boisterous friends are standing in front of Richard Sarvaunt's Restaurant and Bar on "Battle Row" (Railroad Avenue) in Lake Charles. In the 1890s, Battle Row lived up to its name at night and on weekends because of its many saloons and the men who frequented them. Among the people in this photo are a lumberman, a barber, a railroad conductor, the saloon's owner, a policeman, and a man employed to encourage railroad and sawmill workers into saloons. The boy, whom the men called "Moonshine," was employed to run errands. (Courtesy of McNeese Archives.)

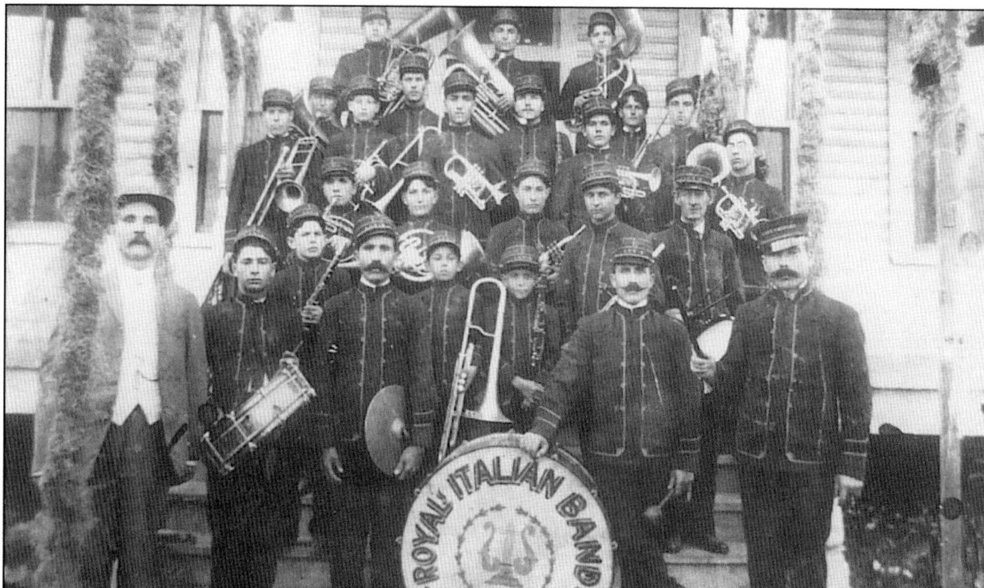

The Royal Italian Band. In 1905, this band assembled for a photograph on the porch of the Pecorino home on the Boulevard in Lake Charles after they finished playing for the wedding of Rosa Pecorino and John Pizzati. The names of band members include the following: Milazzo, Merino, Timpa, Manena, Runte, Piazza, Terranova, DiCarlo, Maggiore, Mancuso, Scalisi, Barras, and Ferrugina. These musicians and a sizable number of immigrants from various southern European countries made their homes in Imperial Calcasieu. (Courtesy of McNeese Archives.)

The Boo Hoo Pie Man. One of the most popular street characters in Lake Charles in the 1920s was William Proshee, a top-hatted basket vendor of 5¢ pies and pastries. Proshee, whose home was on Railroad Avenue, charmed customers into buying his products with his songs. Townspeople loved to hear him sing: "I got a Boo-Hoo muffin an' a Boo-Hoo cake./I got a Tom-Bo pea berry coffee cake./I got icin' an spicin' cake an' Boo-Hoo pie./Eat a Boo-Hoo cake an' you'll boo-hoo an' cry." (Courtesy of McNeese Archives.)

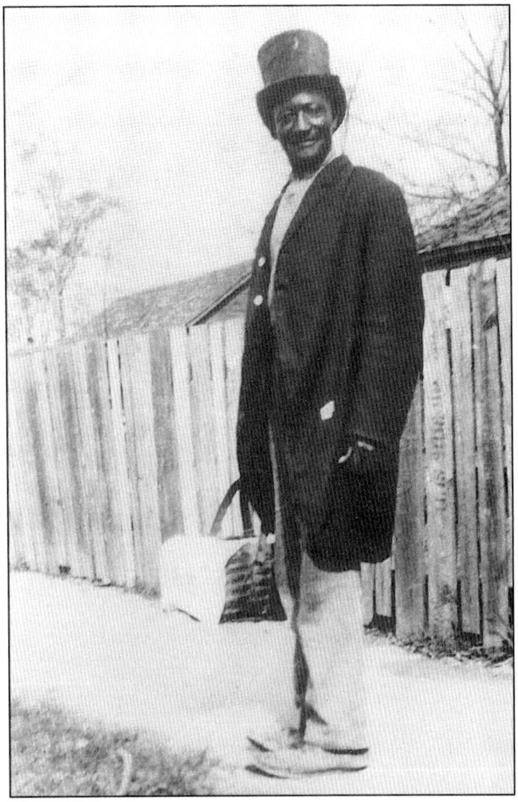

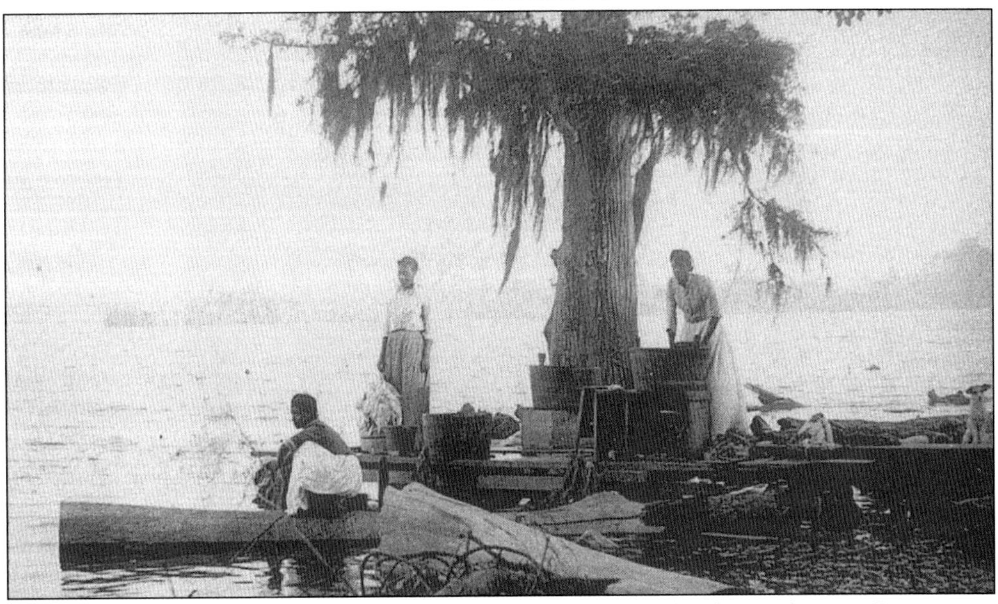

Westlake Laundry. These women washing clothes beside the Calcasieu River were immortalized in 1893 by photographers E.K. and D.P. Sturdevant in their popular "Sturdevant's Views" series. In the days before electricity and public water systems, washing clothes in Imperial Calcasieu had to be done either at a place like this or on a porch where water could be pumped or drawn from a shallow well in a backyard. (Courtesy of McNeese Archives.)

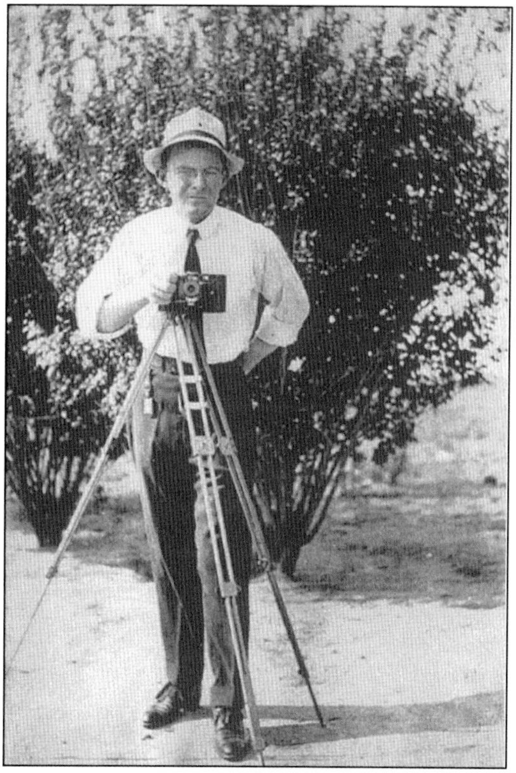

An Early Photographer. In the early 1900s, Charles Davies was one of Imperial Calcasieu's dedicated amateur photographers. On weekends, after working all week on the family farm, he liked to photograph members of his family and interesting local scenes. He did his darkroom work at night during the following week. Without his efforts and those of other photographers like him, there would be no photographic history of old Calcasieu Parish. (Courtesy of Helen Kendall Collection.)

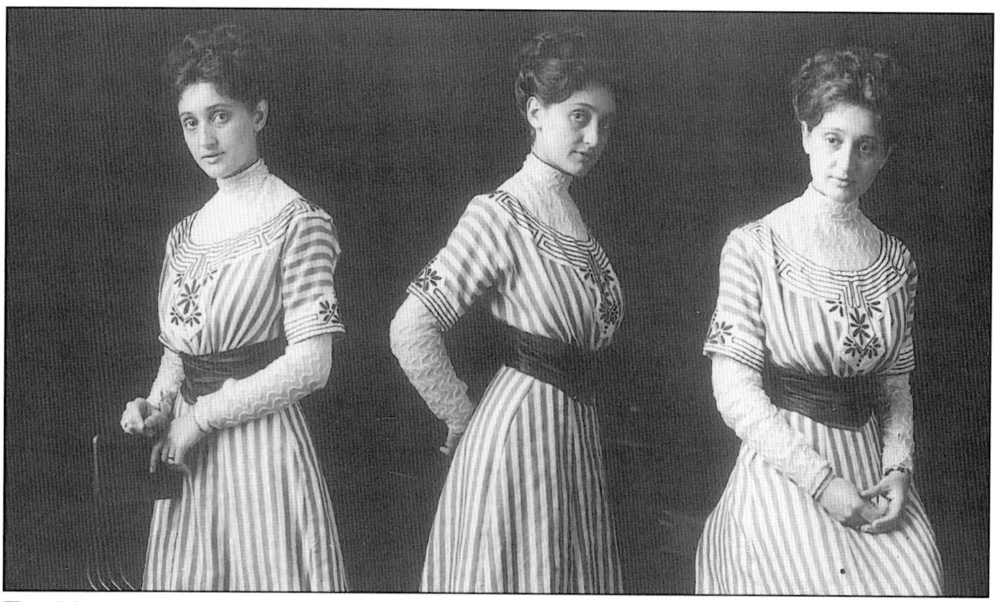

The Mystery Lady on Glass. The identity of this beautiful and once very fashionable lady is now a mystery. To the good fortune of present-day admirers, the glass negative on which these images are recorded was donated to a museum when friends and family members no longer wished to take care of it. Glass negatives require great care because they can be easily scratched or broken, but they make extremely clear photographs. (Courtesy of Imperial Calcasieu Museum.)

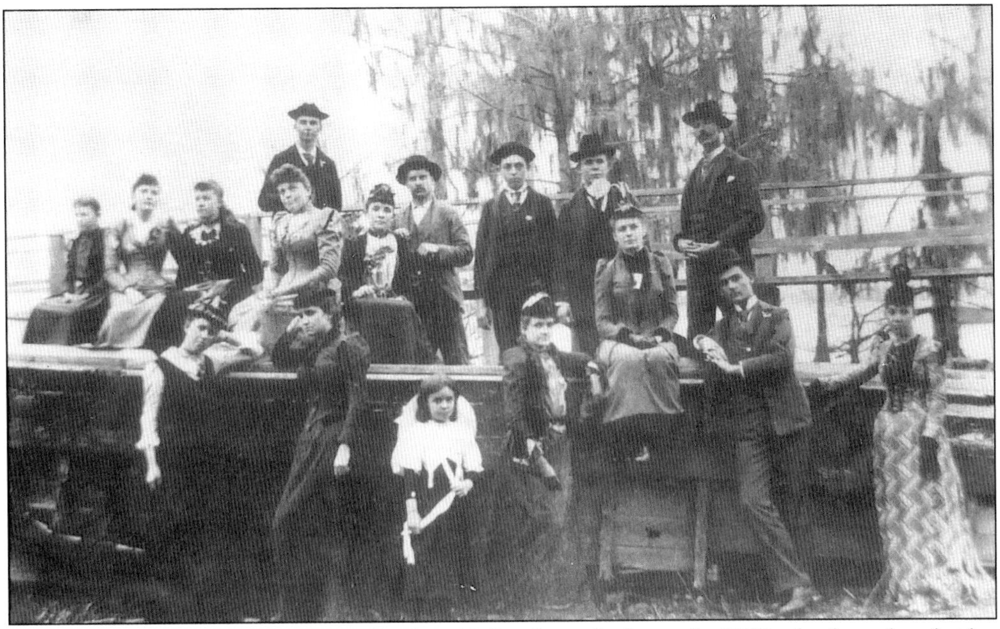

At Lover's Lane Bridge. From the late 1880s through the early 1900s the long foot bridge across scenic Pithon Coulee near the east shore of Lake Charles was a favorite gathering place for young people on Sunday afternoons and other occasions. The young people pictured in this 1890s photograph are gathered at one end of the bridge around the hulk of an old boat that had been beached in a storm. Their chaperon, Mrs. Thomas Wintle, is standing on the far right. (Courtesy of McNeese Archives.)

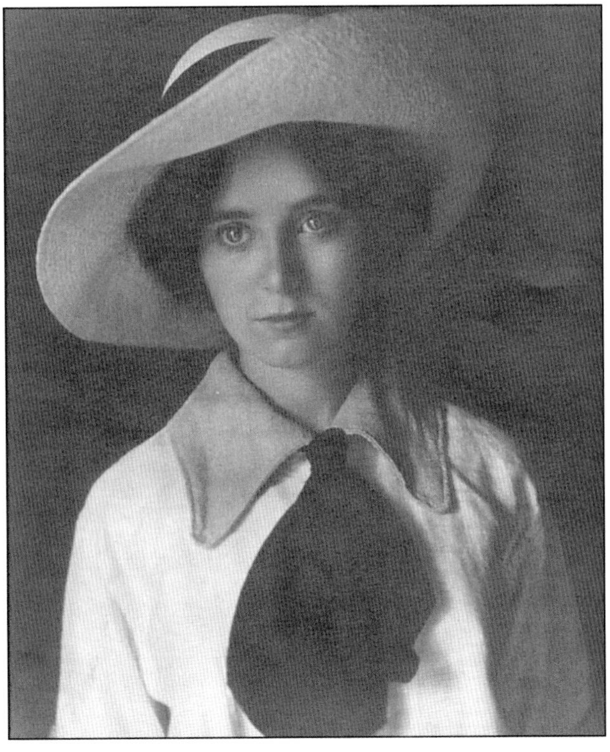

A Photographer's Delight. Emma Davies lived with her parents on a rice farm on the Calcasieu prairie south of Lake Charles when her brother Charles took this photo around 1914. Her haunting eyes foreshadow the sad turn her life would take. She died, a victim of the Spanish flu epidemic of 1918, shortly after her marriage to Angede "Jed" Benoit. (Courtesy of Helen Kendall Collection.)

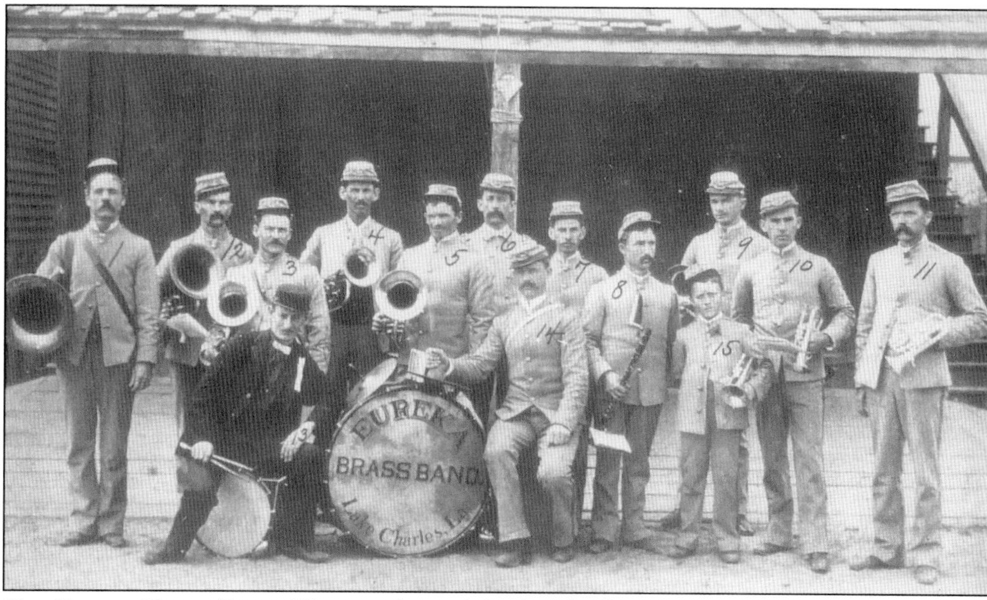

The Eureka Brass Band. The members of this band, all of whom were also members of the Phoenix Volunteer Company of Lake Charles, assembled in front of company headquarters some time in the 1880s for this photograph. For a number of years, the Eureka Brass Band was the only brass band in town and the only one in all of old Calcasieu Parish. Shown here are the following, from left to right: (front row) Louis Runte and Frank Shellman; (back row) Paul Sullivan, unidentified, Ferdinand Roy, Elanson Clark, Steve Sedlock, Dr. W.A. Knapp, Willie Mayo, Rudolph Krause, Ernest Taylor, Walter Moeling, Charles Winterhaler, and D.C. Taylor. (Courtesy of McNeese Archives.)

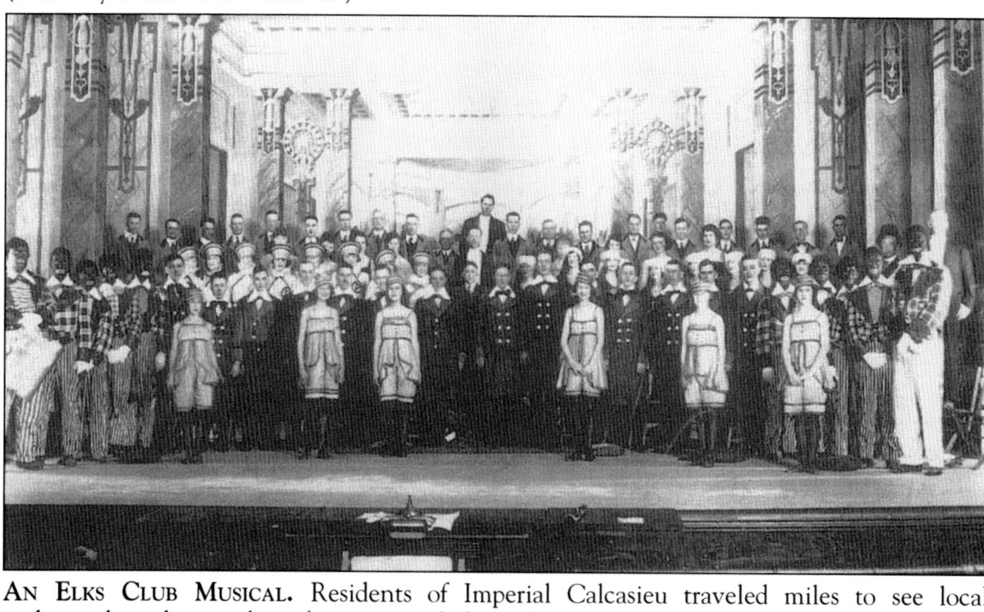

An Elks Club Musical. Residents of Imperial Calcasieu traveled miles to see local and traveling theatrical productions, and they also liked to put on their own shows. This large-cast musical was presented in the Arcade Theater in Lake Charles on February 16 and 17, 1921. The Arcade Theater was built in 1911 and destroyed by fire in 1984. (Courtesy of McNeese Archives.)

EVERYBODY KNEW BEN COLLINS. For 30 years beginning in the 1890s, Ben Collins, shown here in his baseball uniform, supervised electrical work for the local electric company during working hours. During his hours off he played athletics and headed volunteer firefighting efforts. (Courtesy of Zelma Jones and Blanche Suydam Collection.)

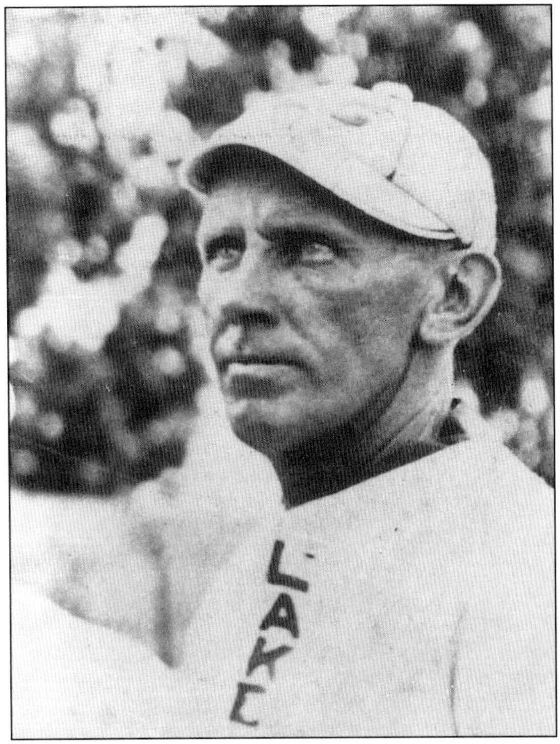

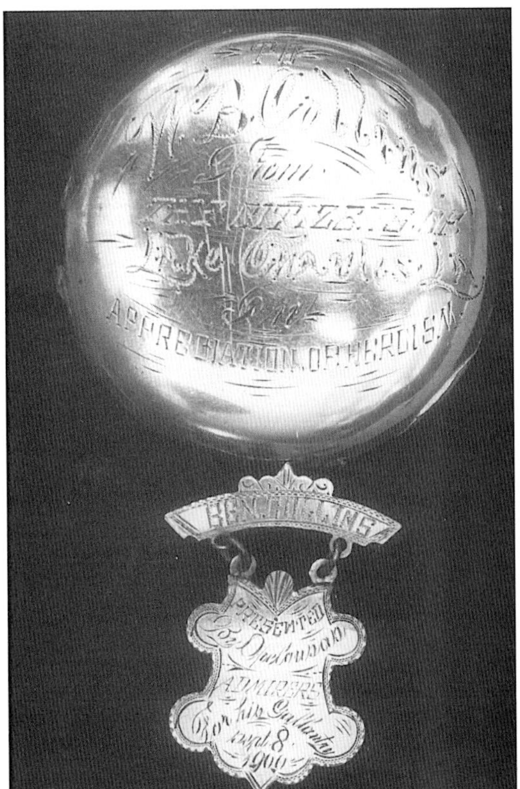

A HERO'S HONORS. On September 8, 1900, Ben Collins dashed out into Lake Charles' main street and stopped a charging runaway horse with an attached buggy, thus saving the daughter of John McNeese from probable serious injury or death. Two groups of bystanders were so struck by his heroism that they presented him with the gold watch and gold medal shown here. In 1925 Ben Collins and two other firefighters— Bill Guillotte and Hollis Vincent—died heroes' deaths while fighting a major fire in downtown Lake Charles. (Courtesy of Zelma Jones and Blanche Suydam Collection.)

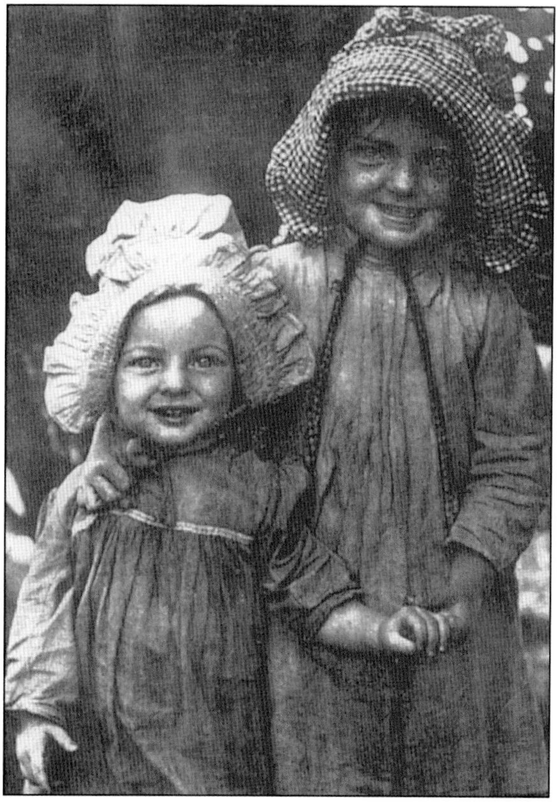

Country Kids. About 1913, when this photo was taken, William Kendall (left) wore a dress along with his older sister, Roberta, in accordance with the custom of that time for dressing very young boys. The children's heavy cotton clothing and bonnets were made at home by their mother or another family member and handed down to all succeeding children until worn out. (Courtesy of Helen Kendall Collection.)

Railroad Builders. From 1879 through the 1920s, Southwest Louisiana was a mecca for men such as these who accepted jobs building and maintaining railroads. After the railroad men completed the Louisiana & Western Railroad between New Orleans and Houston and the Watkins Railroad from Lake Charles to Alexandria, they laid countless miles of tram railroad through Calcasieu's vast long-leaf pine forests for the bustling timber industry. (Courtesy of McNeese Archives.)

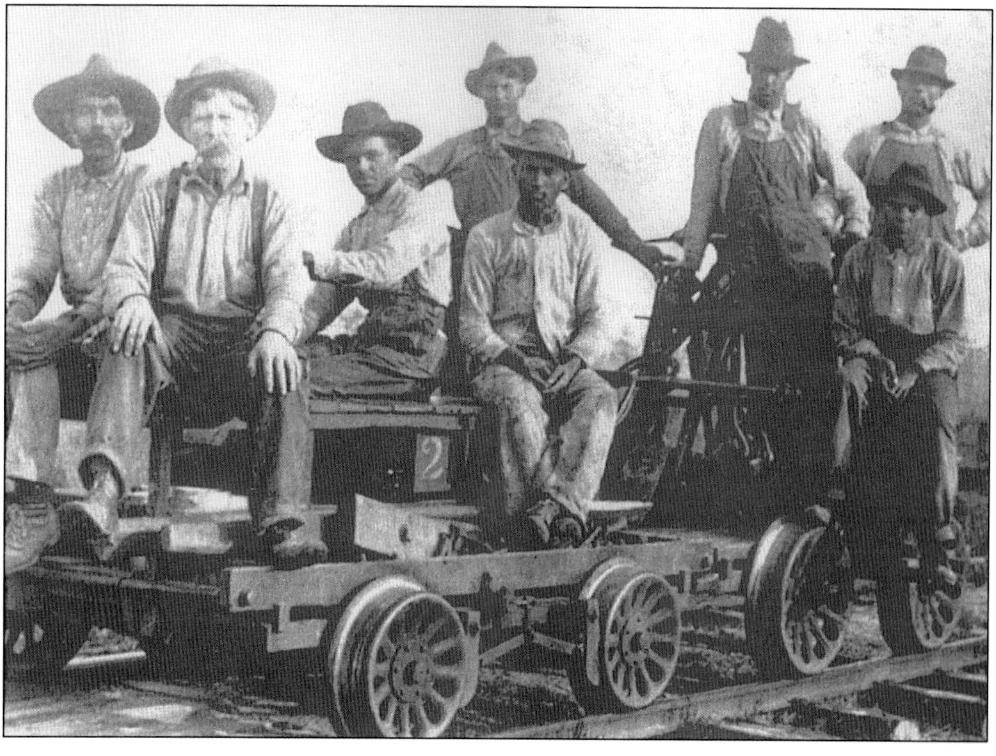

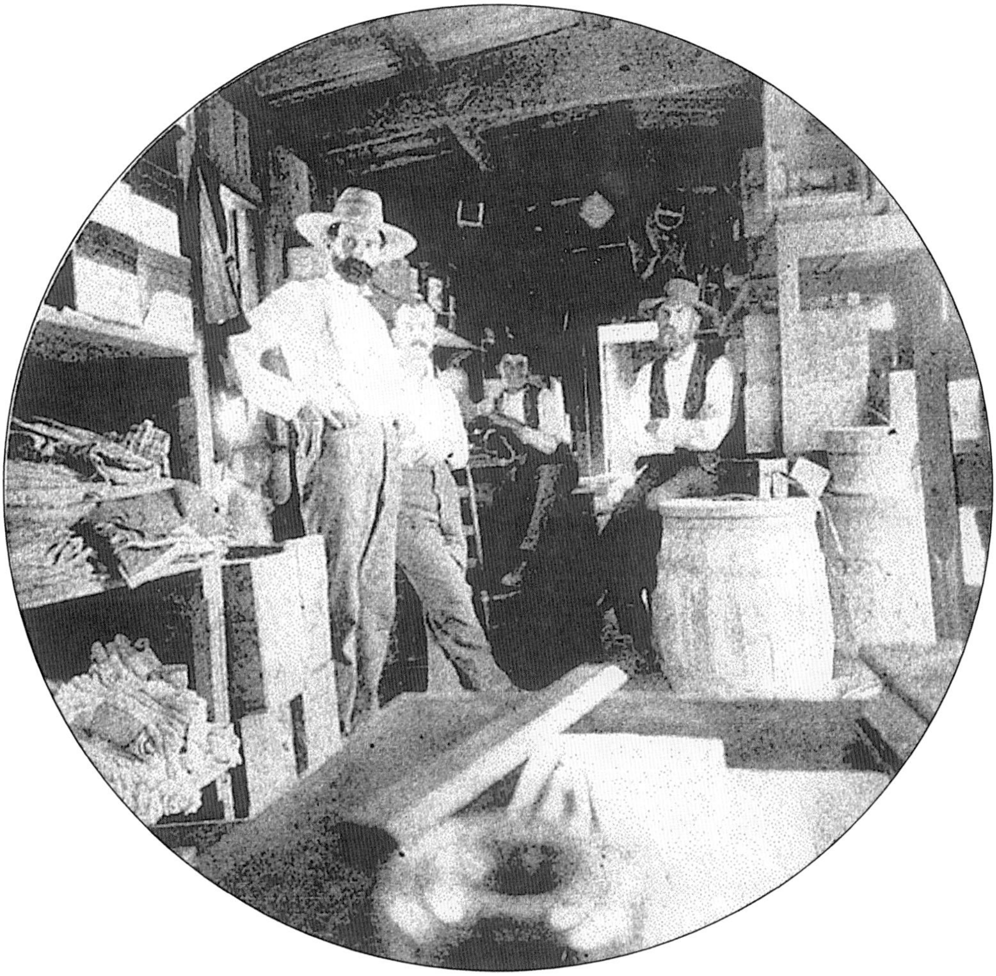

Rice Scholar. Seaman A. Knapp, one of the founders of South Louisiana's rice industry, is shown seated on a barrel, far right, in the old Lake Charles Railroad Commissary not long after he moved to Lake Charles in 1885. Often called the "Professor of Agriculture," he was born in Schroon, Essex County, NY, in 1833 and moved in 1866 to Iowa Agricultural College at Ames, where he became president. Dr. Knapp came to Southwest Louisiana under the sponsorship of Jabez B. Watkins, the land colonizer. He lived in Lake Charles for over 20 years, during which he taught Southwest Louisiana farmers how best to grow rice and was active in business and civic endeavors. In 1897, he accepted a position in the Department of Agriculture in Washington, D.C., where an arch was dedicated to his memory in 1911. In addition to his work with rice and many other accomplishments, he is remembered as the founder of the "corn clubs" that became the Four-H Clubs of America and as the co-founder (with Secretary of Agriculture James F. Wilson) of the Agricultural Extension System of the U.S. Department of Agriculture. (Courtesy of Imperial Calcasieu Museum.)

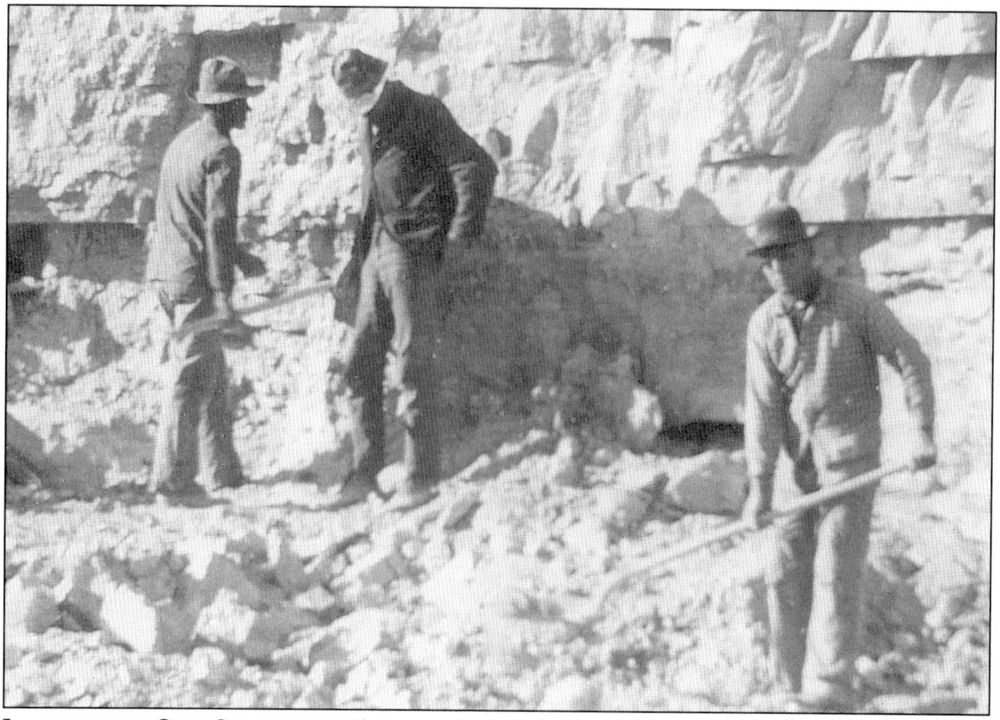

Laboring in Old Calcasieu. These unidentified Union Sulphur Company workers, who probably had a common ethnic background, are representative of thousands who labored in the early industries of Imperial Calcasieu. Union Sulphur employed many Spanish-speaking workers, while Gerstner Field employed some Chinese refugees from the Mexican War. Many African Americans worked in the rice, timber, and lumber industries; many Cajuns worked in agriculture, construction, and oil drilling; and many Scandinavians, in shipbuilding and in the schooner trade. (Courtesy of Imperial Calcasieu Museum.)

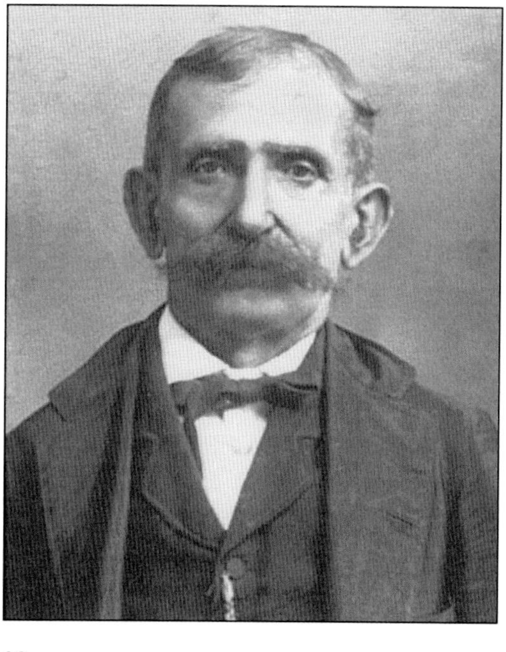

A Colorful French Immigrant. Joseph Cazeaux, a veteran of the Franco-German War, drove a shuttle buggy between the Southern Pacific depot and various Lake Charles hotels during the 1880s and 1890s. While making his rounds, Cazeaux carried many traveling salesmen (called "drummers" in those days) to and from the railroad station. These men liked to tease the little Frenchman. His way of retaliating was to classify all of his male passengers as either "gentlemen" or "drummers." (Courtesy of McNeese Archives.)

Two

COUNTRY LIVING

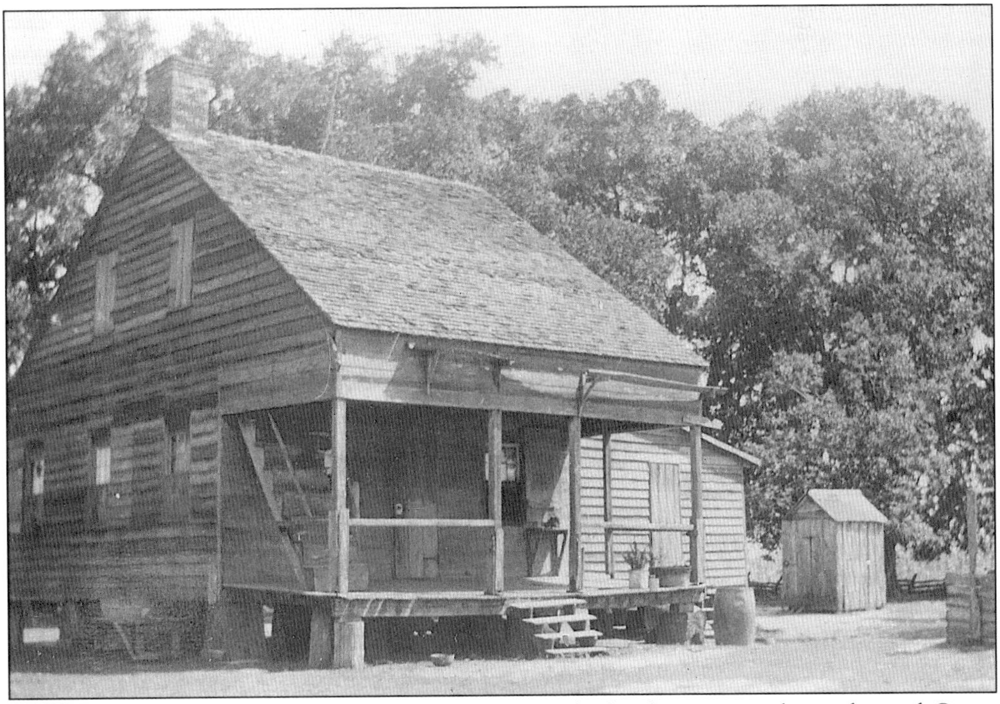

AN OLD CAJUN HOUSE. This house near Hayes was built of cypress in the traditional Cajun style by Arvillion Derouen in 1854, only 14 years after Imperial Calcasieu Parish was carved out of the western part of St. Landry Parish. Derouen was born in 1825 in St. Martin Parish and died in this house on December 17, 1924. When they built this house, Derouen was 25 and his wife was almost 16. Mrs. Derouen also died in her 90s. French-speaking Cajuns, such as the Derouens, settled mostly in the prairie (middle) region of Imperial Calcasieu Parish. (Courtesy of McNeese Archives.)

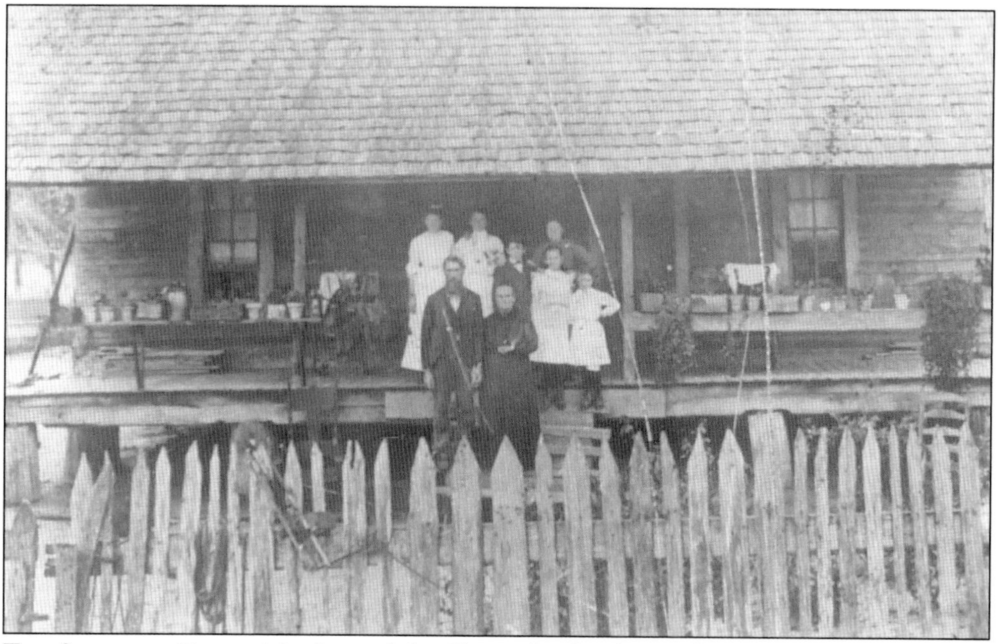

The Shoemake Place. Members of the Shoemake family stand in front of the "dog-trot" hallway of their house on Edgerly Road in this *c.* 1900 photograph. Houses built in this style were favored by the English-speaking settlers from southeastern states who settled mostly in the northern, forested portions of Calcasieu Parish. The dog-trot of this house appears to have been closed off on the far side of the house. (Courtesy of Bill and Dorothy McFatter.)

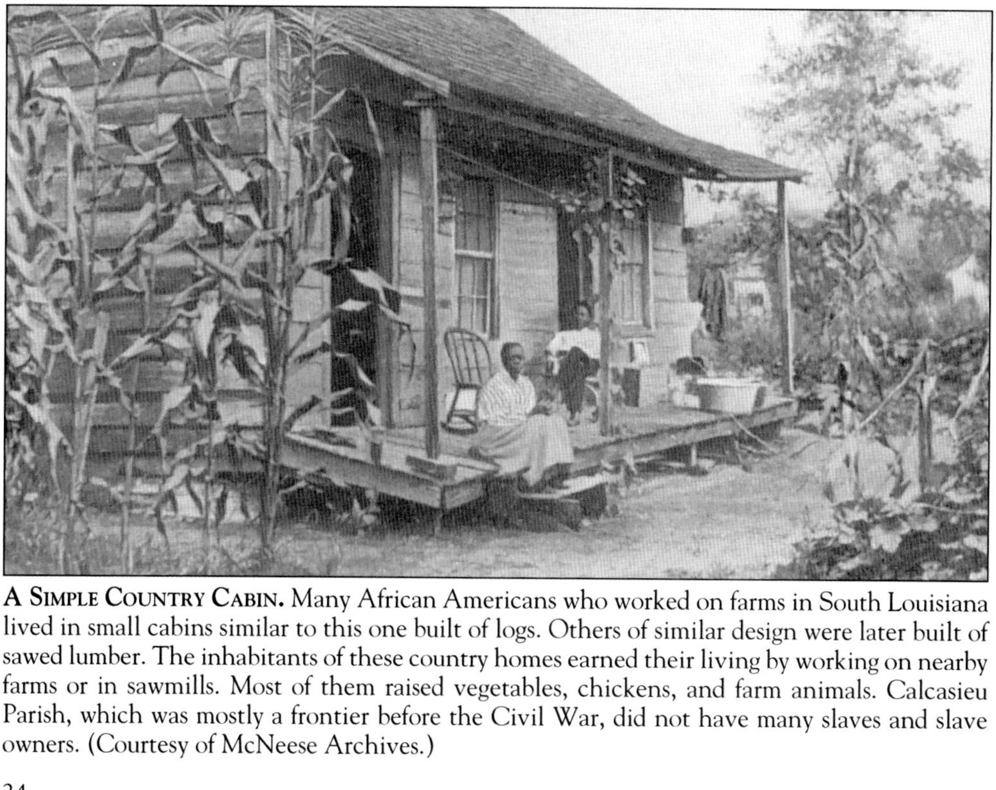

A Simple Country Cabin. Many African Americans who worked on farms in South Louisiana lived in small cabins similar to this one built of logs. Others of similar design were later built of sawed lumber. The inhabitants of these country homes earned their living by working on nearby farms or in sawmills. Most of them raised vegetables, chickens, and farm animals. Calcasieu Parish, which was mostly a frontier before the Civil War, did not have many slaves and slave owners. (Courtesy of McNeese Archives.)

A Prairie Farm Family. In this 1912 photograph, Charles and Helen (Davies) Kendall are standing with their first two children at their farm home near Chalkley, southeast of Lake Charles. Charles was born in Illinois, and Helen near Morgan City. Charles died 19 years after this photo was taken, shortly before the birth of the couple's eighth child. Helen then became a teacher and raised her large family with the aid of her parents. (Courtesy of Helen Kendall Collection.)

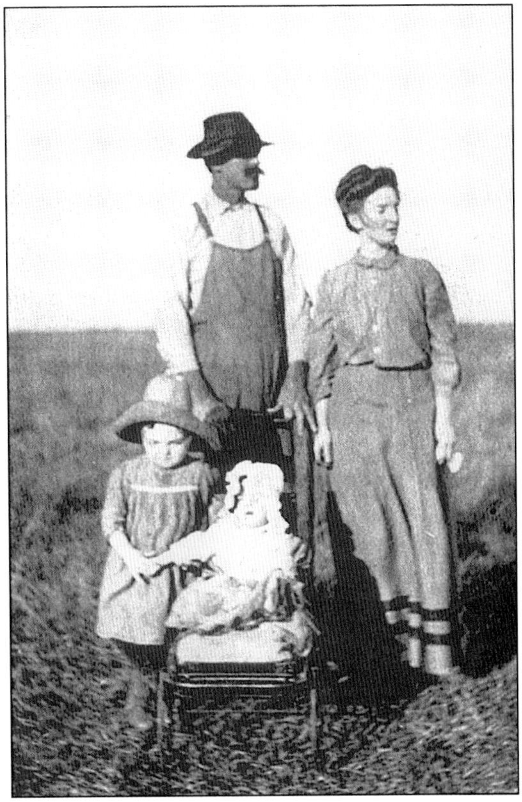

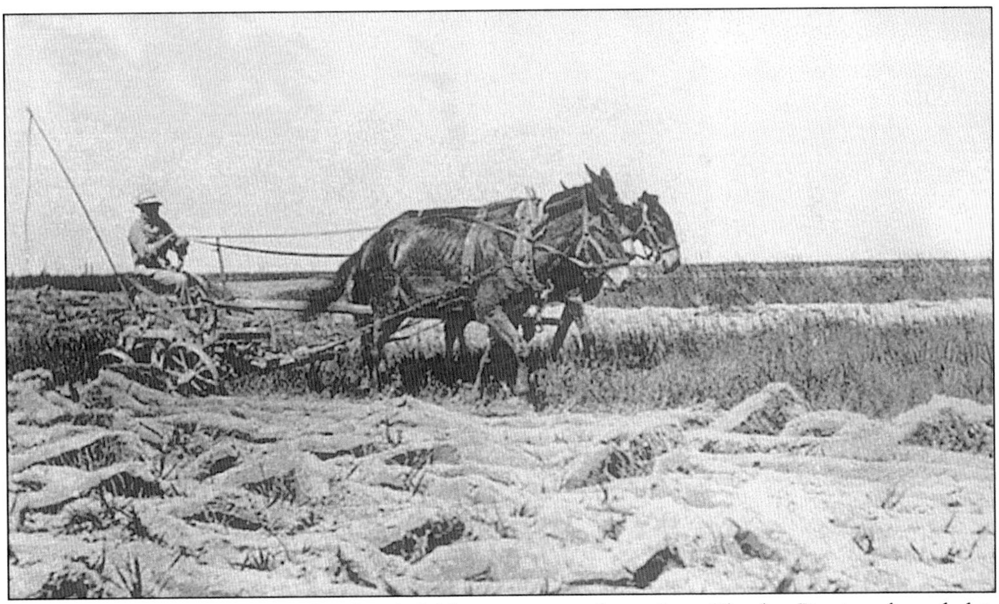

Prairie Plowing. Strings of sod roiled like uneasy snakes when Charles Davies plowed this prairie field in preparation for planting the family's rice crop around the year 1905. When steam tractors became more common, farmers like Davies sometimes hired tractor owners to plow their fields for them. Payment for this service and water provided by a canal company was made from the crop loan or from a share of the harvest. (Courtesy of Helen Kendall Collection.)

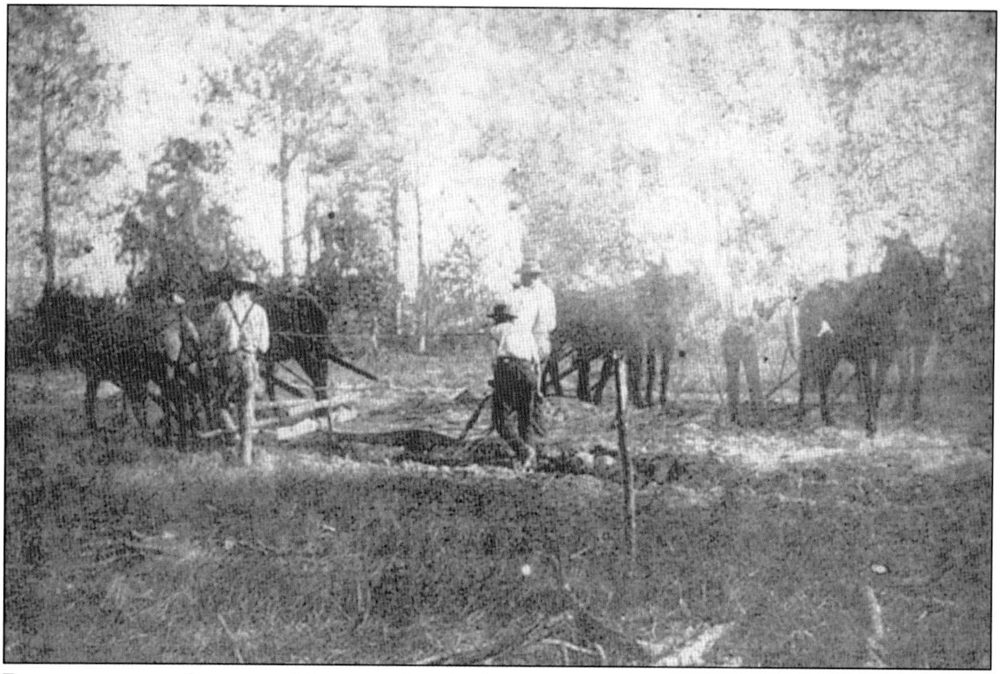

Plowing in the Cutover. Homesteaders in the northern, forested parts of Imperial Calcasieu had to clear their land of trees and stumps before they could hitch up their mules for the difficult plowing, seen in this photograph. The trees that once stood on this land would have been used first to build the houses, barns, and fences of these farmers and then for other purposes. (Courtesy of Imperial Calcasieu Museum.)

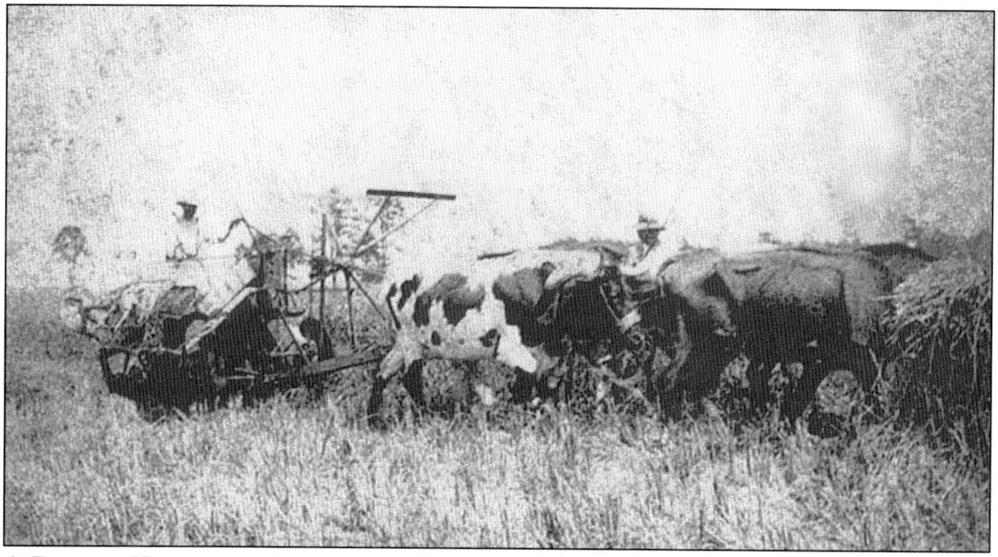

A Deering Harvester. A strange combination of old and new farming methods was used to harvest the rice crop shown in this photo. The machine being used is a Deering Harvester of the type that arrived in Lake Charles in the summer of 1888 on 22 railroad cars from Chicago. About 1,000 rice farmers and businessmen applauded the arrival of these machines and the speeches of Professor S.A. Knapp of Lake Charles and S.L. Cary of Jennings, who had encouraged farmers to update their rice farming methods. (Courtesy of McNeese Archives.)

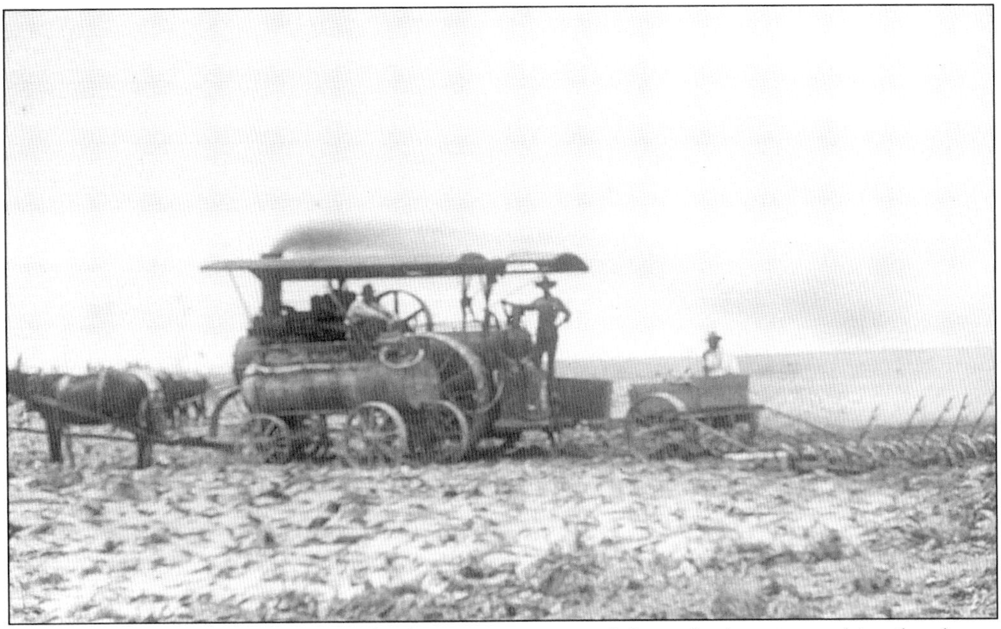

Steam Power. The prairies on which rice was grown did not look quite so big after huge, steam-powered tractors pulling gang plows were introduced to subdue them. The operator of this tractor, which was used in the Welsh area, has stopped to take on water and fuel from a wagon being pulled by horses. (Courtesy of McNeese Archives.)

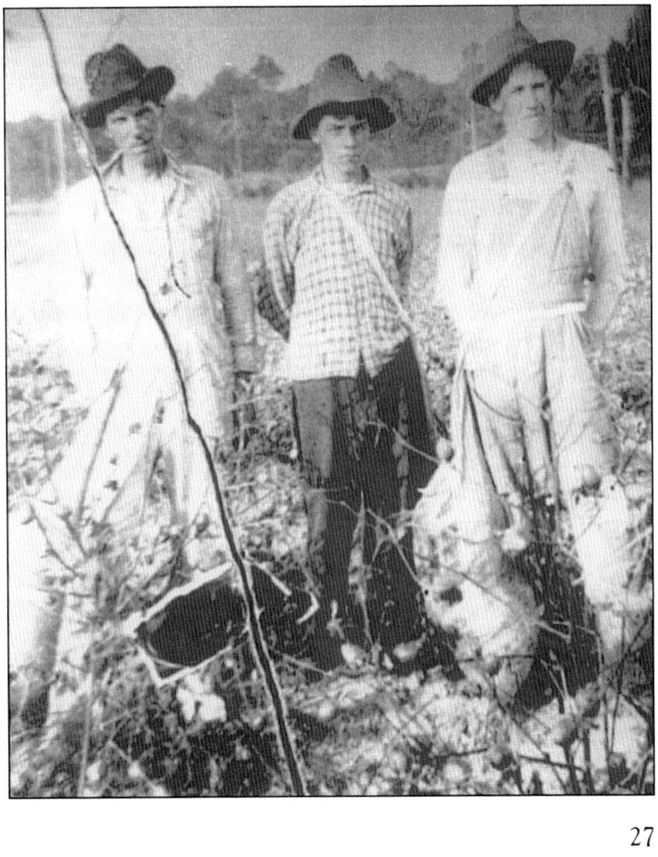

Cotton Pickers. In the days before mechanized cotton pickers, just about every young person who grew up on a small farm in Imperial Calcasieu had to spend many long, hot days bent over and dragging a cotton sack in the family's fields. Cotton was grown successfully on both the prairies and in cutover lands of old Calcasieu Parish.

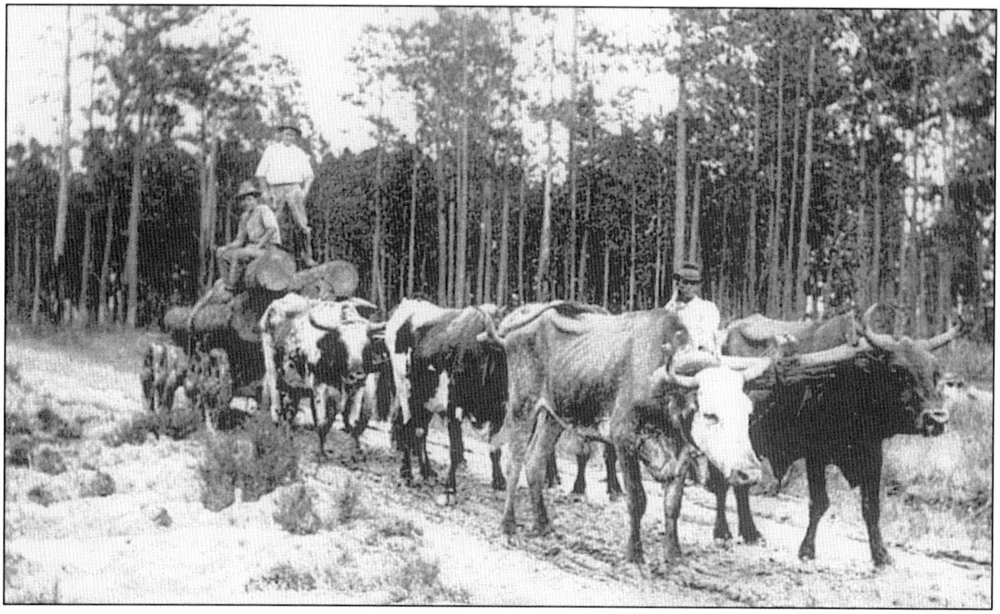

Log Haulers. In this photograph a number of huge, longleaf yellow pine logs are being hauled to a mill by workmen who will either sell the logs to the mill or have them sawed into lumber for their own use. Oxen, although slow, were favored over mules and horses for this kind of work because of their great strength, endurance, and calm natures. They were used in logging into the 1920s. (Courtesy of Bill and Dorothy McFatter.)

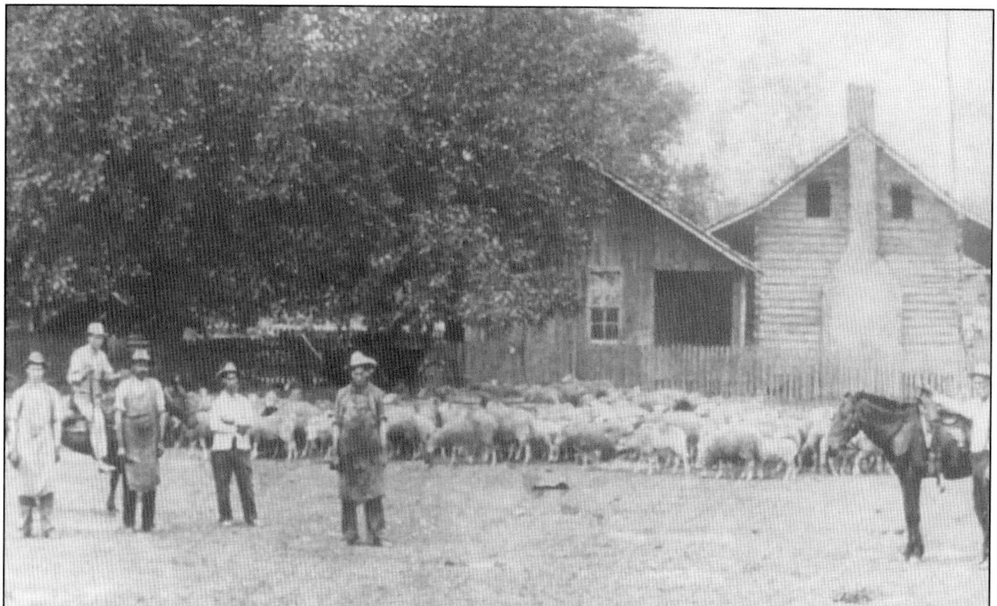

Sheep Ranchers. The agriculture of Imperial Calcasieu was so diverse in the early 1900s that it even included large sheep ranches, such as the one shown here. These ranches were most numerous on cutover timber lands in the areas around DeRidder, DeQuincy, and Merryville. In the background, note the log house to which a house built of sawed lumber has been attached. (Courtesy of Patty McFatter Singletary.)

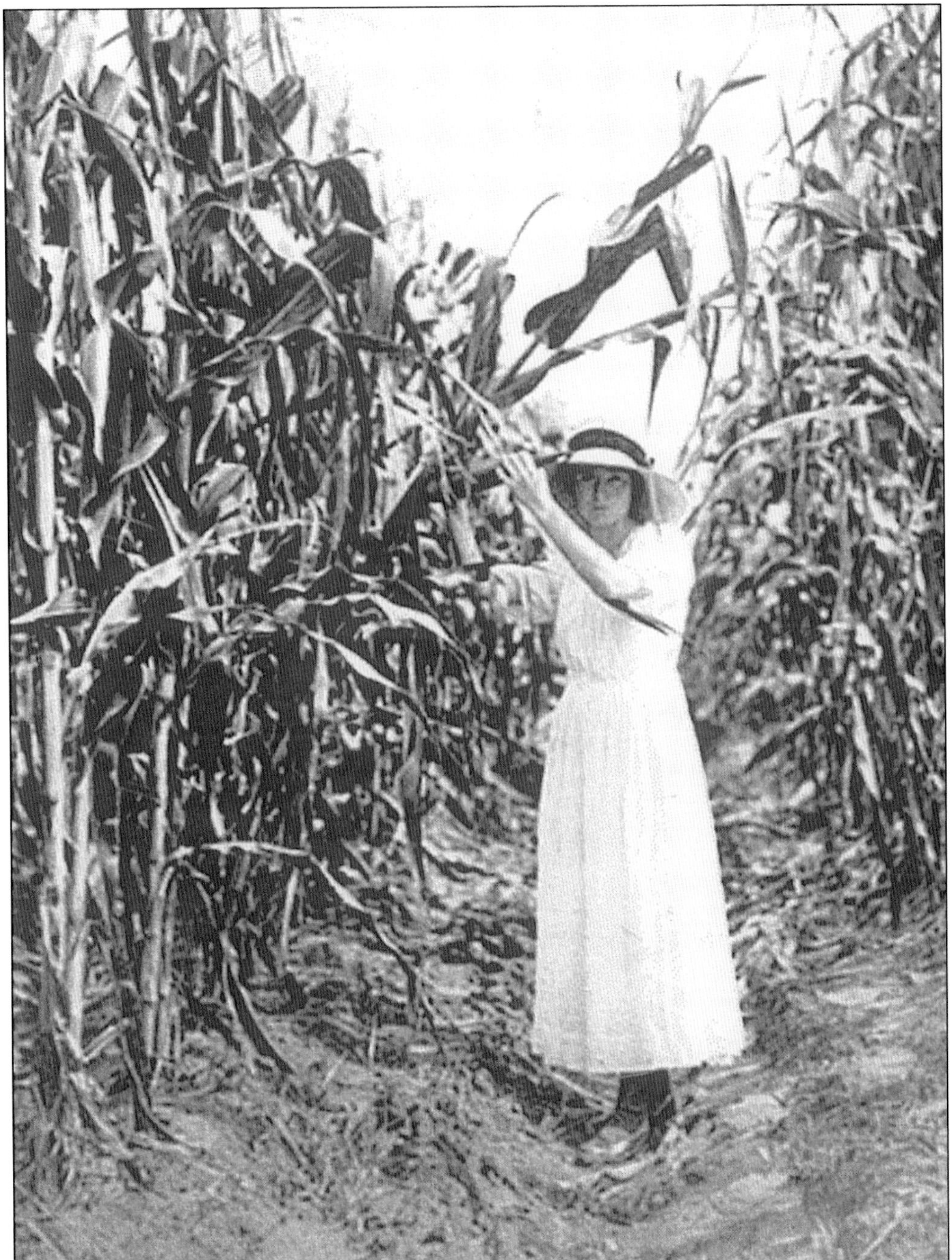

TALL CORN, LONG EARS. Emma Davies appears to be gathering a few ears of her father's and brother-in-law's corn for the family's Sunday dinner in this photo taken around 1916 on the family's farm south of Lake Charles. How did they make it grow so tall? One neighbor said he often saw David Davies hoeing in his garden before sunrise by the light of a kerosene lantern. (Courtesy of Helen Kendall Collection.)

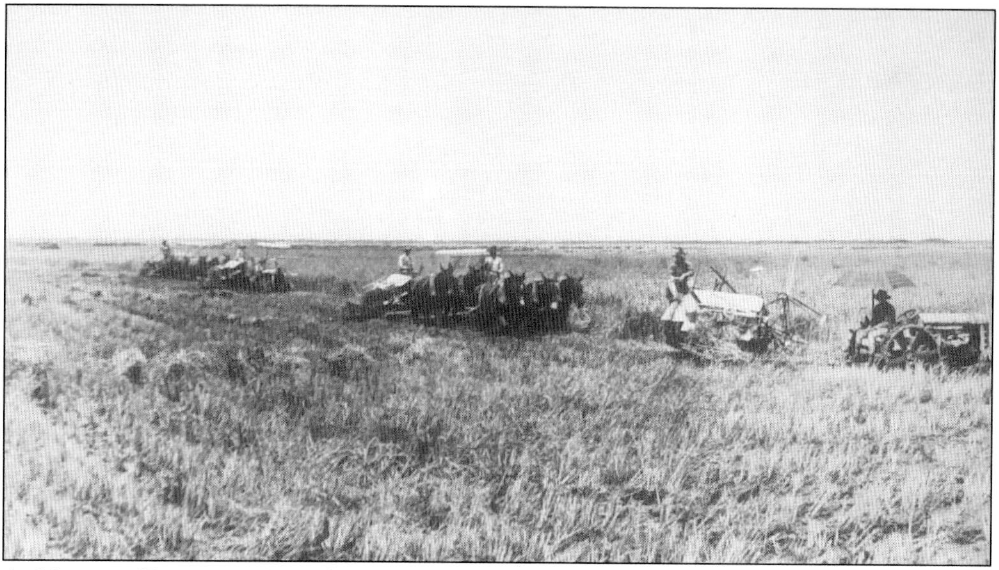

A Modern Tractor. A modern, steel-wheeled tractor heads the lineup of Deering-type harvesters being used in this 1920s rice harvest. In a few years tractors like this would be replaced by rubber-tired tractors that were even more powerful, and animal power would become a thing of the past on large farms. (Courtesy of Imperial Calcasieu Museum.)

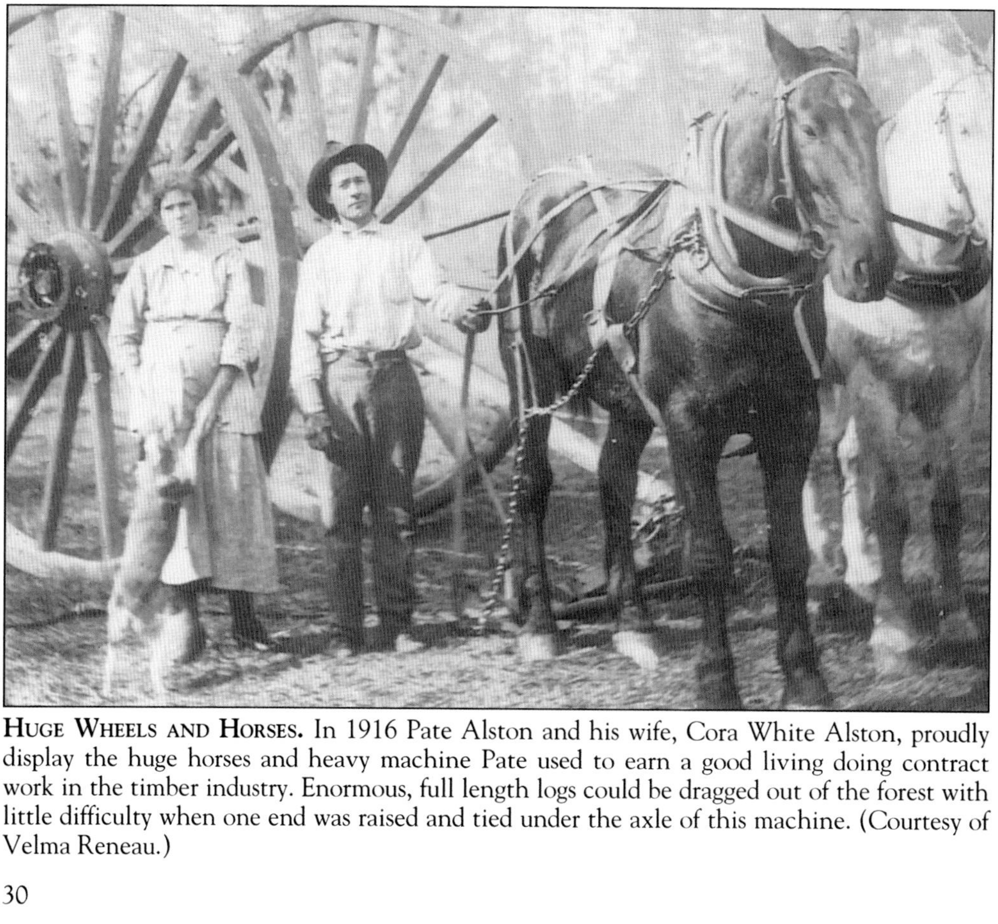

Huge Wheels and Horses. In 1916 Pate Alston and his wife, Cora White Alston, proudly display the huge horses and heavy machine Pate used to earn a good living doing contract work in the timber industry. Enormous, full length logs could be dragged out of the forest with little difficulty when one end was raised and tied under the axle of this machine. (Courtesy of Velma Reneau.)

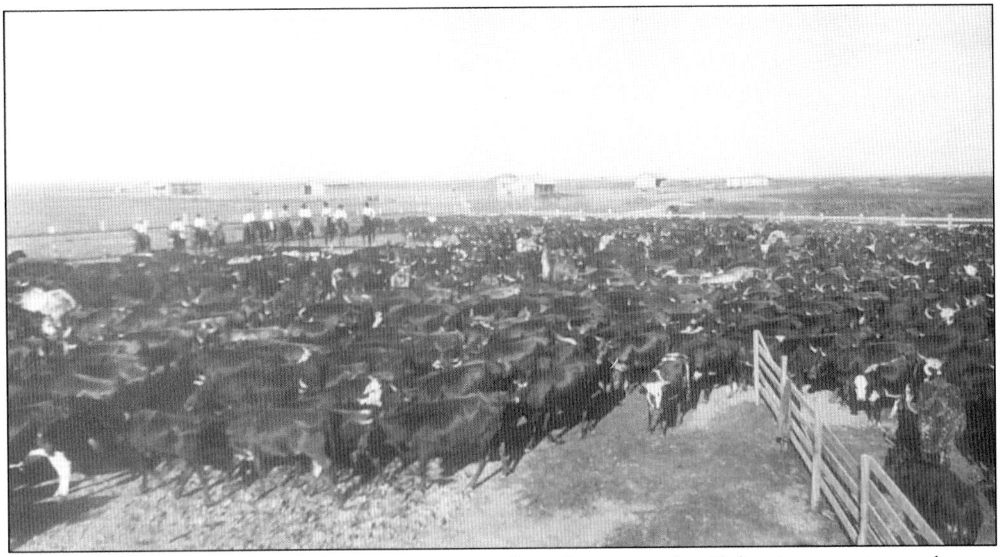

A Cattle Roundup. Before there were any roads or fences on the Calcasieu prairie, cattlemen got together and rounded up free-ranging herds each year. During these roundups each owner claimed his new calves and branded them by identifying the calf's mother. The roundup in this photo is believed to have taken place on a large private ranch in west Calcasieu, south of the towns of Sulphur and Vinton. Cattle in this region grazed on the prairie during warm months and in the marsh during the winter. (Courtesy of Imperial Calcasieu Museum.)

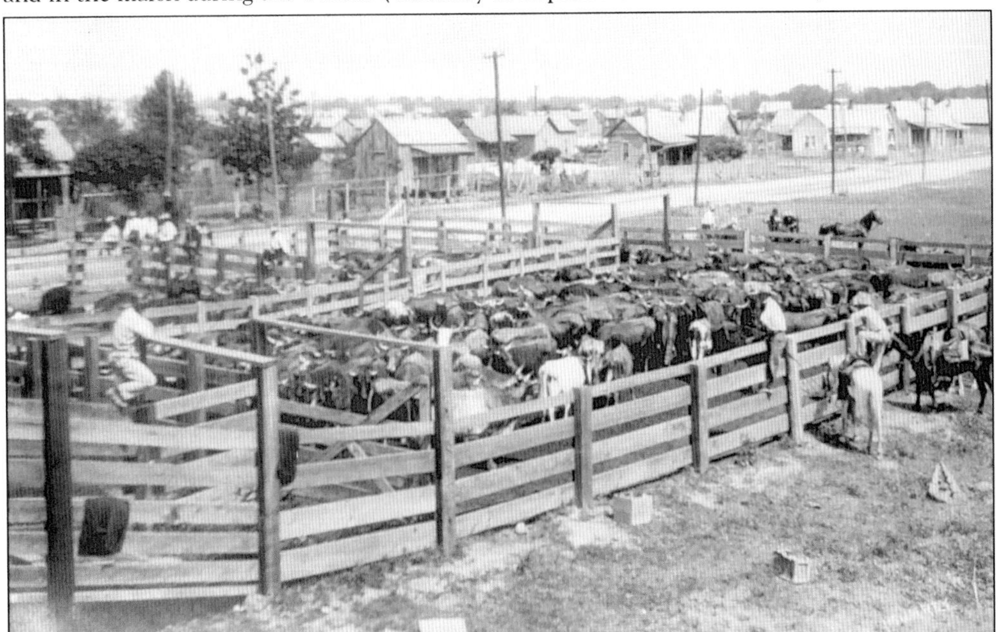

Cattle Pens and Urban Housing. As time passed and cattle raising became more sophisticated, Calcasieu cattlemen learned the value of ridding cattle of disease-carrying ticks by "dipping" the cows in narrow troughs filled with chemically treated water and by vaccinating them to prevent diseases. This 1920s photo shows west Calcasieu cattlemen preparing a herd for market. Note the old-time, modest-income housing in the background. (Courtesy of Imperial Calcasieu Museum.)

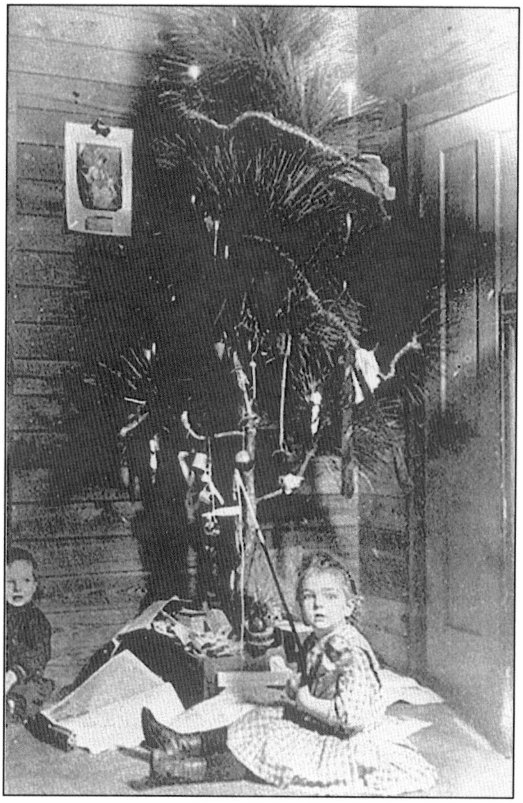

A Country Christmas. Country children enjoyed Christmas even though their tree and gifts seem meager by modern standards. In this photo taken about 1914, Billy and Roberta Kendall are in the process of opening a couple of presents under a pine Christmas tree. In the early 1900s, most Calcasieu farm children received some fruit, a bit of candy, and a couple of inexpensive gifts for Christmas. (Courtesy of Helen Kendall Collection.)

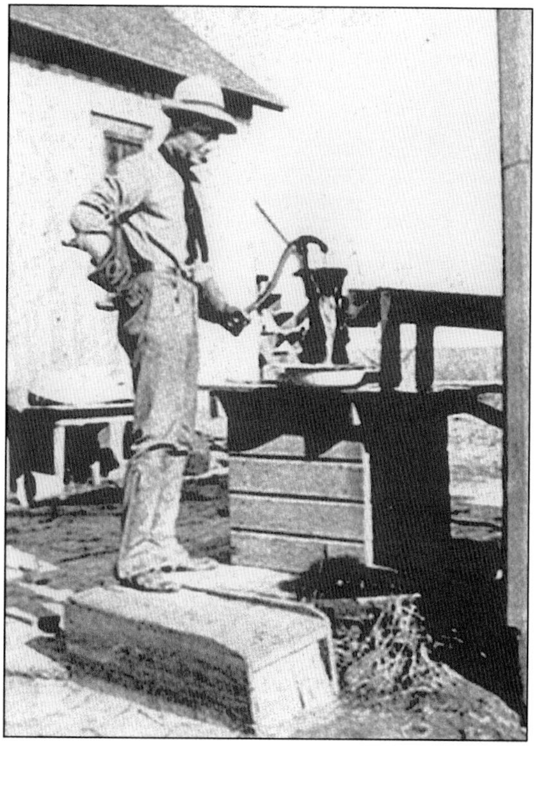

Easy Water. One of the blessings of Calcasieu Parish was that water was within easy reach of almost every home just by drilling or digging a hole about 15 to 20 feet straight down. In this photo taken around 1915, Charles Davies is shown getting a basin of water from a hand-operated pitcher pump. (Courtesy of Helen Kendall Collection.)

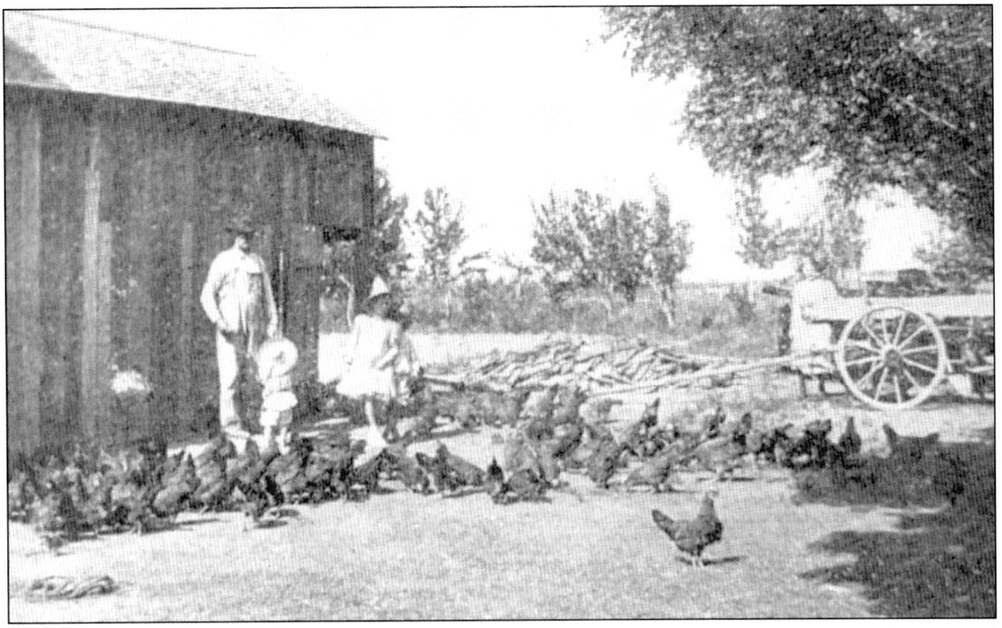

Barnyard Gold. Chickens were as good as gold to every old-time Calcasieu Parish farmer and his family because they provided eggs and meat, which could be either consumed or traded. Chickens could also be raised easily with corn and other grains produced on the farm. (Courtesy of McNeese Archives.)

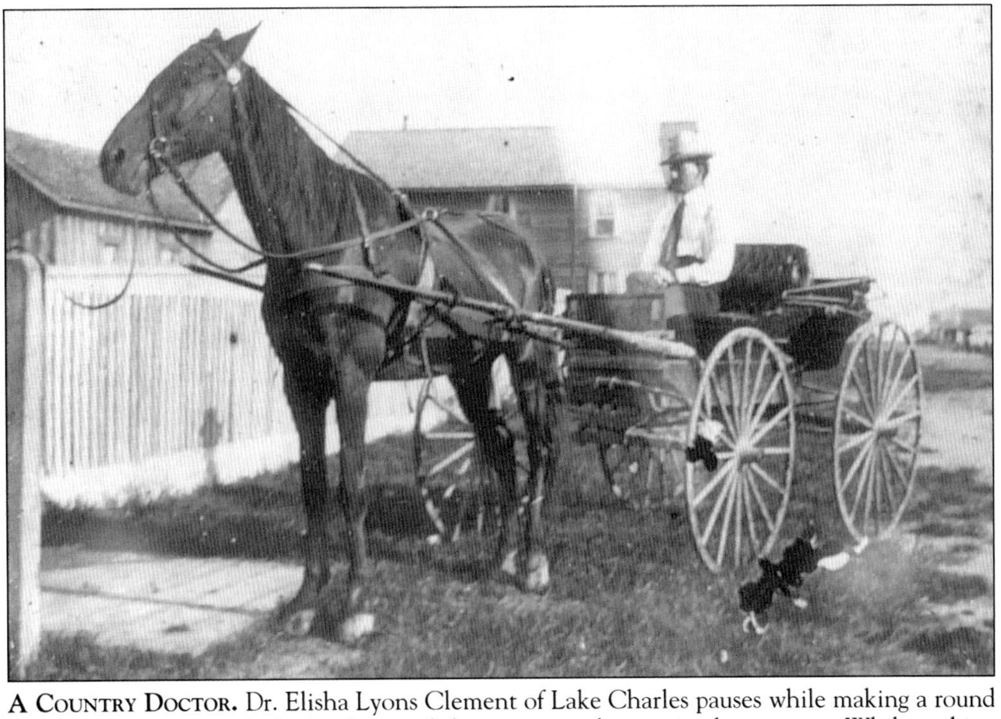

A Country Doctor. Dr. Elisha Lyons Clement of Lake Charles pauses while making a round of house calls, some of which often took him many miles out in the country. While making country calls during hunting season, Dr. Clement took along his dog and gun just in case he spotted some worthy game. (Courtesy of Imperial Calcasieu Museum.)

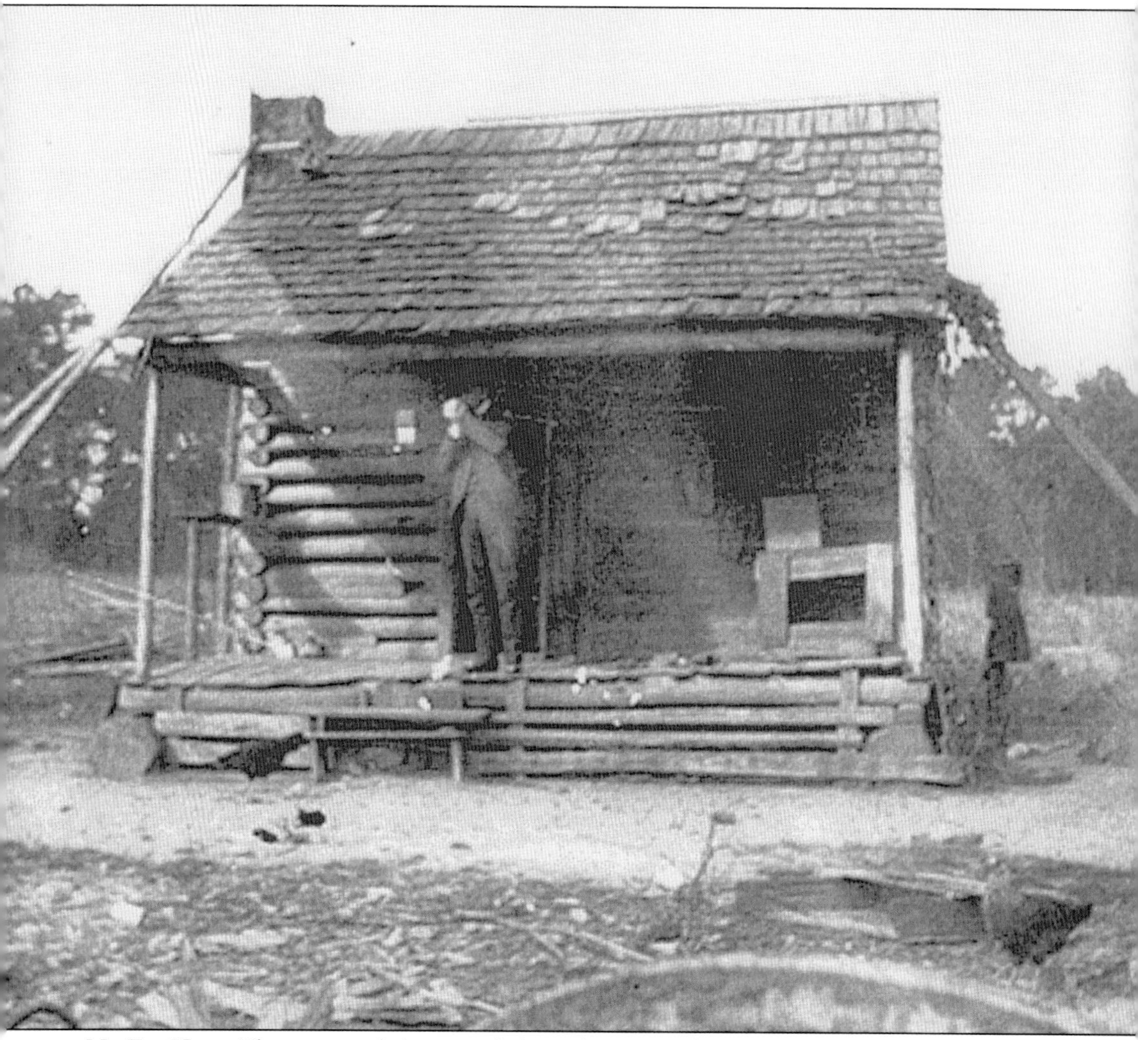

NO FEE HERE. The unnamed physician lighting his pipe as he emerges from this log cabin in the Niblett's Bluff area in 1902 probably had little hope of collecting his fee, unless he could catch one of the chickens seen in the lower right corner of this photograph. (Courtesy of Imperial Calcasieu Museum.)

Three

Town Life

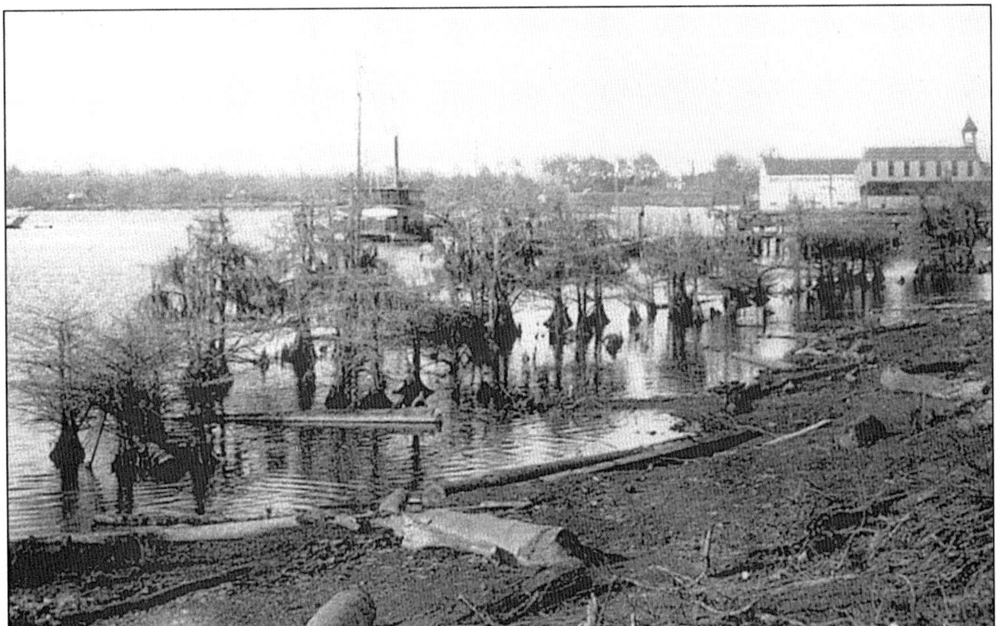

A Town Is Born. One of the strongest points in favor of establishing a town on the east side of Lake Charles, which was named after Charles Sallier, was the site's link by water with points up and down the Calcasieu River and the river's connection with the Gulf of Mexico. This 1893 photograph of the east shoreline of Lake Charles depicts what the shoreline looked like to the town's earliest residents. The tall object is the stack of the ferry *Hazel*, which is docked at its Pujo Street landing. (Courtesy of Imperial Calcasieu Museum.)

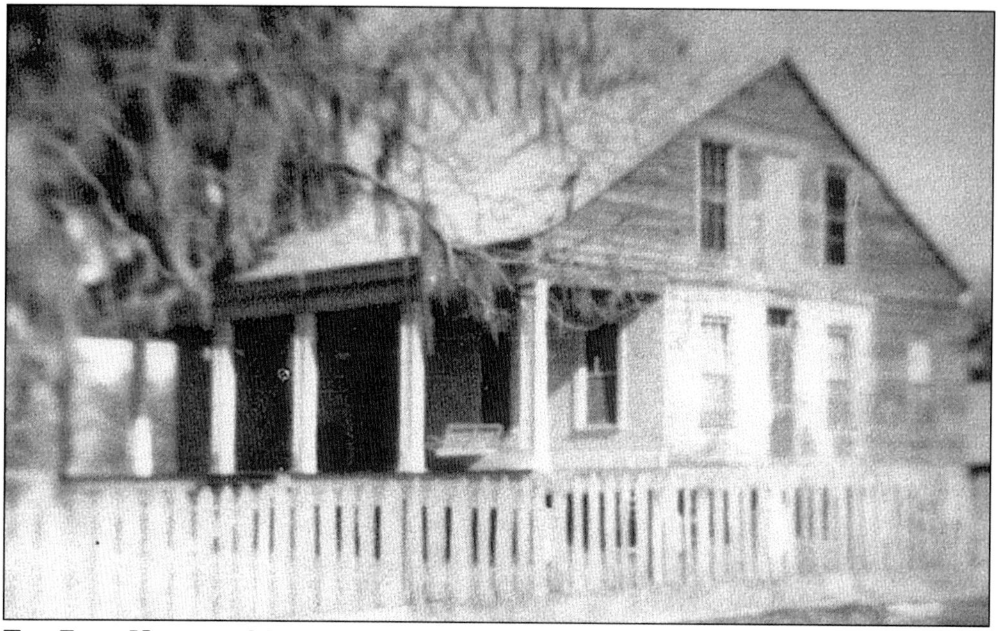

The First House in Mermentau. Jean Castex founded the village of Mermentau when he built this house and a trading post on the western bank of the Mermentau River in the mid-1800s. Later, he built a larger house and a store across the river where the town is located today. The Mermentau River was the eastern boundary of Calcasieu Parish before the subdivision that took effect January 1, 1913. Castex died on August 13, 1900. (Courtesy of Lynn and Eva Bourdier.)

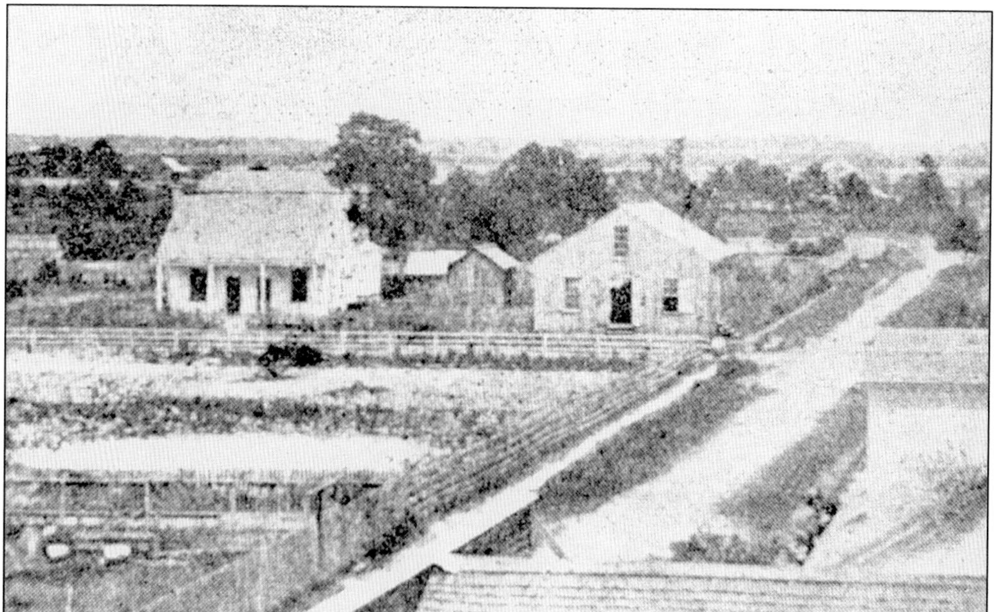

A Sparsely Settled Place. Only a few houses had been built directly east of "downtown" Lake Charles when this photo was taken in the 1870s. The lane leading off to the right would eventually become Pujo Street. In less than 20 years, the area covered by this photo would be filled with streets, houses, trees, and a few businesses. (Courtesy of McNeese Archives.)

LOOKING SOUTHEAST. By 1882, the town of Lake Charles had begun to sprawl from its central hub on the eastern shore of the lake. This photo was taken from the old city hall tower, looking toward the southeast. In the early days, every private dwelling was built of wood, the resource that propelled the town's economy. (Courtesy of McNeese Archives.)

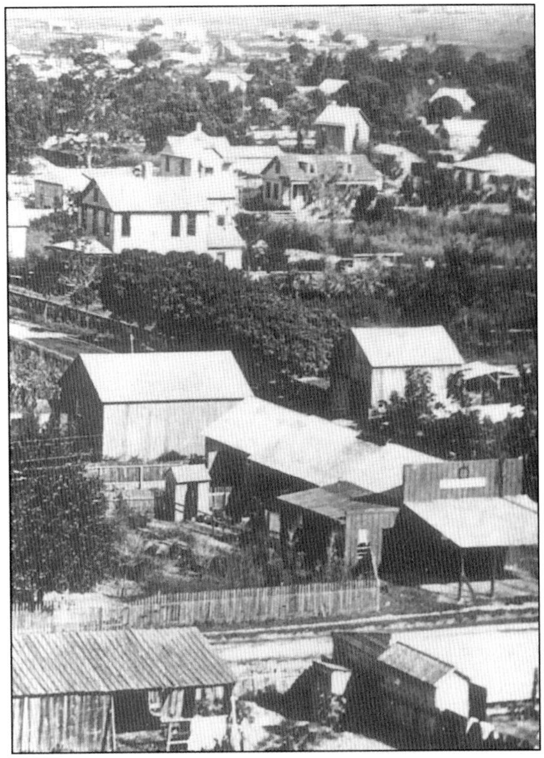

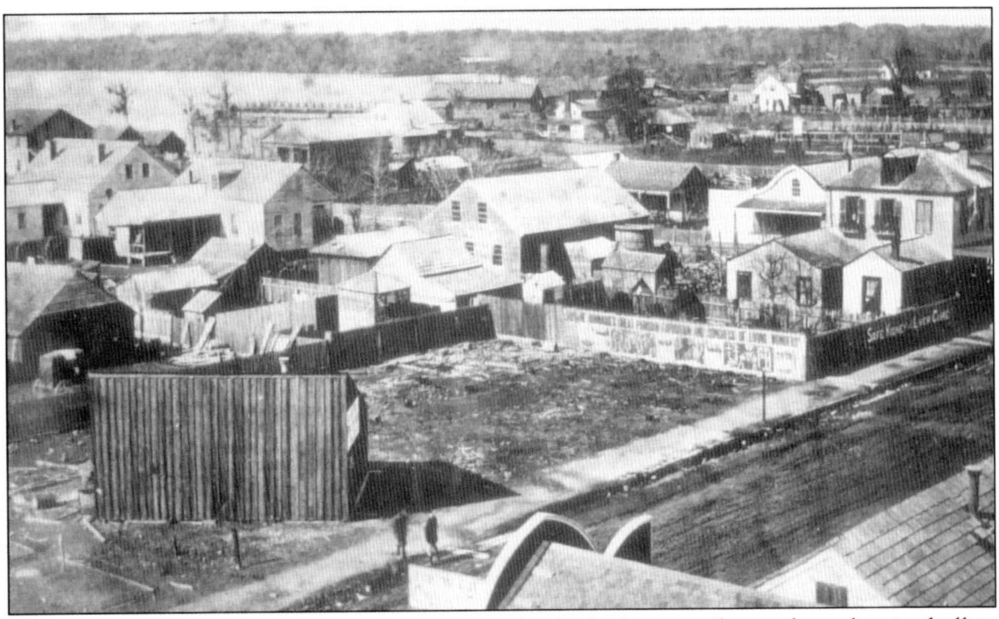

LOOKING NORTHWEST. An aerial view of Lake Charles looking northwest from the city hall in 1882 shows wooden frame stores, hotels, and residences, as well as the northeast corner of the lake. The oddly placed building in the left foreground was a photographer's studio, which was built to direct steady northwestern light through a skylight for good photographic lighting. The writing on the fence in the right foreground advertised a traveling show that was coming to town. (Courtesy of McNeese Archives.)

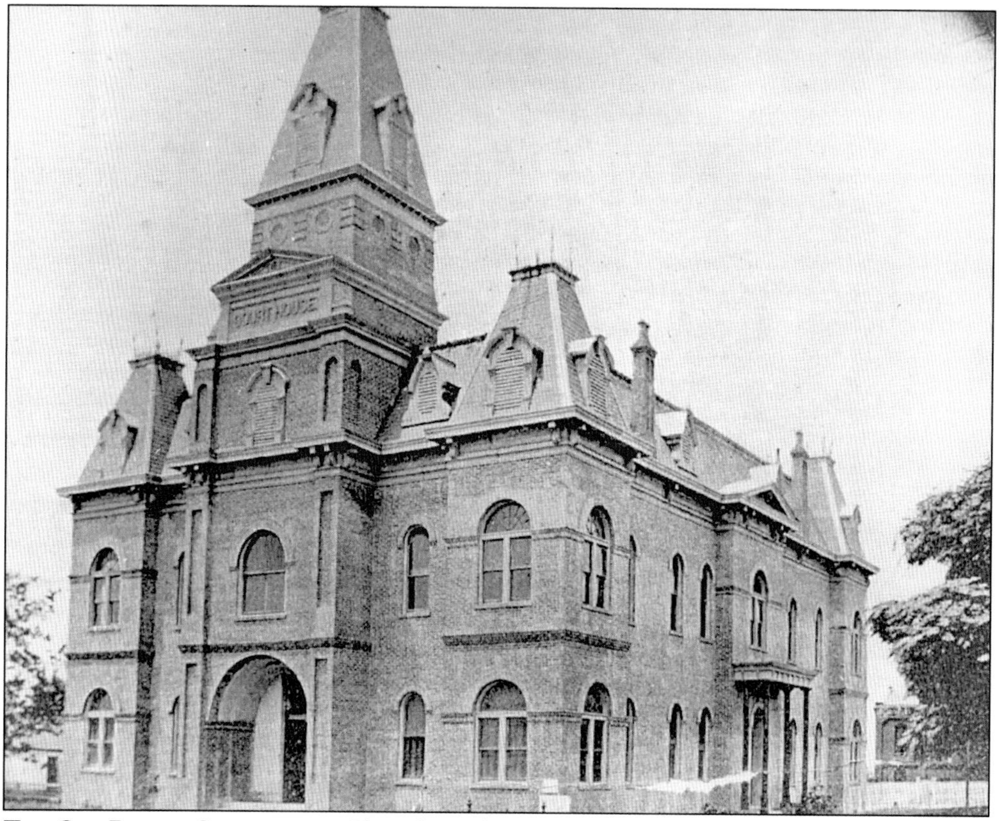

The Old Parish Courthouse. This photo shows the Calcasieu Parish Courthouse that was built in 1890, before it was enlarged and given a new front in 1902. South Court Street ran down to the lake on the left side of this building, and North Court ran down to the lake on the right. Along each of these streets were located prominent hotels and large residences. Some of these buildings and this courthouse were destroyed in the great Lake Charles fire of 1910.

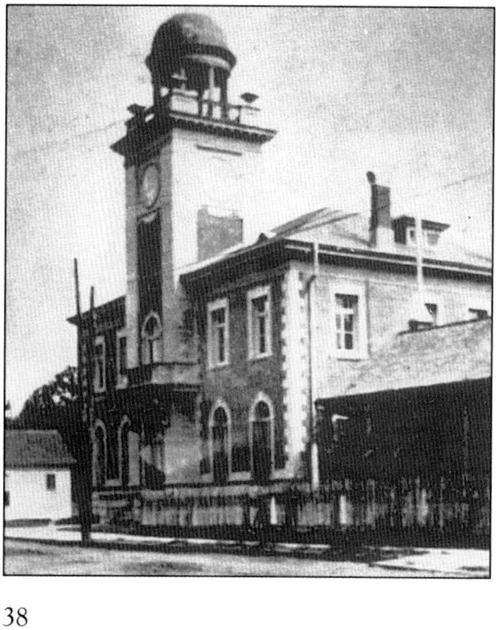

The Old Lake Charles City Hall. This is the old Lake Charles City Hall as it appeared in 1882. It was located across Ryan Street from the parish courthouse before being destroyed, along with 100 other buildings, by the great fire of 1910. Many old aerial photos of Lake Charles were taken from the tower of this building. (Courtesy of McNeese Archives.)

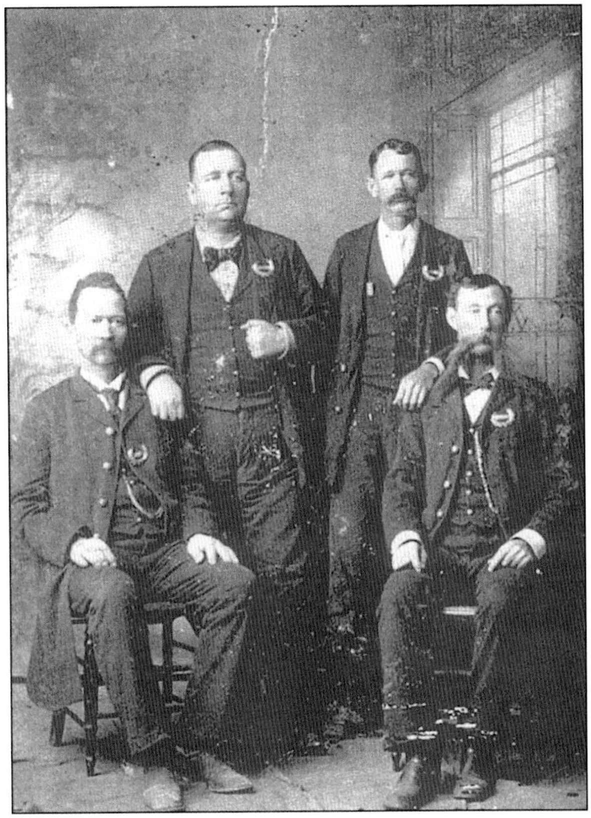

The Early 1900s Police Force. In the early 1900s the four stalwart members of the Lake Charles police force sat for this group photo. They are as follows, from left to right: (seated) Jeff Lyons and Henry Roy; (standing) Shellby Gauthier and Jake Rigmaiden. At that time, Lake Charles was a rowdy place on weekends when its many saloons on Ryan Street and Railroad Avenue ("Battle Row") produced fights, shootings, and other disturbances. (Courtesy of McNeese Archives.)

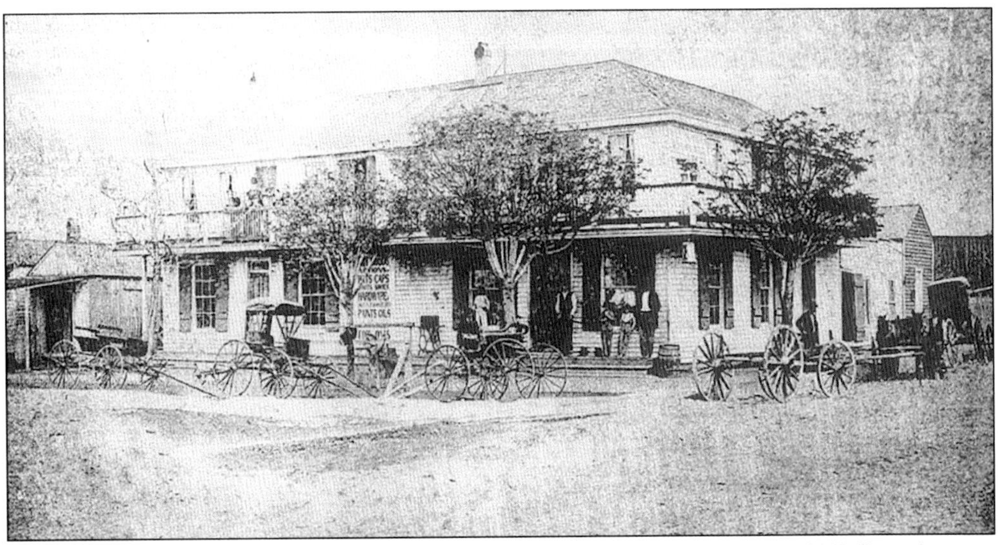

Bryan's Store. A popular Lake Charles place to shop during the 1880s was J.W. Bryan's store. This store sold a wide variety of household goods, plus items as large as wagons and buggies, and was located across from the courthouse on the corner of North Court and Ryan Streets. During the 1870s, when Bryan's and a few other stores were the only ones in town, the only large stores in the area were located in Galveston, TX. (Courtesy of Imperial Calcasieu Museum.)

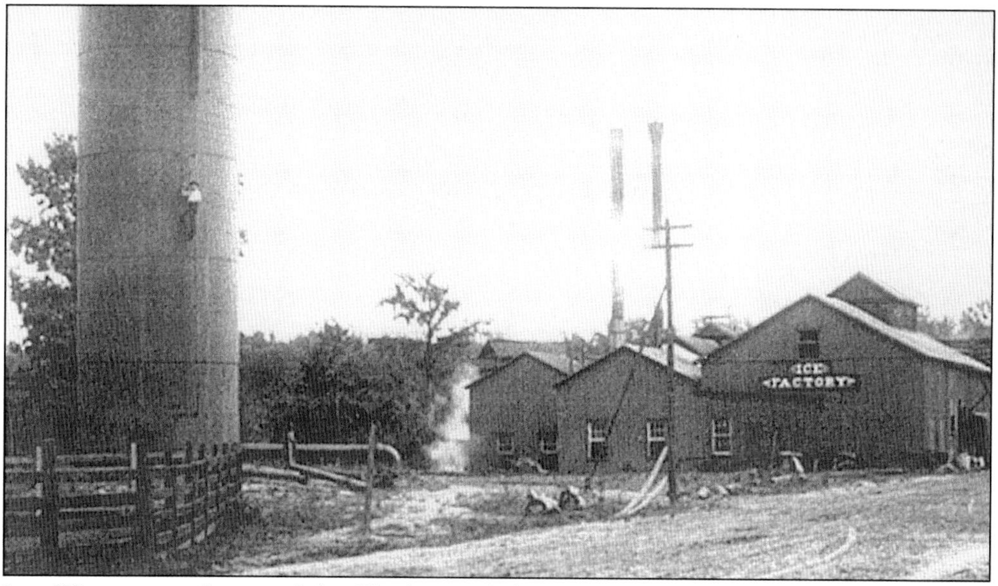

ICE, WATER, AND LIGHTS. Lake Charles needed ice in the 1880s, so J.A. Landry founded a company to fill this need. Then Landry's company added electricity, water, gas, and trolley service during a period of about ten years. The name of the company was changed to reflect the service provided, but it was commonly known as the Lake Charles Ice, Lights and Water Company. This 1893 photo shows the firm's North Ryan Street water tower, ice factory, and electric power plant represented by the twin smoke stacks in the background. (Courtesy of Imperial Calcasieu Museum.)

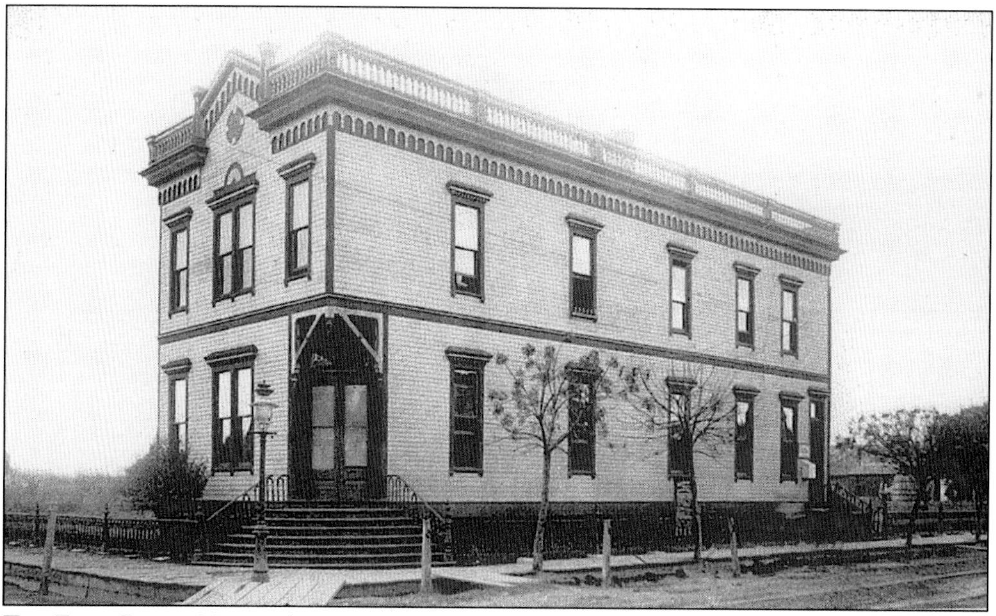

THE FIRST BANK. J.B. Watkins, the land owner and developer of thousands of acres and the builder of the first railroad leading northward out of Lake Charles, built the parish's first bank in 1884. It was located on what is now the southwest corner of Broad and Hodges Streets. It was built in what was called the Norwegian-style architecture and decorated with the best available furnishings at that time. (Courtesy of McNeese Archives.)

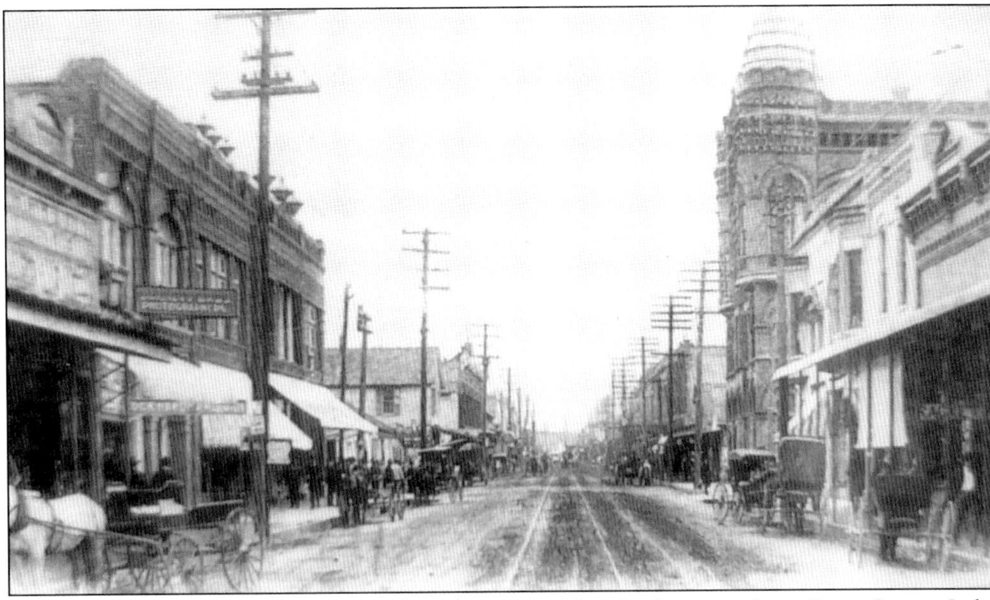

Dirt Main Street. By 1903, when this photo was taken looking north on Ryan Street, Lake Charles had a mule-powered trolley, electric power lines to all of its offices and businesses, and an imposing brick structure housing the Calcasieu Bank on the east side of the street—but no paving. The paving of downtown Ryan Street was completed in 1907. (Courtesy of McNeese Archives.)

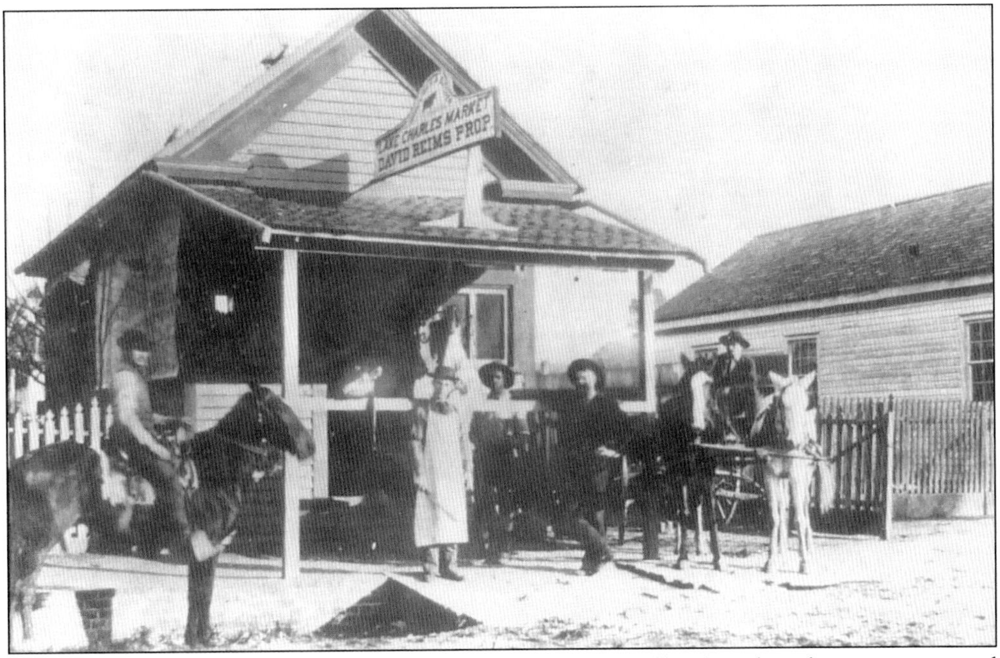

Reims' Meat Market. In the 1880s, David Reims and some of his friends and customers paused for a photograph taken in front of his shop in downtown Lake Charles. Reims learned the butcher's trade in New Orleans and opened his Lake Charles shop in 1881. In addition to fresh meat and sausage, he sold fresh vegetables and fruit which were shipped in daily by railroad from New Orleans. (Courtesy of McNeese Archives.)

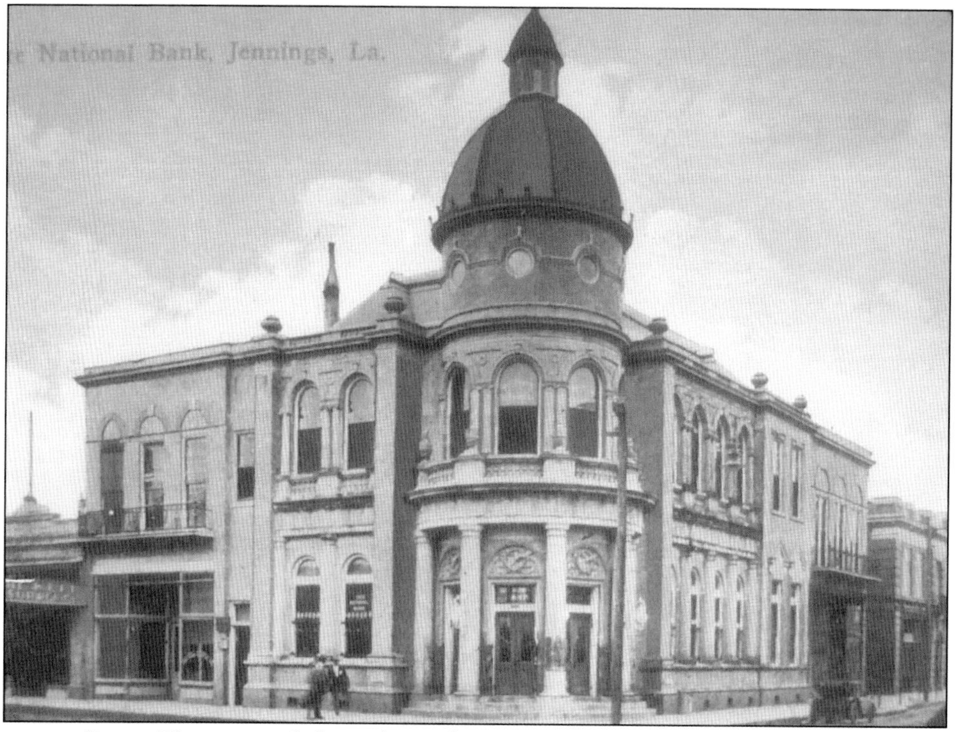

JENNINGS BANK. This postcard photo shows the impressive front of the State National Bank of Jennings. S.L. Cary, who is called the "father of Jennings," said Jennings only had two families, a store, and a railroad depot when he arrived there from Iowa in 1883. His promotion of growing rice by the methods suggested by Prof. S.A. Knapp made banks like this one both necessary and profitable. (Courtesy of Imperial Calcasieu Museum.)

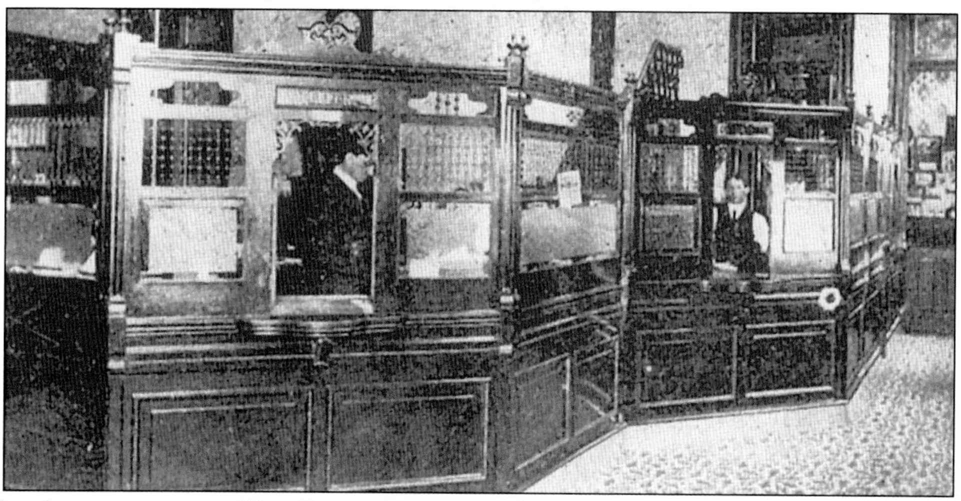

THE INTERIOR OF THE NEW BANK. Assistant cashiers W.H. Simmons (in the foreground) and Louis Prager readied their tellers' cages for business in 1902 when this photo was taken in the new building of First National Bank of Lake Charles. The bank was founded in 1889 and operated in a smaller building until this structure was completed. It was often called "the stone bank" because of the huge imported stones used in its construction. (Courtesy of McNeese Archives.)

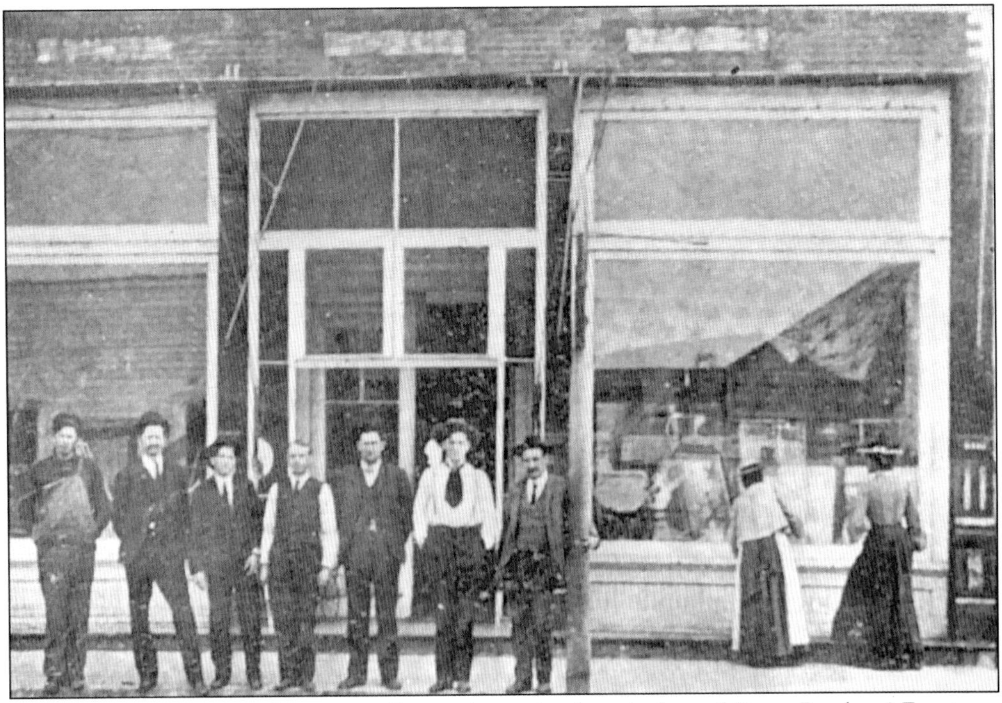

LOAFING AND WINDOW SHOPPING. Pretty things in the window of Scott Brothers' Furniture Store attracted some ladies in 1902, while some gentlemen enjoyed visiting on the sidewalk with their friends. Other stores that could be visited at this time included Mrs. Oppenheimer's Cut-Rate Store, which was popular with rural folk; Harry Miller's Grocery; and the J.S. Smith Music Store, which carried the latest Edison cylinder phonographs. (Courtesy of McNeese Archives.)

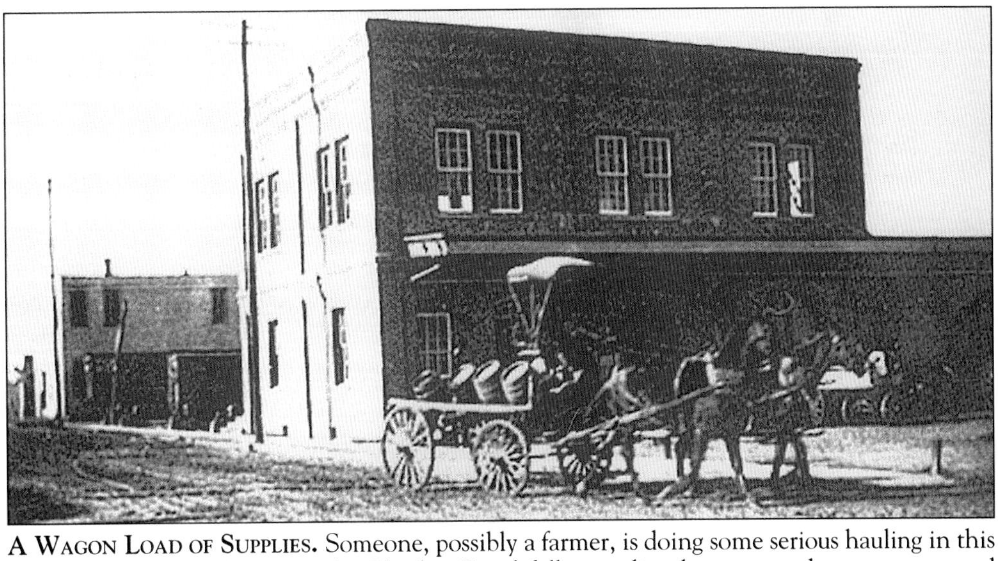

A WAGON LOAD OF SUPPLIES. Someone, possibly a farmer, is doing some serious hauling in this early 1900s photo taken in Lake Charles. Rural folk traveling by team and wagon measured in hours and sometimes days the time required to make a trip to town and back. This meant that all of the goods that would be needed for a very long time had to be carried in one load. (Courtesy of Helen Kendall Collection.)

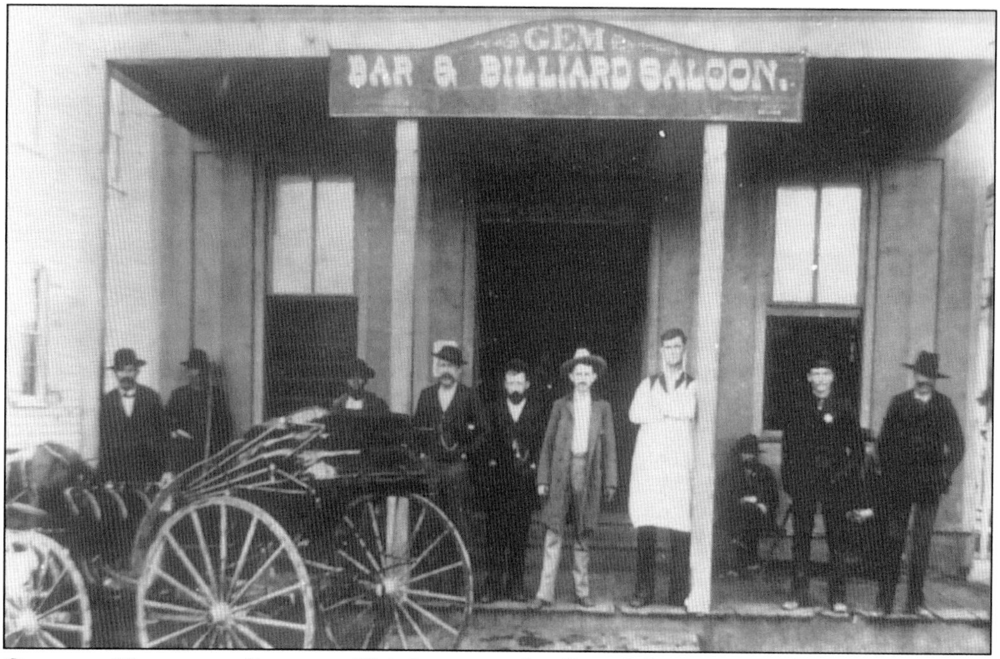

One of a Number of Saloons. This lineup at the Gem Saloon is typical of the lineup one would expect to find in a saloon in a frontier town like Lake Charles. In 1900, around the time this photo was taken, a huge mob from many saloons gathered in front of the old courthouse and then attacked the door of the parish jail with a battering ram, trying to get at a prisoner. When shots were fired and a deputy sheriff was killed, the mob sobered up and went home. (Courtesy of McNeese Archives.)

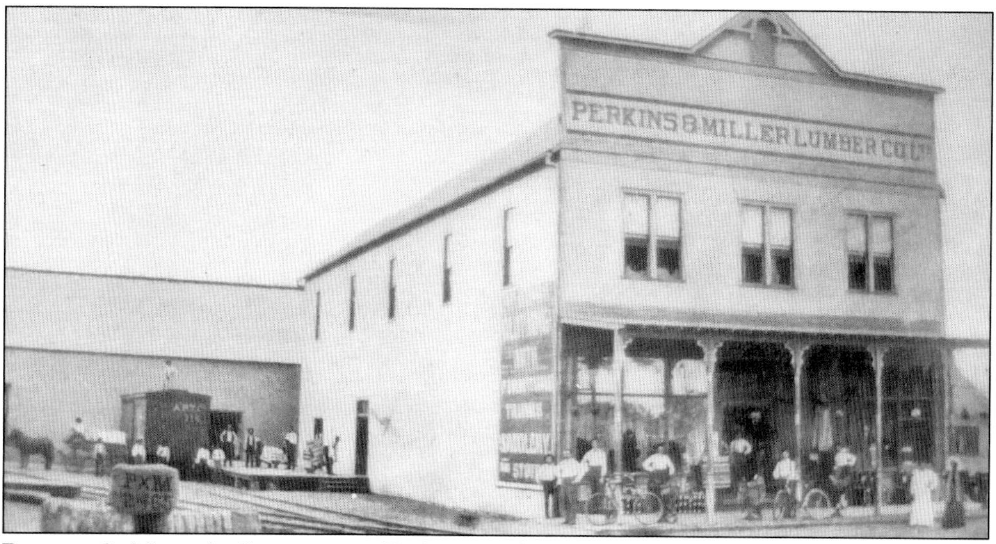

Perkins & Miller's Commissary. To keep workers from taking time off to go to town for supplies, sawmill owners set up commissary stores near their mills such as the one pictured here in 1905 in Westlake. These stores carried all of the employees' basic shopping needs and took special orders to be filled in larger towns. Customers had to ask clerks for goods in most commissary stores because they were kept behind long counters. Commissary stores made credit available to all employees. (Courtesy of McNeese Archives.)

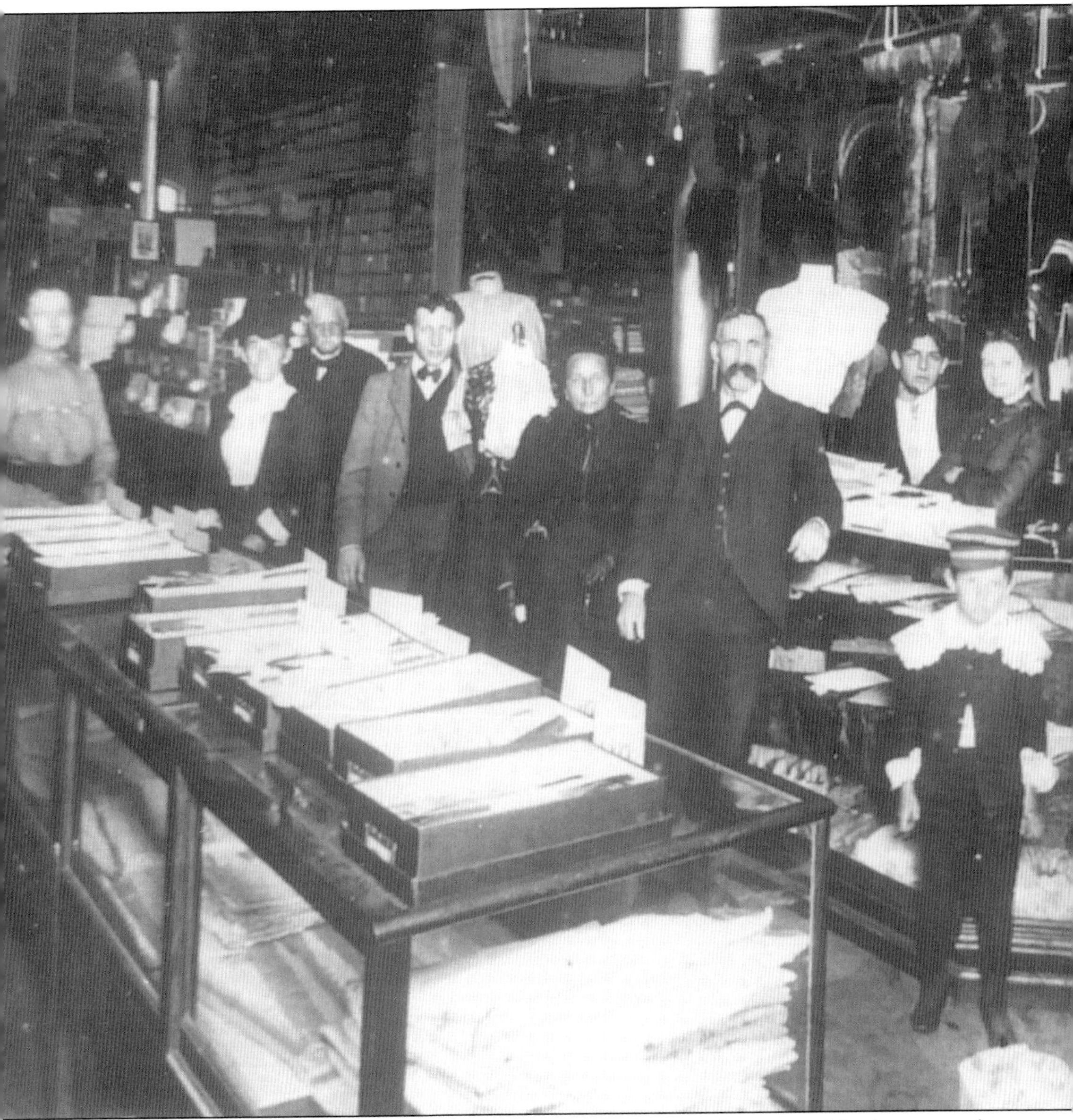

INSIDE KAUFMAN'S STORE. Leopold Kaufman, store owner, is the man with the mustache in this early 1900s scene inside his general merchandise store in downtown Lake Charles. Kaufman arrived in Calcasieu Parish by buggy in September 1879 and opened this store shortly thereafter. In the years before banks, his store carried on banking operations. He was one of the organizers of Temple Sinai and was known for his non-sectarian charities. He was also one of the organizers of the First National Bank, which opened in 1889. In 1901, Kaufman sold this store and devoted his energy to real estate development. At the time of his death at age 85 in 1937, he owned a number of Ryan Street properties, including the Kaufman Building. (Courtesy of McNeese Archives.)

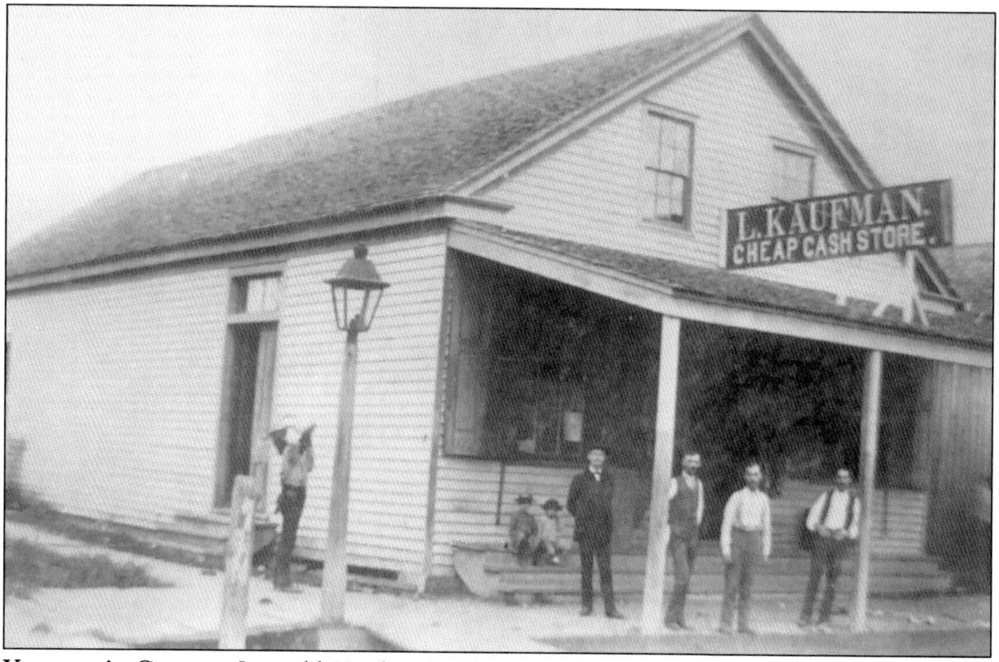

KAUFMAN'S CORNER. Leopold Kaufman's Cheap Cash Store was located on the southeast corner of Ryan and Broad Streets in early Lake Charles. The men in this 1882 photo are, from left to right, George Wells, Will Gayle, John Blancas, and Leopold Kaufman. Some of the niceties provided for shoppers shown in this photo include the kerosene street light on the pole, the wooden bridges across the streets' open ditches, the roof over the wooden sidewalk, and the steps across the front of Kaufman's store where tired people could rest. (Courtesy of McNeese Archives.)

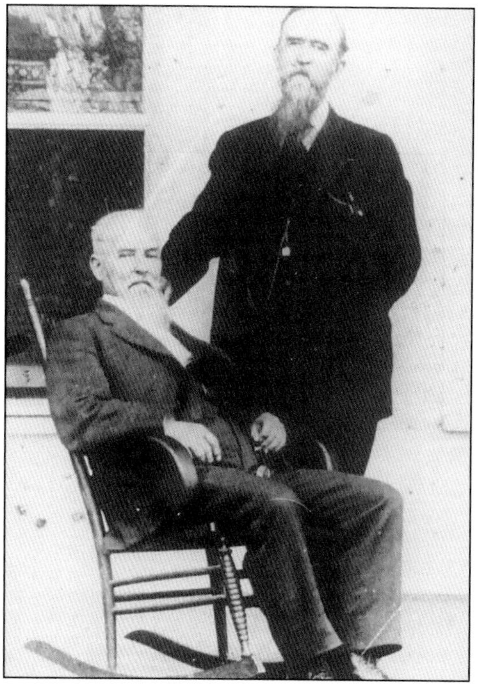

TWO EARLY PHYSICIANS. Dr. Erastus Lyons (seated) and Dr. C.L. Richardson were two of the many respected physicians who treated patients from their Lake Charles offices. This photo was taken in 1889. Other early area doctors included Dr. T.H. Watkins and Dr. Abram H. Moss, also of Lake Charles; and Dr. Frederick Erbelding of Cameron. (Courtesy of Imperial Calcasieu Museum.)

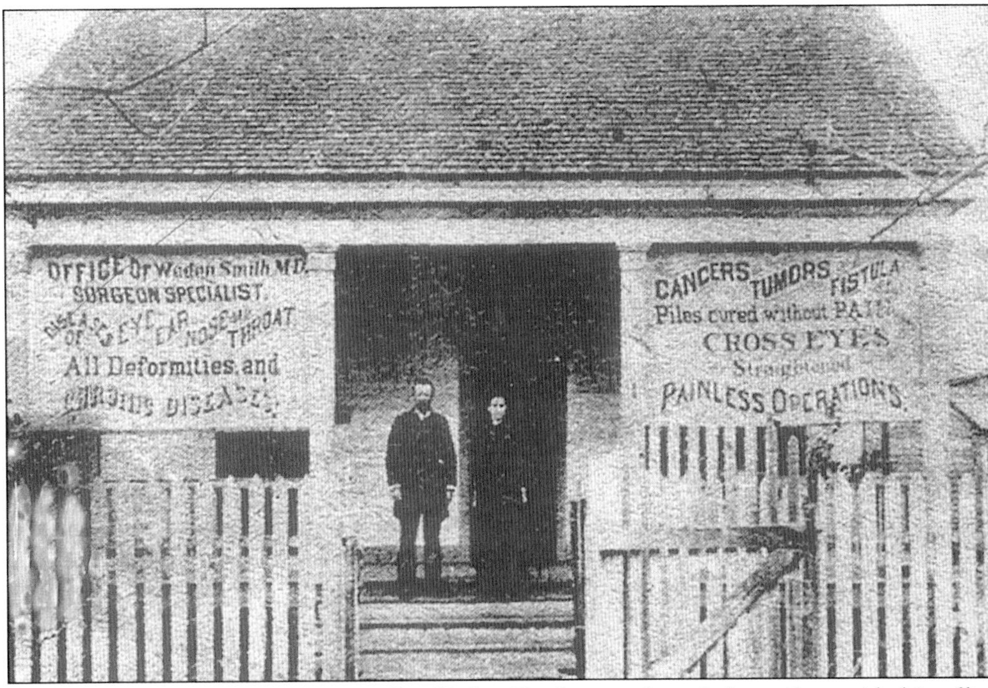

MIRACLE DOCTOR. Dr. Weden Smith of Lake Charles stands with his wife outside his office in this 1880s photo. His sign proclaims him to be a "Surgeon Specialist [who treats] Diseases of eye, ear, nose and throat, all deformities and chronic diseases, cancers, tumors, fisula [sic]. Piles cured without pain. Cross eyes straightened. Painless Operations." (Courtesy of Imperial Calcasieu Museum.)

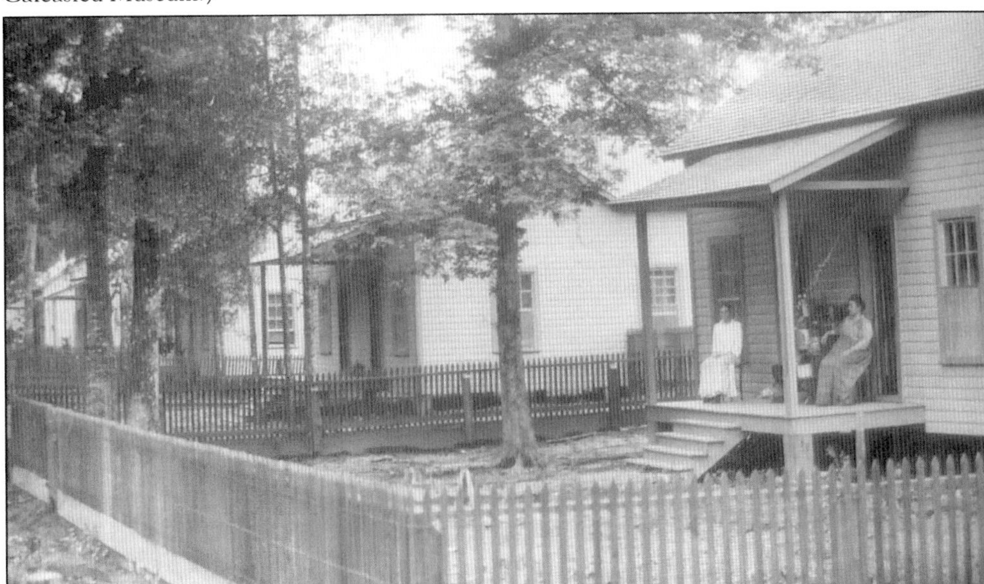

COMPANY HOUSING. Seen in this early 1900s photograph, company housing at Sulphur Mines included long, neat lines of frame cottages with picket fences. Some of the other company towns in Imperial Calcasieu were Elizabeth, Oakdale, Longville, Merryville, Bon Ami, Ragley, and DeQuincy. (Courtesy of Imperial Calcasieu Museum.)

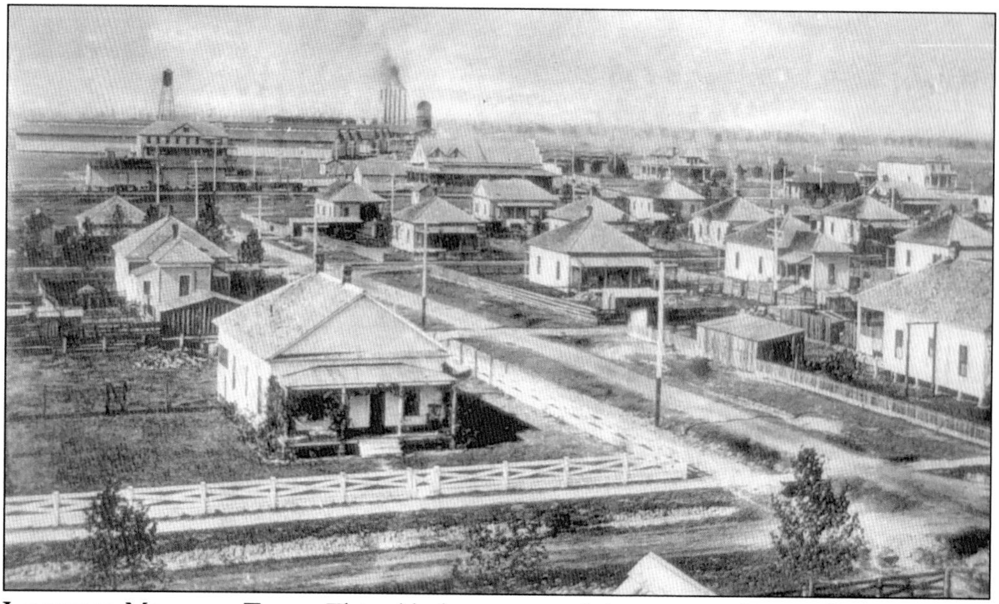

LONGVILLE MILL AND TOWN. This old photo postcard shows part of Longville built by the Long-Bel Lumber Company, as it looked at its peak around the year 1918, when it had about 3,000 residents. In the distance on the left are the buildings housing the company headquarters and commissary. The huge mill is in the distant background. The town was built during the years 1906–1907. The mill was destroyed by fire in 1921, but the company continued partial operations with a hardwood flooring mill until 1929. (Courtesy of McNeese Archives.)

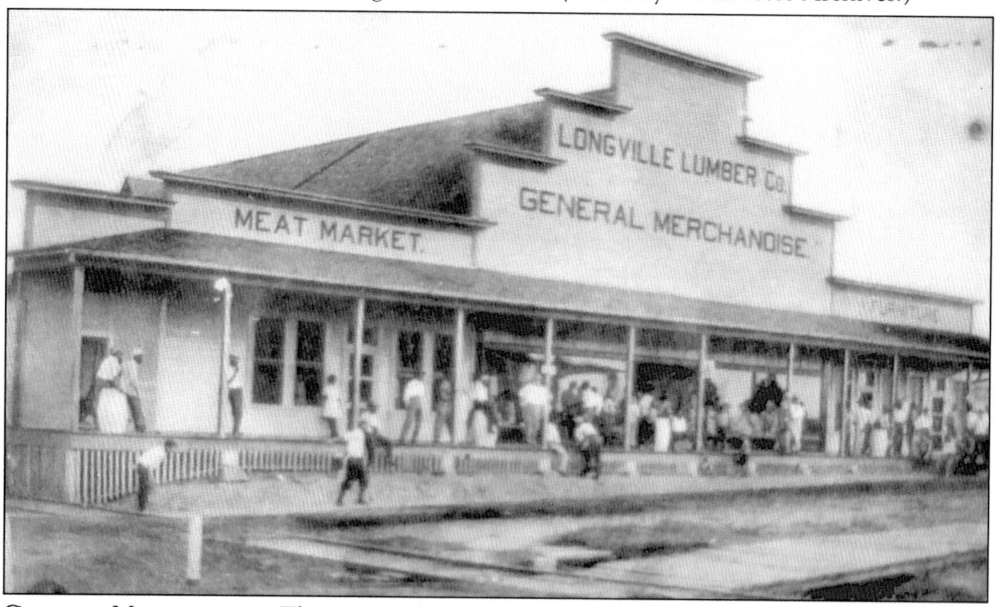

GENERAL MERCHANDISE. The Longville General Merchandise Store, or commissary, was the old-time equivalent of a modern super-store. This store carried everything from meats to furniture and served as a gathering place for employees and their families after work and on weekends. When the timber ran out in the 1920s, stores like this one and towns like Longville withered away into tiny villages or disappeared completely. (Courtesy of Imperial Calcasieu Museum.)

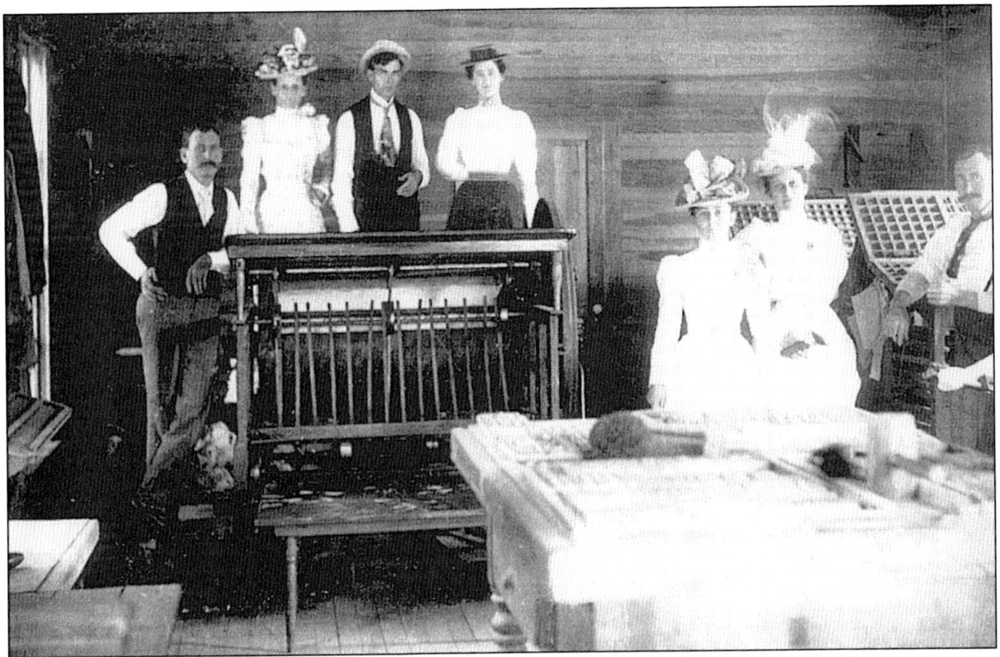

THE *LAKE CHARLES PRESS*. Progressive towns have always found newspapers to be essential in their growth. In this 1900 photo, the editor of the *Lake Charles Press*, members of his staff, and their wives are shown in the newspaper's office. William Sterling, the editor, is on the far right. (Courtesy of McNeese Archives.)

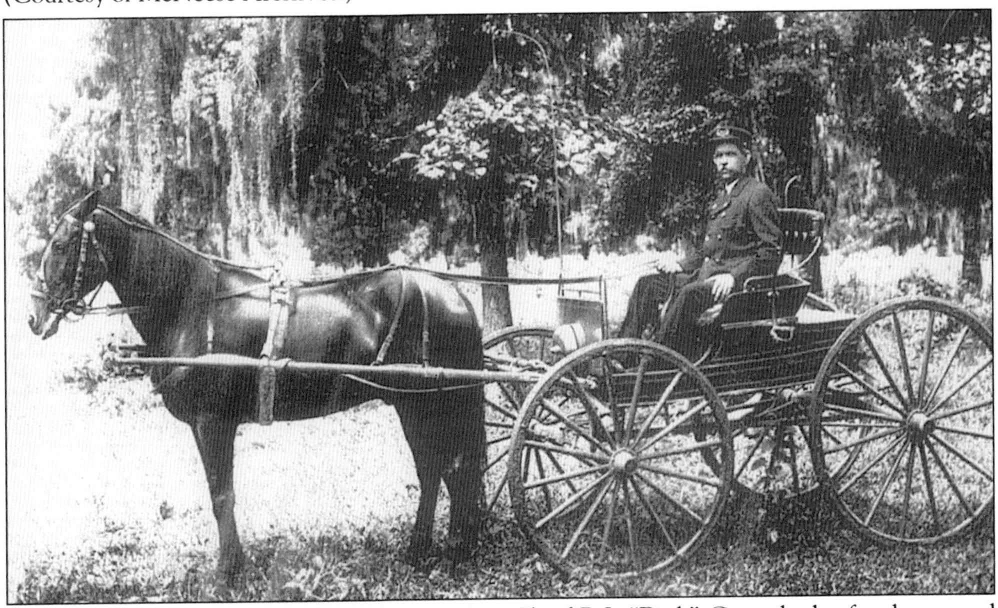

THE FIRE CHIEF AND BELL. Lake Charles Fire Chief R.J. "Dick" Gunn had a fast horse and a sturdy rig so that he could arrive at fires before the firemen whose efforts he would have to direct. Gunn served as fire chief from 1890 to 1908 and from 1910 to his death in 1914. Note the alarm bell mounted on the dashboard of the chief's buggy. In 1906 Gunn exchanged his horse and buggy for a motorized rig. He was not chief during the big fire of 1910. (Courtesy of McNeese Archives.)

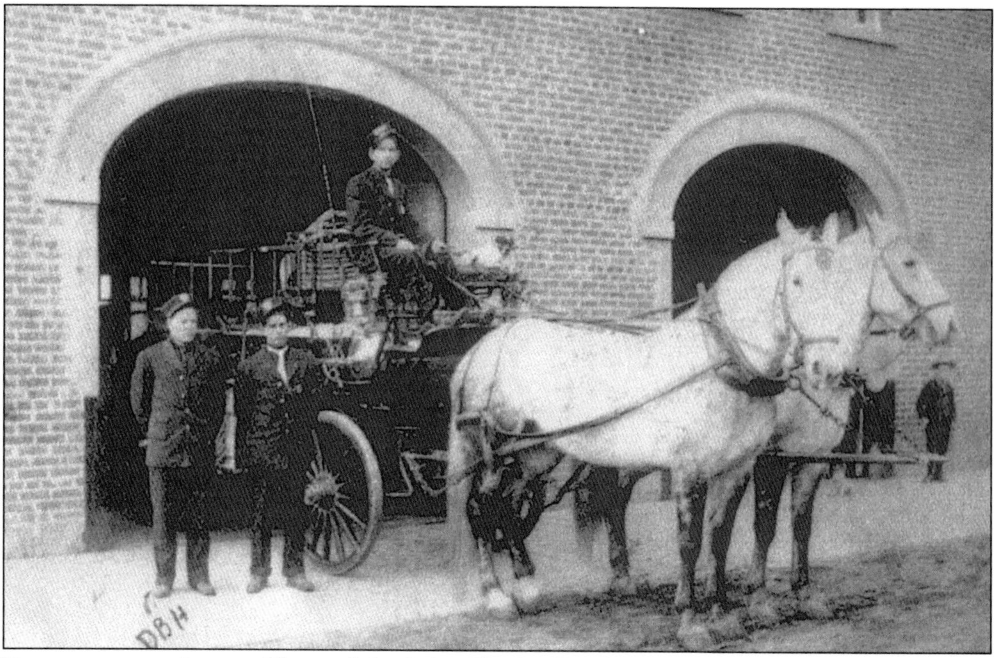

READY FOR THE ALARM. Three of the Lake Charles Fire Department's six paid firefighters are shown with their magnificent horses in this photo, taken around 1905 at Fire Station No. 1. The station, located on the corner of Cole and Iris Streets, was destroyed in the great fire of 1910. After that fire, the city purchased a horse-drawn steam pumper, which was replaced by motorized fire trucks in 1913. (Courtesy of McNeese Archives.)

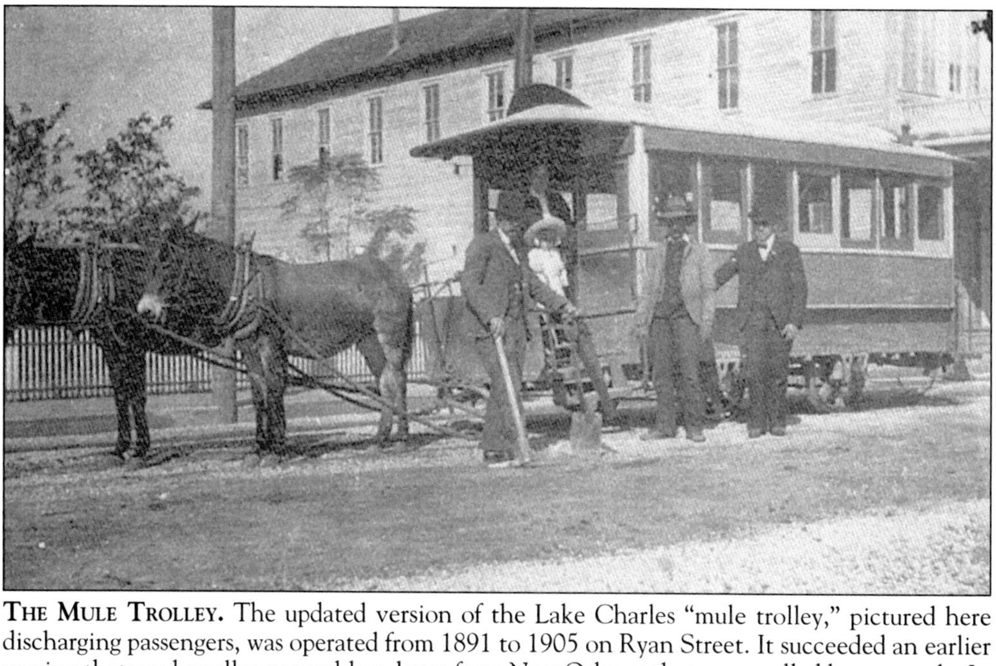

THE MULE TROLLEY. The updated version of the Lake Charles "mule trolley," pictured here discharging passengers, was operated from 1891 to 1905 on Ryan Street. It succeeded an earlier version that used smaller, second-hand cars from New Orleans that were pulled by one mule. In 1905 the mule trolley was replaced by an electric system that was operated on two sets of tracks. (Courtesy of Imperial Calcasieu Museum.)

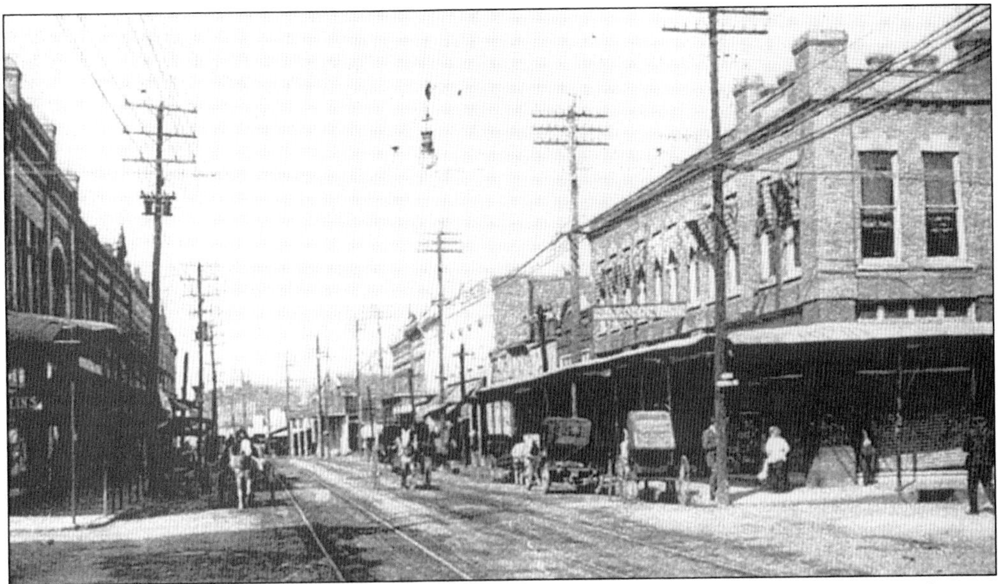

Main Street Improvements. The booming timber, oil, sulphur, and rice industries of Calcasieu Parish helped Lake Charles upgrade its main street as shown in this 1915 photograph. By this time, the improvements included an underground drainage system to replace the open ditches, paving, an electric trolley system, plus electricity, gas, water, and telephones. (Courtesy of Imperial Calcasieu Museum.)

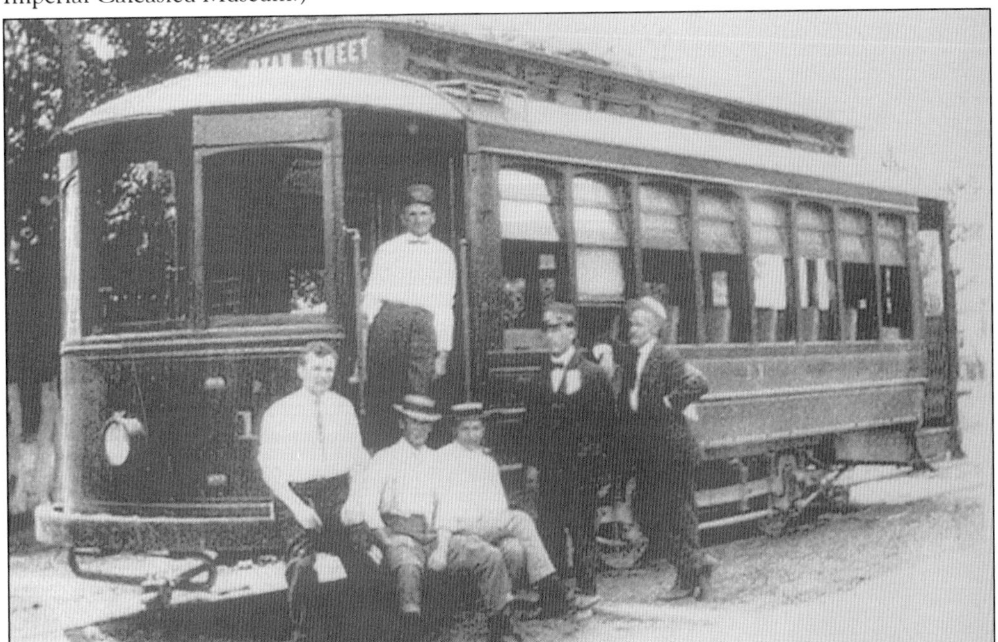

The Electric Trolley Line. An electric trolley system, with cars such as the one shown here, served Lake Charles passengers in various parts of town from 1905 to 1926. Ryan Street had a double set of tracks, but single tracks served Shell Beach Drive, Hodges Street, and Kirkman Street. The electric system was replaced by gasoline-powered buses in 1926. (Courtesy of McNeese Archives.)

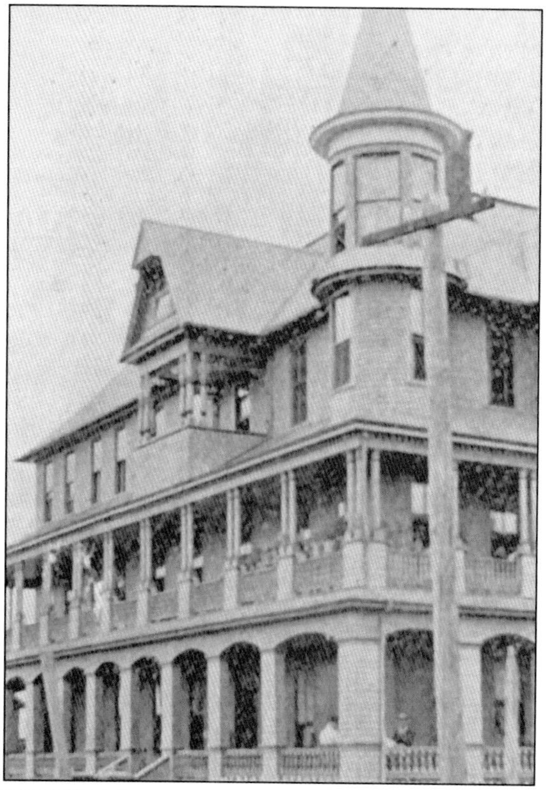

The Enormous Wooden Howard Hotel. The Howard Hotel, or "Howard House" as it was called in its day, was an enormous wooden structure that could accommodate dinner parties, musical or literary programs, and overnight guests all at the same time during the 1890s and early 1900s. The hotel's livery stable could accommodate up to 100 horses. The hotel burned to the ground on October 14, 1903, from a fire that originated in the kitchen. (Courtesy of McNeese Archives.)

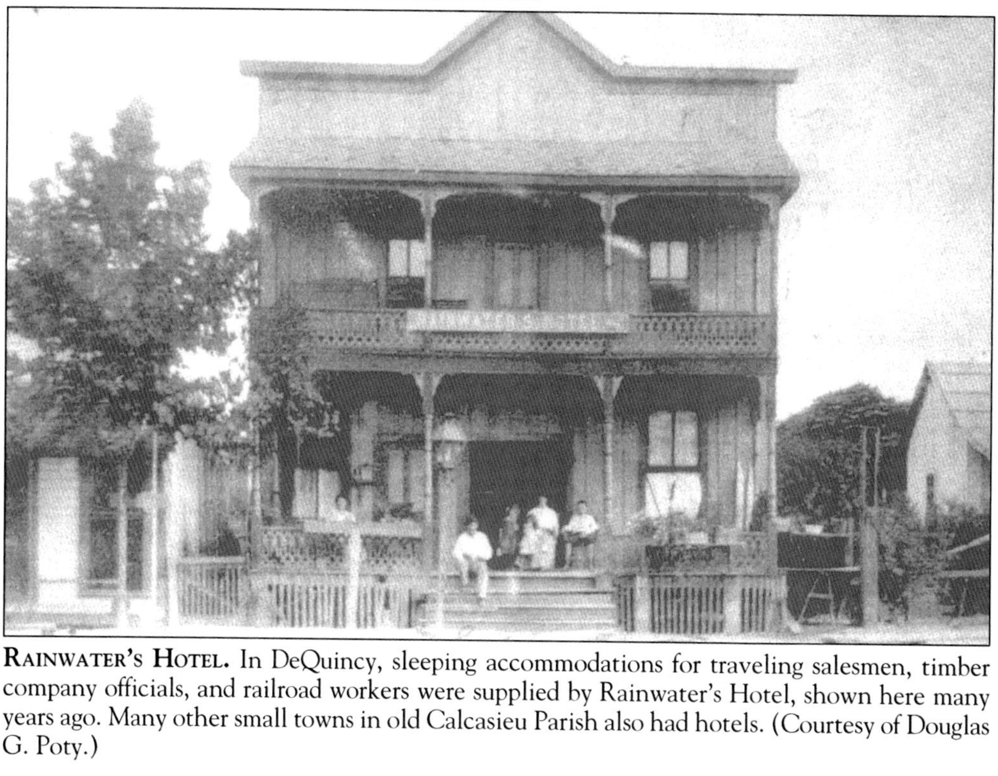

Rainwater's Hotel. In DeQuincy, sleeping accommodations for traveling salesmen, timber company officials, and railroad workers were supplied by Rainwater's Hotel, shown here many years ago. Many other small towns in old Calcasieu Parish also had hotels. (Courtesy of Douglas G. Poty.)

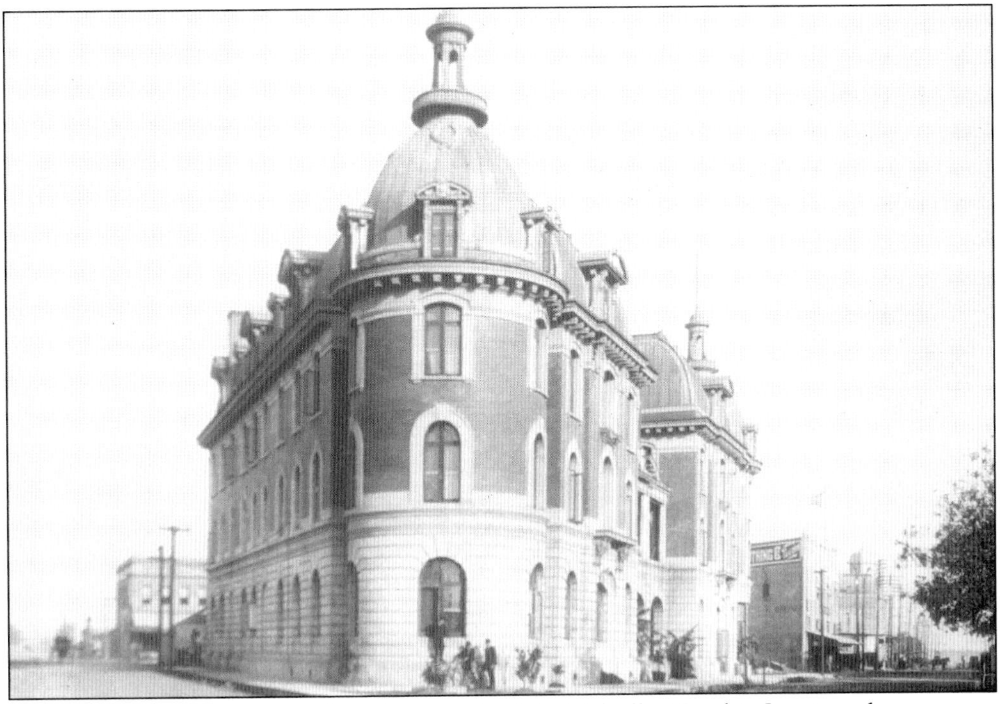

The Mahaffey Hotel. This 1909 photograph of the Mahaffey Hotel in Jennings demonstrates the phenomenal growth of that town in the first 15 years of its existence. S.L. Cary, the town's founder, said Jennings had only two houses when he arrived there in 1883. The rapid expansion was based largely upon the growth of the rice industry and the influx of Midwesterners Cary encouraged to settle in the area. (Courtesy of Imperial Calcasieu Museum.)

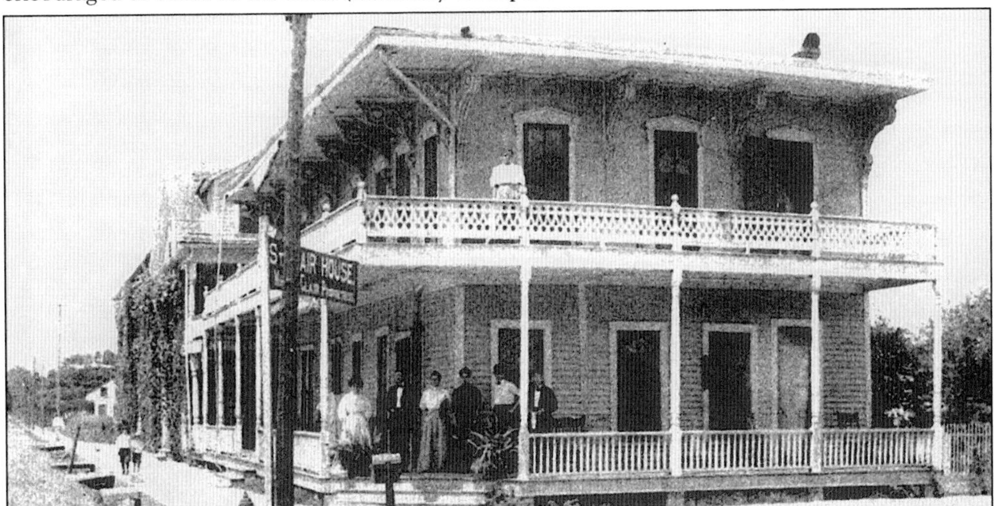

One of Many Boardinghouses. St. Clair House, shown here with its owner and residents assembled on its long galleries, was one of many boardinghouses in Lake Charles during the early 1900s. In those days, boardinghouses served the function presently served by both apartment houses and cafes. Note the elaborate ornamental woodwork that was popular at this time. (Courtesy Imperial Calcasieu Museum.)

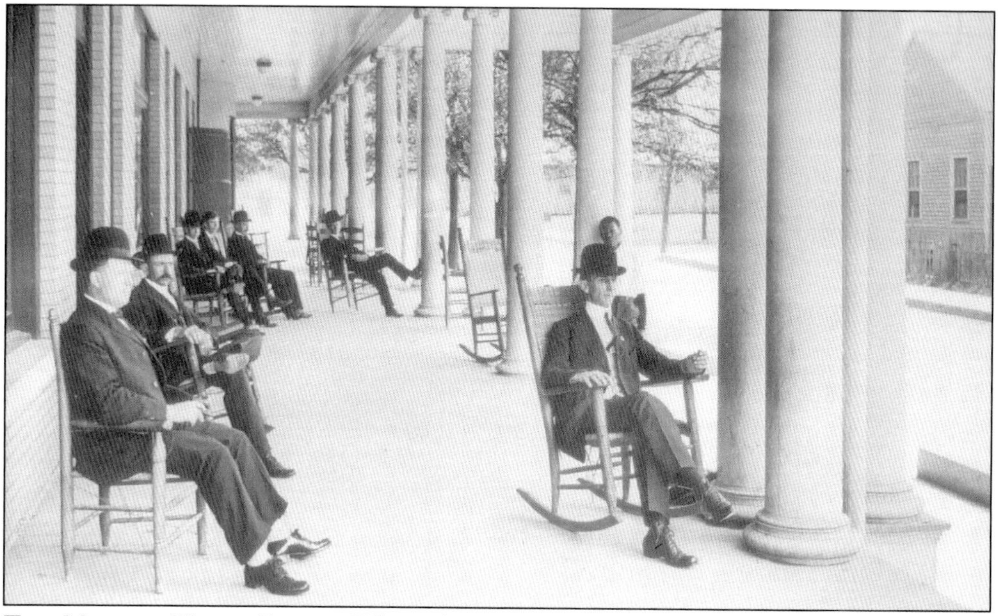

THE MAJESTIC HOTEL PORCH. When the Howard Hotel burned in 1903, Lake Charles businessmen immediately began making plans to replace it with another hotel that would be recognized as one of the finest in the South. The result was the Majestic Hotel, which was completed in 1905. The men in this 1909 photo are enjoying the hotel's long, columned front porch. (Courtesy of Imperial Calcasieu Museum.)

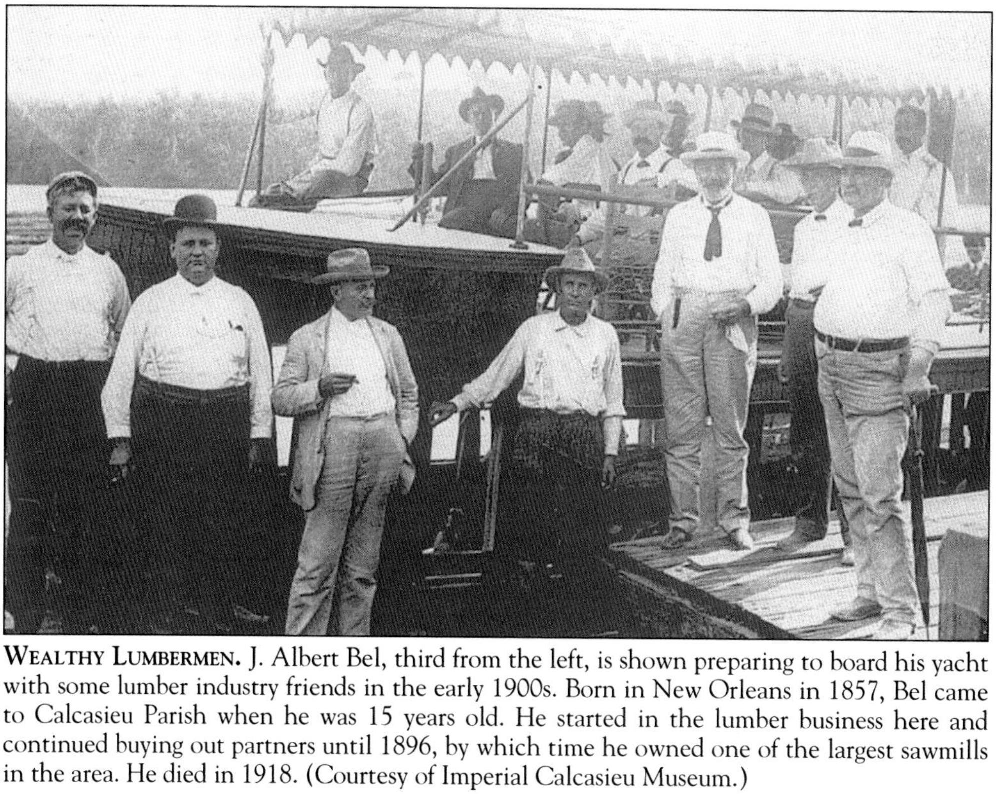

WEALTHY LUMBERMEN. J. Albert Bel, third from the left, is shown preparing to board his yacht with some lumber industry friends in the early 1900s. Born in New Orleans in 1857, Bel came to Calcasieu Parish when he was 15 years old. He started in the lumber business here and continued buying out partners until 1896, by which time he owned one of the largest sawmills in the area. He died in 1918. (Courtesy of Imperial Calcasieu Museum.)

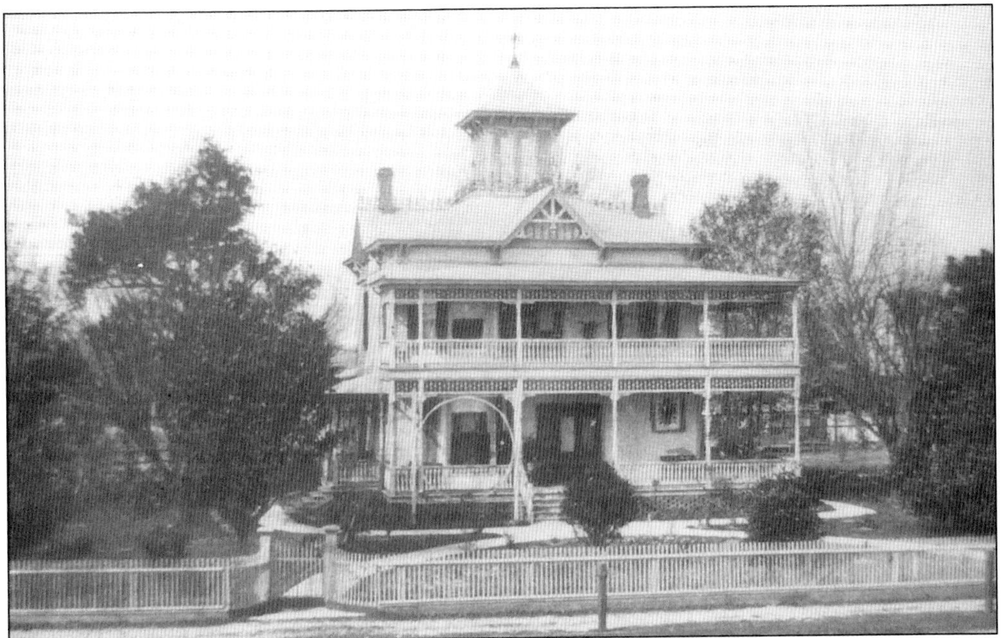

THE J.A. BEL RESIDENCE. This huge residence at 527 Mill Street, shown as it appeared in 1905, was built as the home of lumber industrialist J. Albert Bel. It is one of the larger examples of an architectural style adopted and refined by Bel and other persons who had houses built in Lake Charles during the lumber era. The house was torn down in 1951, and its lumber was used in building Boys' Village near Iowa. (Courtesy of McNeese Archives.)

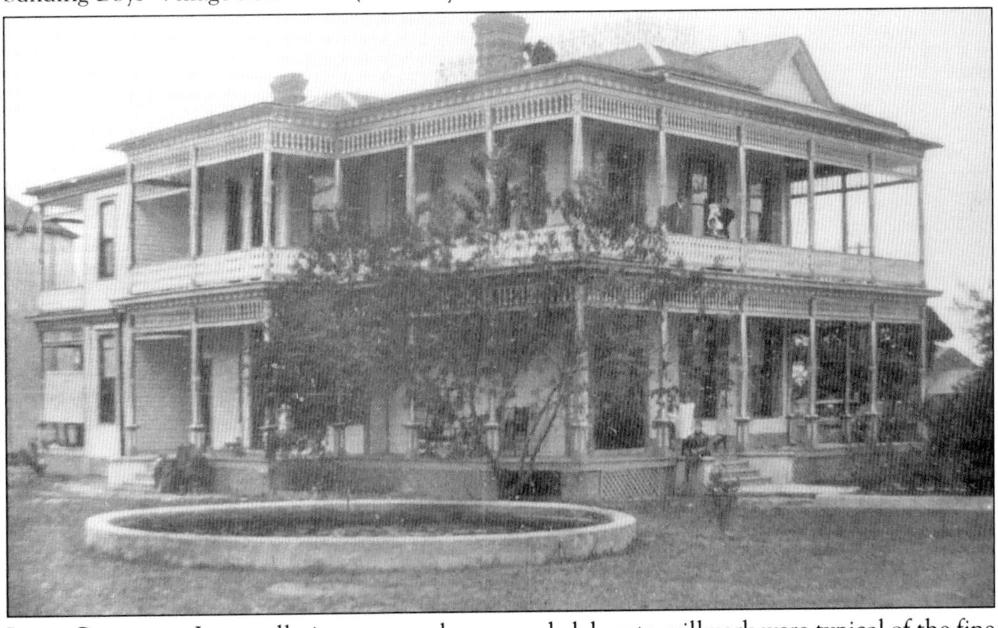

LONG GALLERIES. Long galleries, many columns, and elaborate grillwork were typical of the fine houses built of longleaf yellow pine and cypress by people whose wealth was generated, either directly or indirectly, by the timber industry. This Lake Charles house, shown in 1905, was owned during its lifespan by three men—Dr. J.C. Munday, Joseph Elstner and James Gardiner—before it burned down in 1919. (Courtesy of McNeese Archives.)

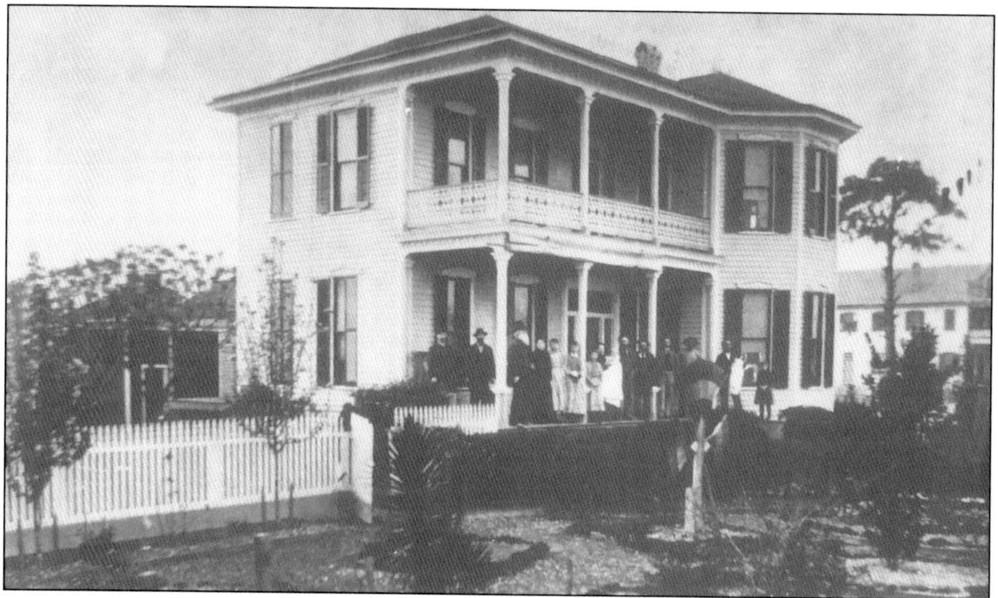

A Westlake Residence. Capt. Fred Wehrt, owner of the ferry boat *Hazel*, and members of his family assembled on his gallery for this photograph taken in 1890. Captain Wehrt's house overlooked Lake Charles from the west side of the lake. In addition to owning a fine house, he had a large garden, grape arbors, and many kinds of fruit trees. The hurricane of 1918 tore down the arbors and trees and wrecked this house. (Courtesy of McNeese Archives.)

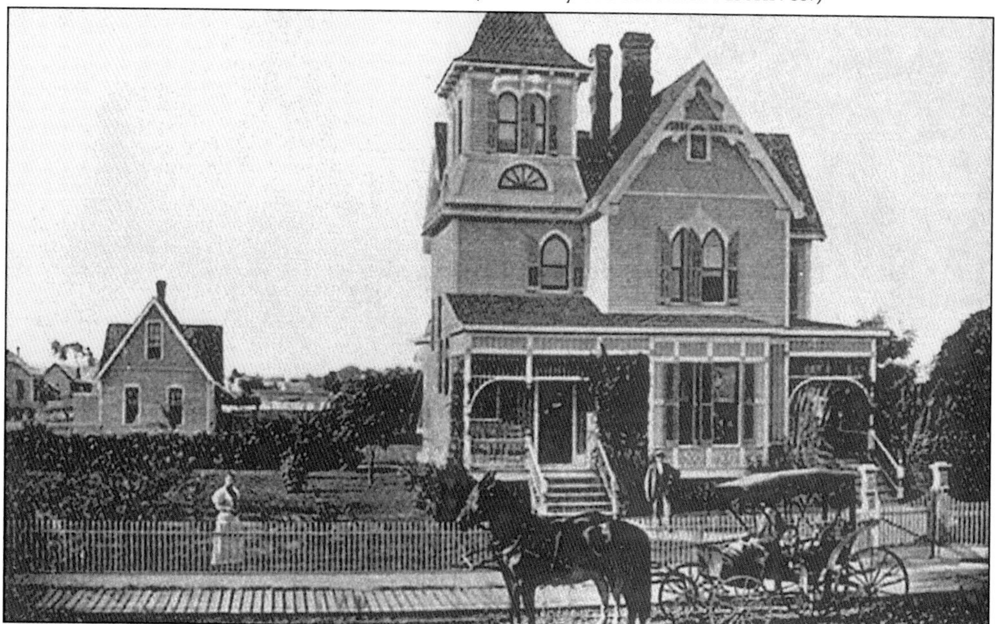

A Lumberman's Residence. The R.H. Nason residence on the corner of Broad and Ford Streets in Lake Charles was a neat house of fanciful architectural design. Nason was one of the "Michigan men" capitalists who moved to Calcasieu Parish in the 1880s. In 1883 Nason bought the old Daniel Goos mill property and established the sawmill that was later sold to Bradley-Ramsey. Note the wooden sidewalks, dirt street, and absence of large trees. (Courtesy of McNeese Archives.)

Four

Transportation

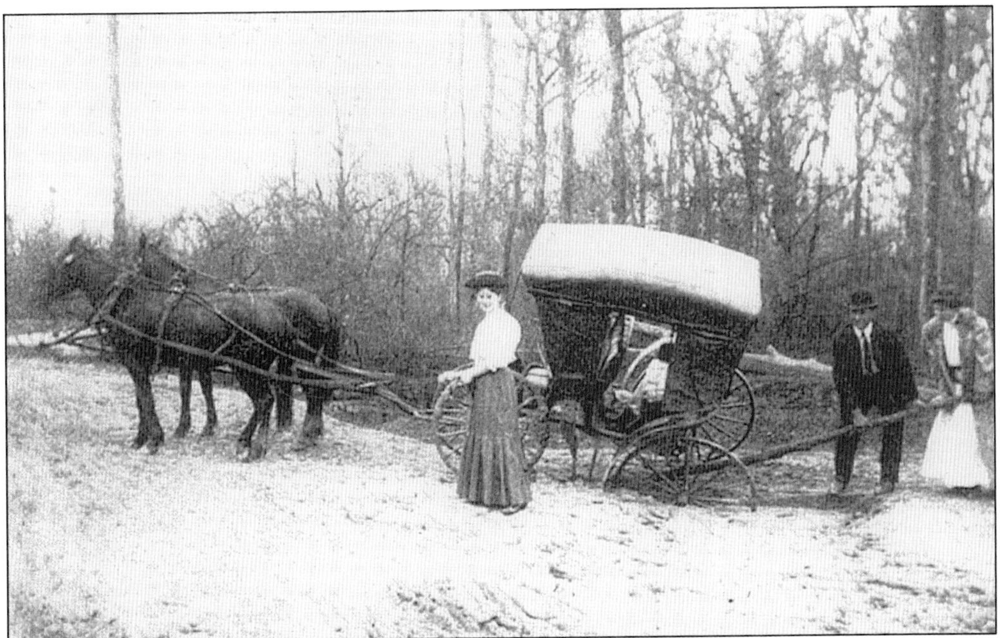

Bad Roads. Travel was slow and filled with uncertainties throughout Imperial Calcasieu Parish in the 1890s, as is shown in this photo. During the 1890s, all roads in the parish were dirt. In the earliest days of the parish, the Police Jury, the parish's governing body, attempted to keep the roads passable by appointing "road overseers" and ordering various male residents to serve a certain number of days each year doing road work. (Courtesy of Imperial Calcasieu Museum.)

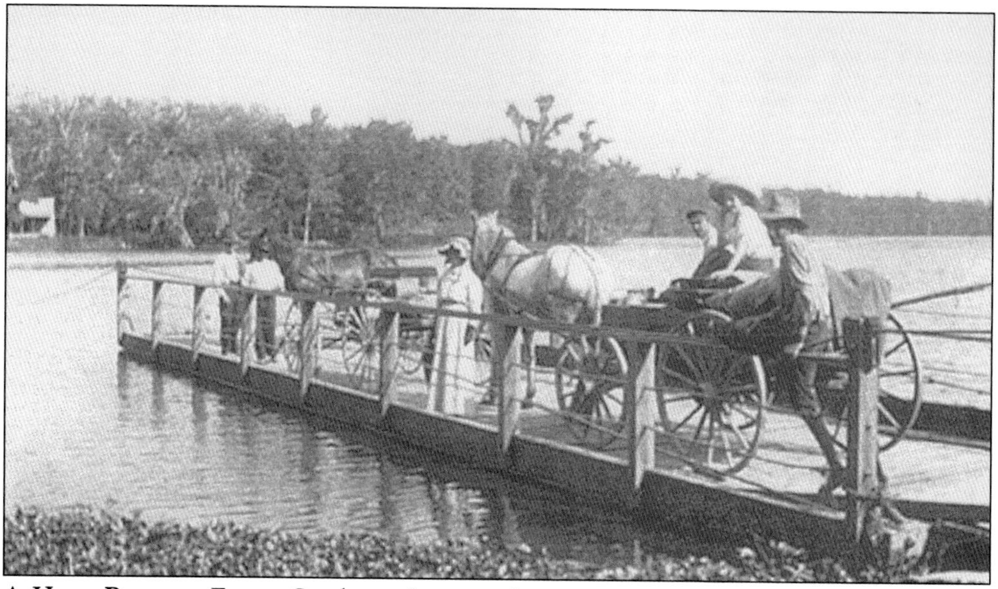

A HAND-POWERED FERRY. Southwest Louisiana's numerous waterways were broad and deep, making ferries like this one across the Calcasieu River a necessity in the days before bridges. The operator of this 1890s ferry probably charged his passengers a small fee and hoped they would help him pull the rope that moved the ferry across the river. If not, the crossing could take all day. (Courtesy of Bill Day.)

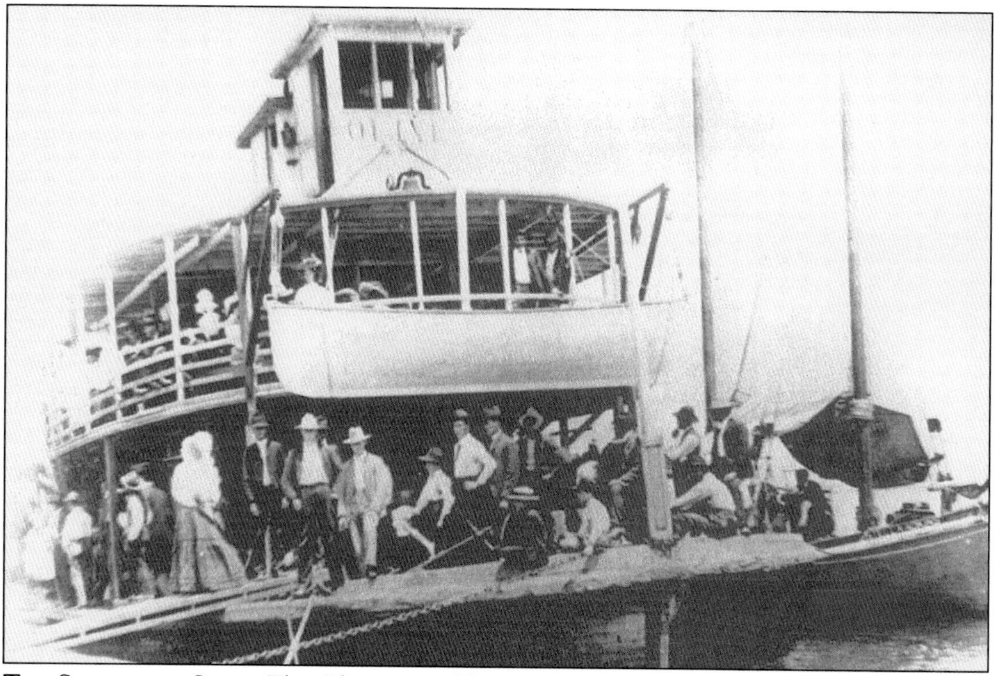

THE STEAMBOAT OLIVE. The *Olive*, owned by Capt. George W. Caldwell of Mermentau, is shown discharging passengers at Grand Chenier in marsh-bound Cameron Parish in this early 1900s photo. Around this time, in addition to the *Olive*, other boats like the *Ramos* and the *Borealis Rex* were operated on the Calcasieu, while the *Pelican* was operated on the Sabine River. (Courtesy of Oma and Clifford Caldwell.)

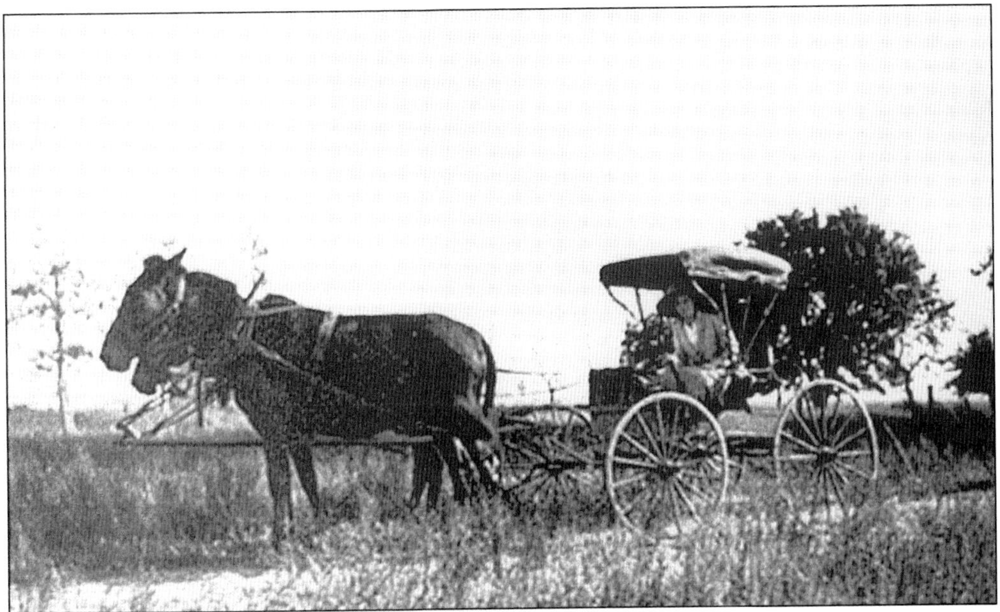

STANDARD TRANSPORTATION. Buggies such as this one were the standard means of transportation in Southwest Louisiana until around 1915, when they began to be replaced by automobiles. This c. 1907 photo shows Helen Davies in her family's best buggy. During the years prior to the coming of automobiles, most roads were actually only hard-packed dirt trails that became very soft in rainy weather. (Courtesy of Helen Kendall Collection.)

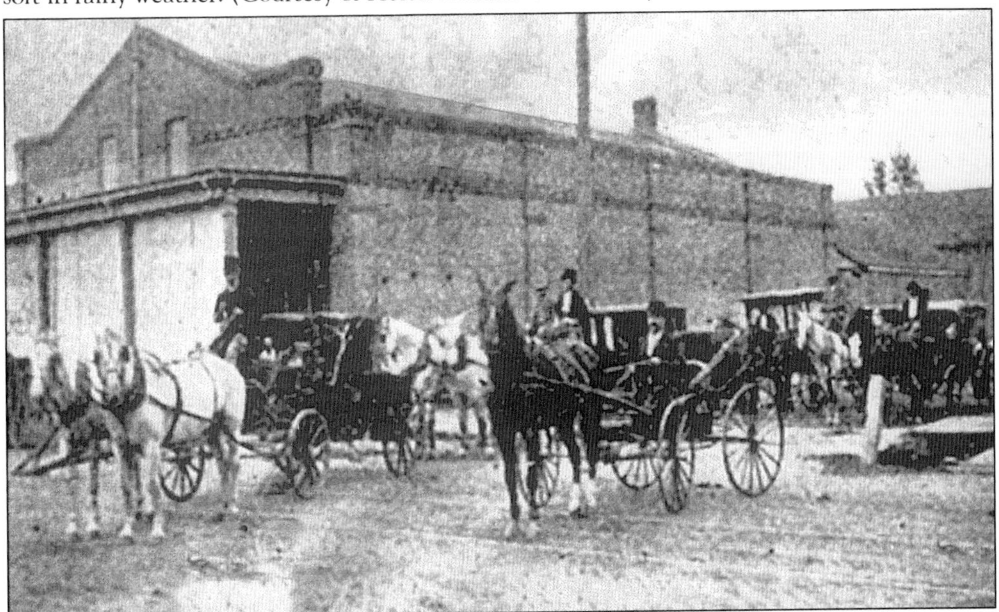

LIVERY STABLES. Every sizable town had several livery stables in the horse and buggy days. The Lake Charles Livery, Feed and Sale Stables, owned by D.R. Swift (shown here), provided services that included undertaking and embalming, the sale of all kinds of coal, and the sending of hacks to all trains (day or night) and to funerals as shown in the 1898 letterhead engraving shown here. Other Lake Charles liveries about that time were the W.A. Kirkwood Livery Stable and the Trotti Livery Stable. (Courtesy of McNeese Archives.)

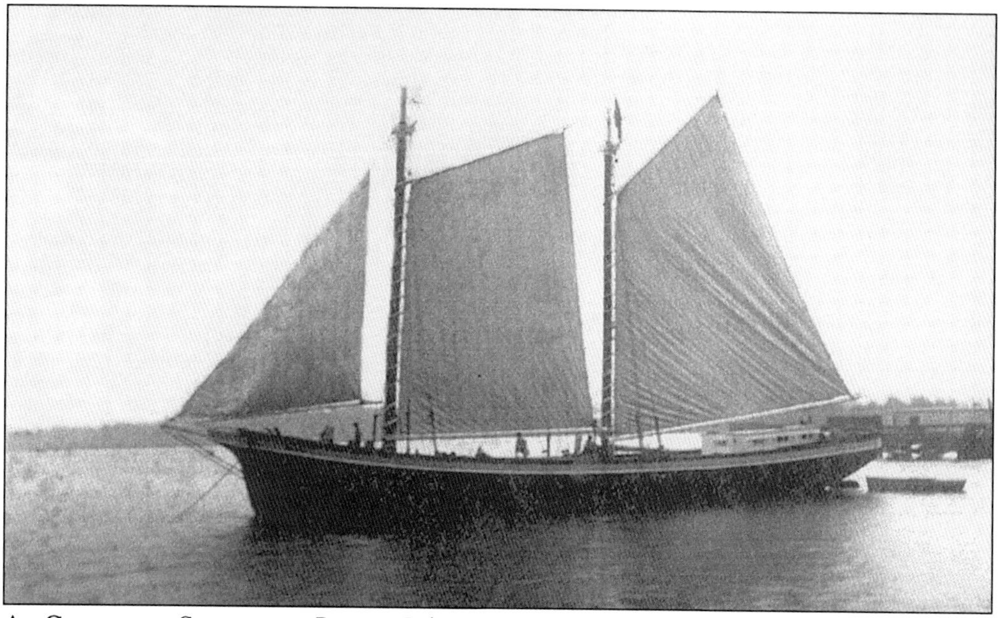

A Calcasieu Schooner. Pretty Calcasieu River trade schooners such as this one photographed near Clooney's Shipyard were built locally and operated between Lake Charles and Galveston from the 1860s to the early 1900s. The vessels ranged from 60 to 95 feet in length and from 16 to 30 feet in width, had masts that were 40 to 90 feet tall, and carried between 50,000 to 125,000 board feet of lumber per schooner. (Courtesy of Imperial Calcasieu Museum.)

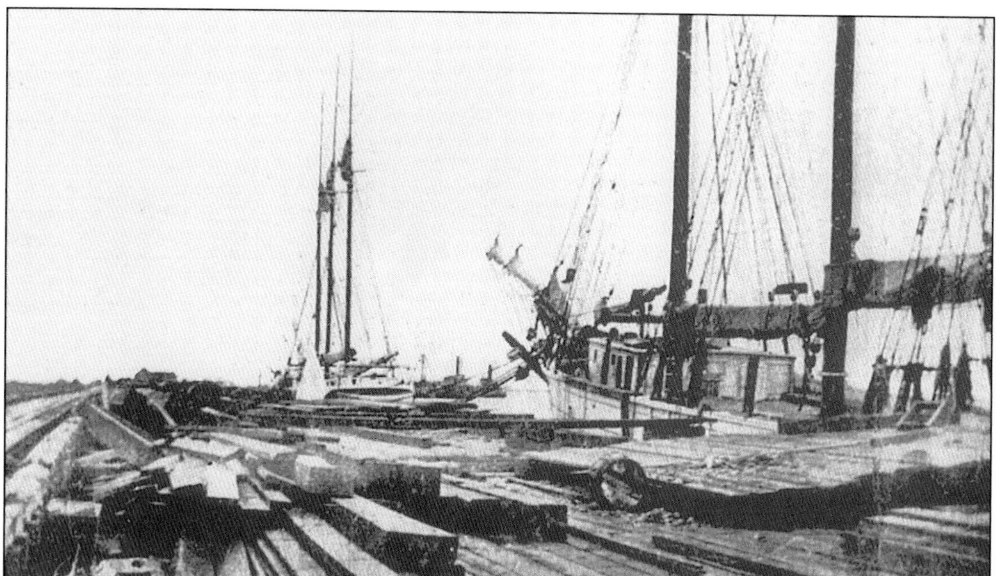

Loads of Lumber. Two Calcasieu lumber schooners are being loaded at the foot of Division Street in Lake Charles in this 1888 photo. In 1934, retired captains Frank Ford and A.F. Dobbertine could still name 70 schooners they had known that carried lumber from Calcasieu to Galveston between the years 1871 and 1895. Schooners continued to be used to transport lumber even after the coming of railroads because they could be operated by as few as two sailors and required no overhead for fuel. (Courtesy of McNeese Archives.)

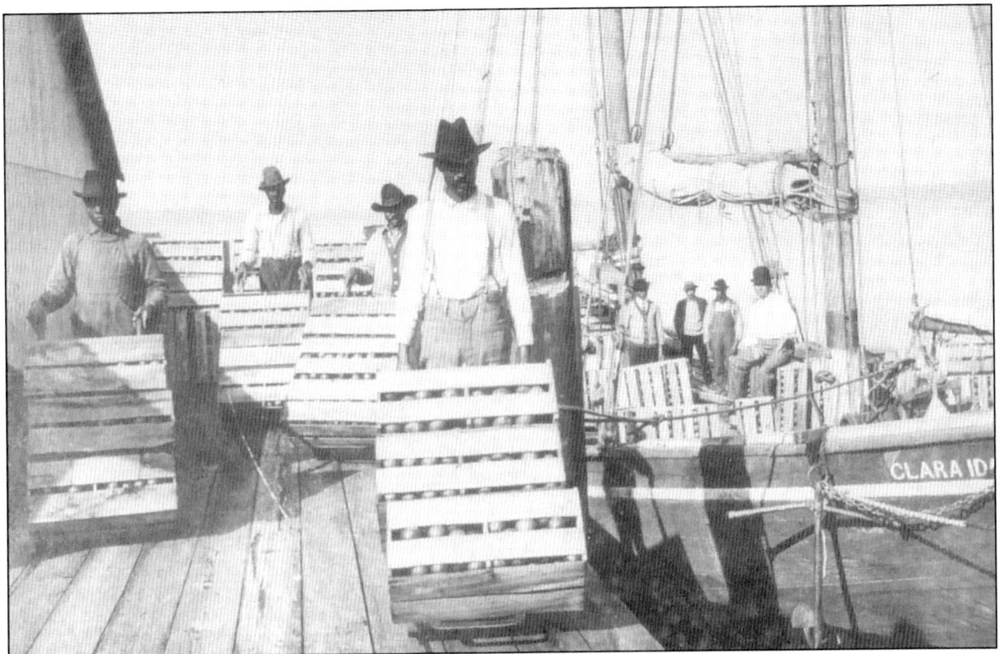

Unloading Oranges. Stevedores are unloading Cameron Parish oranges from the schooner *Clara Ida* in this photo taken at a Lake Charles wharf *c.* 1900. Some of the main items transported by schooner were Calcasieu lumber, Cameron oranges, and trade goods from Galveston, TX. From the earliest times to the coming of the railroad in 1880, Lake Charles was more closely linked with Galveston than it was with any other city because of the schooner trade. (Courtesy of Anne Phillips.)

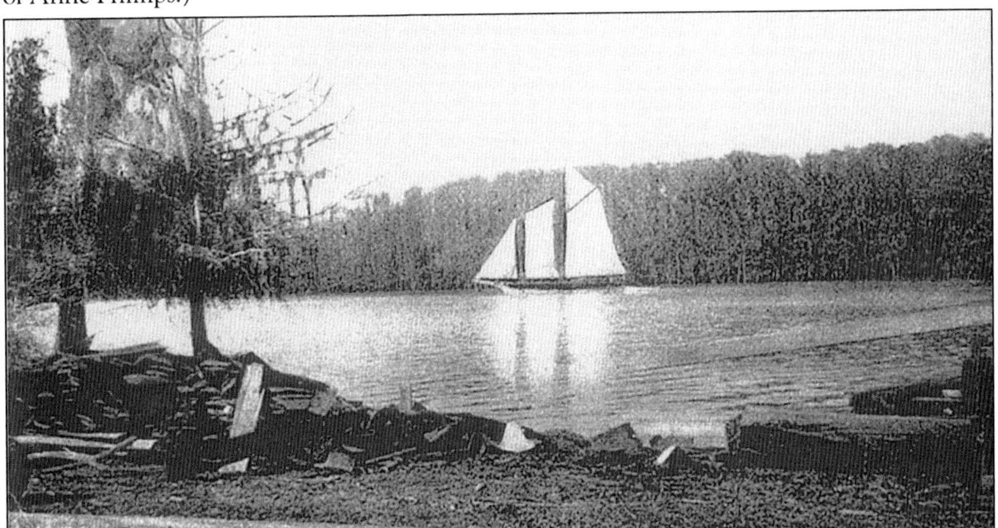

Headed for Galveston. Schooners usually enjoyed tranquil passages up and down the tree-lined sections of the Calcasieu River. However, they were exposed to storms, groundings, and other hazards while crossing Big Lake, the Calcasieu bar, and the Gulf of Mexico. Periodic hurricanes and winter storms were their greatest hazard. In 1871, for example, eight Calcasieu schooners were heavily damaged or sunk in a hurricane that hit near Galveston. (Courtesy of McNeese Archives.)

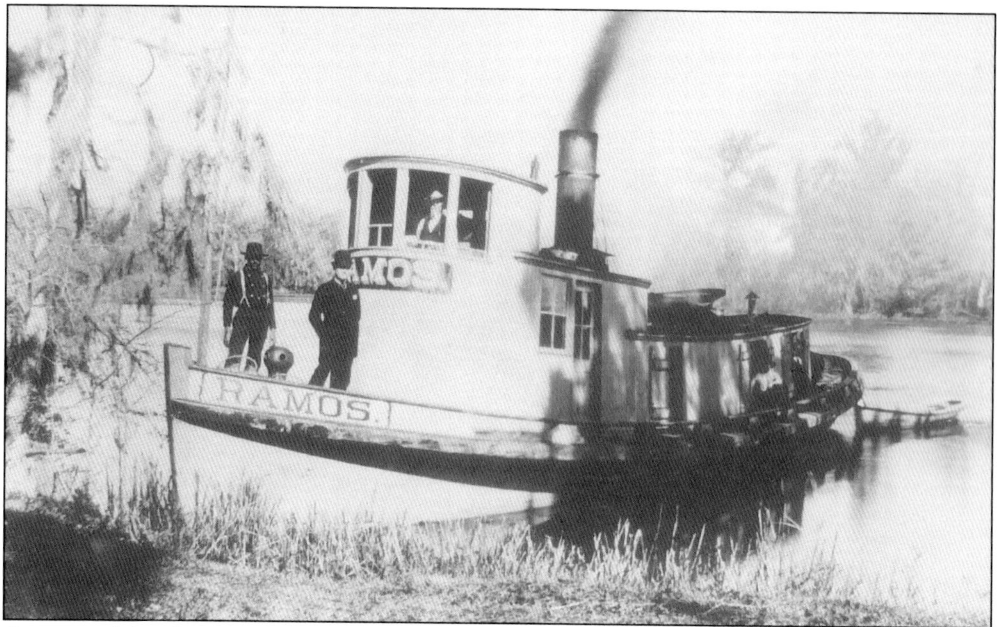

AN EARLY MAIL BOAT. The steam-powered tug *Ramos* made regular trips from Lake Charles to Leesburg (Cameron) beginning in the middle 1870s. On a return trip to Lake Charles on May 24, 1879, the *Ramos* was struck by a violent squall and she sank about a mile south of Lake Charles. Six passengers drowned in the mishap. The following week sailors working from two schooners raised the *Ramos*, which was then repaired and put back into operation. (Courtesy of Imperial Calcasieu Museum.)

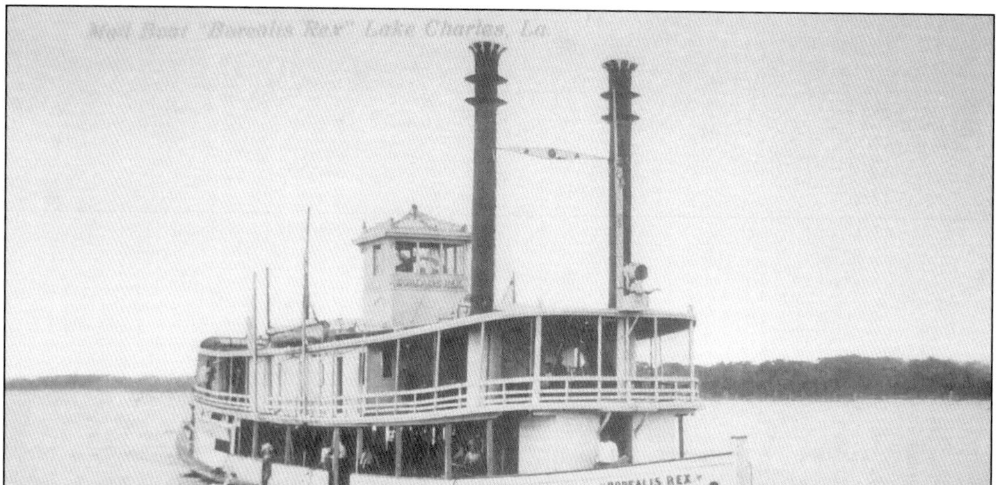

THE FAMOUS *Borealis Rex*. The best-remembered Calcasieu River packet was the *Borealis Rex*, a stern-wheeler built in Minnesota in 1888 and brought to the Calcasieu River in 1905. It replaced another smaller and slower packet, the *Romeo*. The *Rex* was 121 feet long and 22 feet wide. This steamboat sank during the 1918 hurricane, was raised and refitted, and continued in service until 1930. (Courtesy of Imperial Calcasieu Museum.)

A STEAMER ON THE RIVER. In 1893, the Sturdevant brothers, E.K. and D.P., captured much of the charm of the Calcasieu River and the satisfaction felt by those who used it in this photograph, which was one of their popular "Sturdevant's Views." The boat is a steam-powered propeller tug. Note the two men toasting their good fortune in the foreground. (Courtesy of Imperial Calcasieu Museum.)

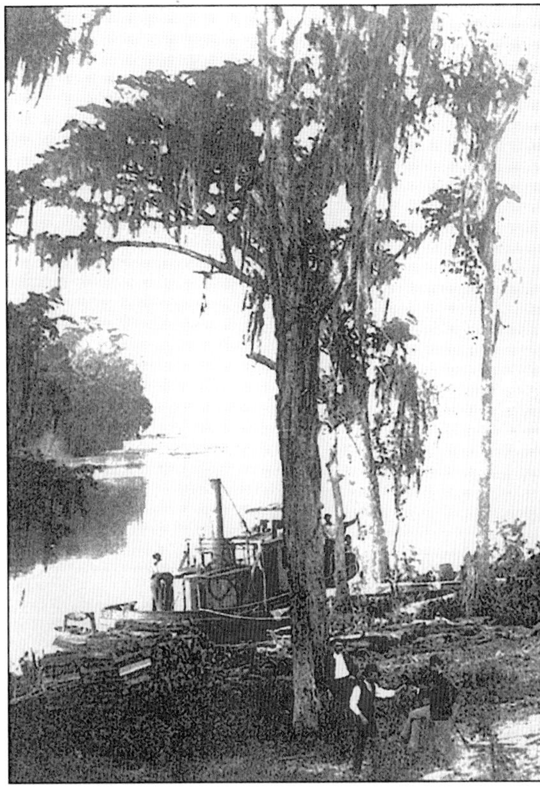

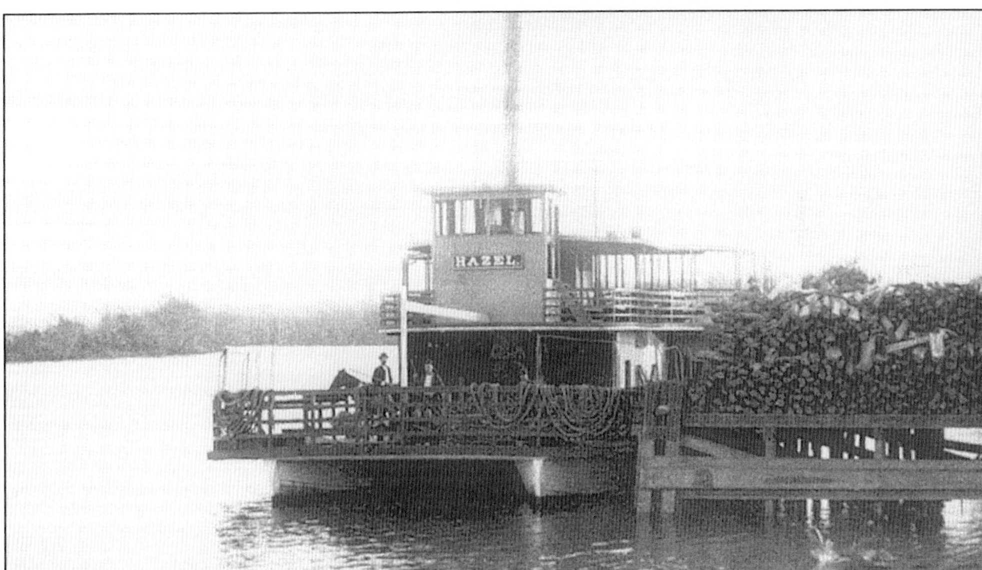

A LAKE CHARLES FERRY. The steam propeller ferry *Hazel* is seen tied up at its Westlake landing in this 1893 photo. The wooden structure mounted across the bows of the *Hazel's* twin hulls was used to ferry horses and buggies. Named for the daughter of Capt. Fred Wehrt, the owner, the *Hazel* was used in regular service between Lake Charles and Westlake from 1888 to 1917. The *Nettie*, owned by Capt. Green Hall, preceded the *Hazel*, starting service at this crossing in 1879. (Courtesy of Imperial Calcasieu Museum.)

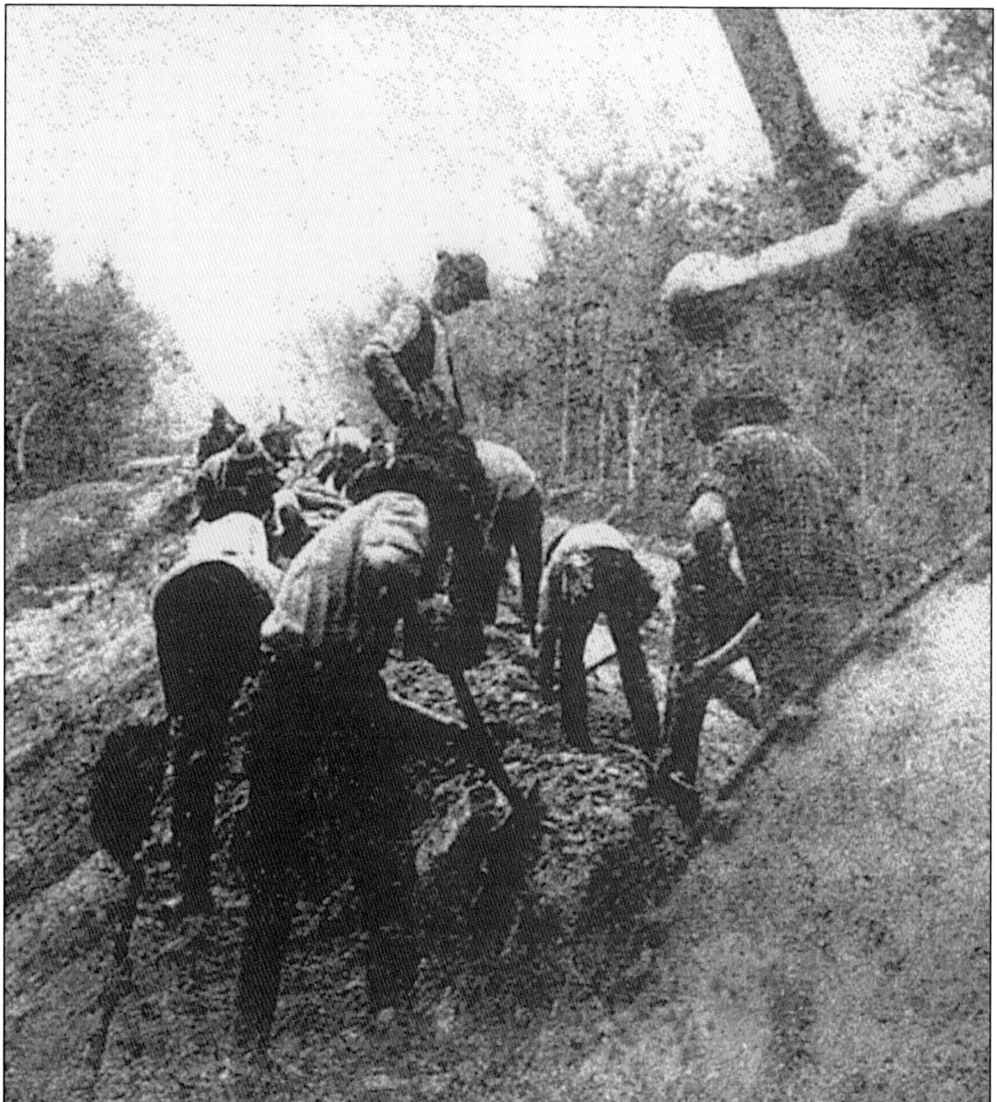

RAILROAD BUILDERS. Every back is bent as railroad workers toil under the wary eyes of their foreman in this *c.* 1880 photo taken during the construction of the first railroad across Calcasieu Parish. This road was constructed by Louisiana & Western (later known as Southern Pacific) as the final link connecting New Orleans and Houston. Note the front of a locomotive, thought to be the *Sabine*, in the right foreground of the image. (Courtesy of Imperial Calcasieu Museum.)

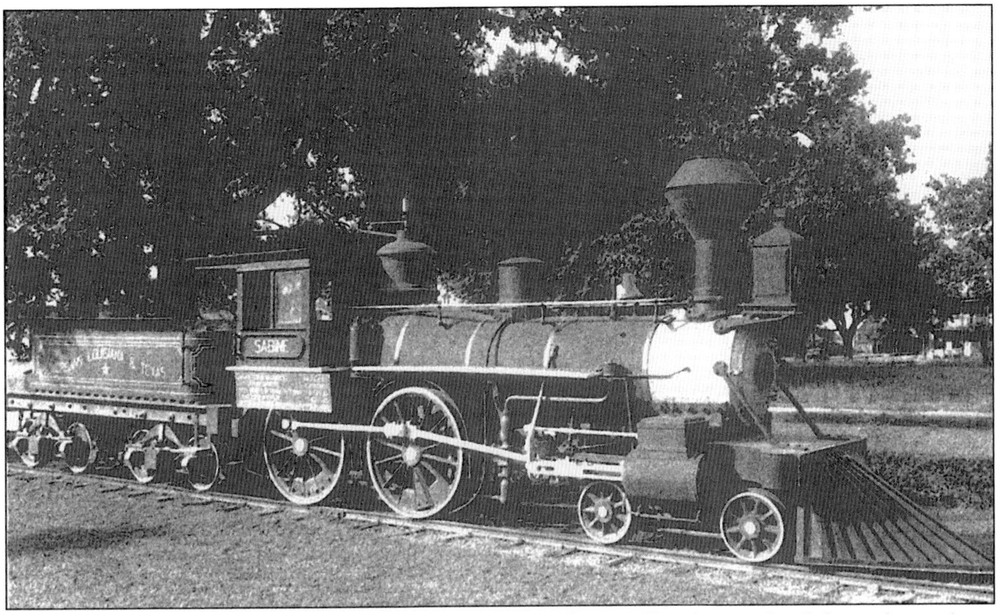

The Sabine. The first railroad locomotive to serve Calcasieu Parish was the *Sabine*, shown here in the last photo taken before Southern Pacific donated the locomotive to the World War II scrap-iron drive in 1942. This engine brought the first train into Lake Charles on April 7, 1880, and was used in regular service in Southwest Louisiana for a number of years afterwards. (Courtesy of McNeese Archives.)

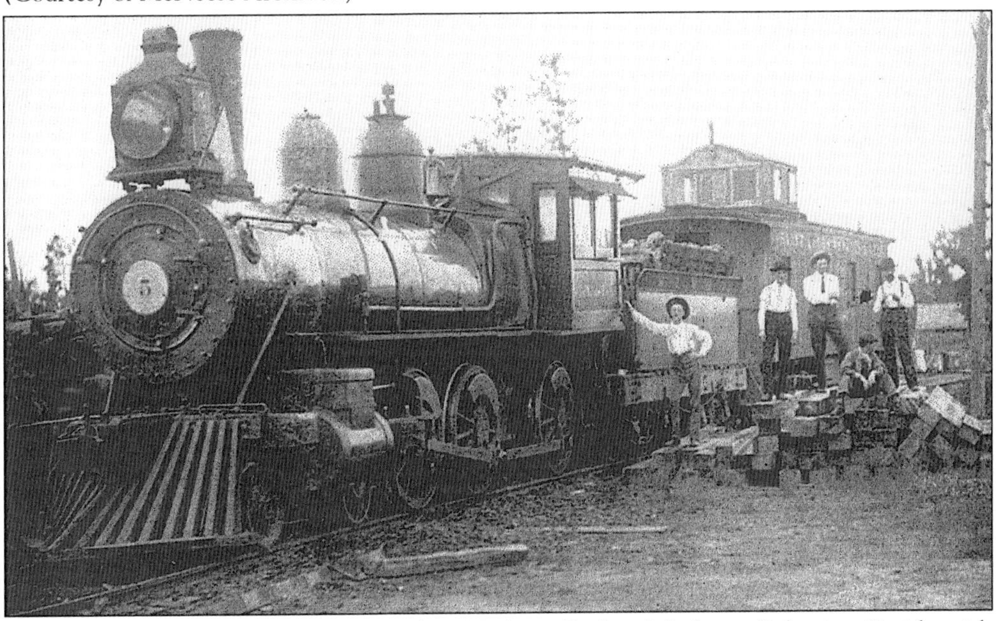

The First North-South Train. The Watkins Railroad linking Calcasieu Parish with Alexandria was completed in 1892 when this train rolled into Lake Charles. Note the decorative flags on each side of the headlight. The 107-mile Watkins Railroad was built by land entrepreneur J.B. Watkins as part of his plan for developing Southwest Louisiana. The Watkins Railroad later became part of the Missouri-Pacific system. (Courtesy of Imperial Calcasieu Museum.)

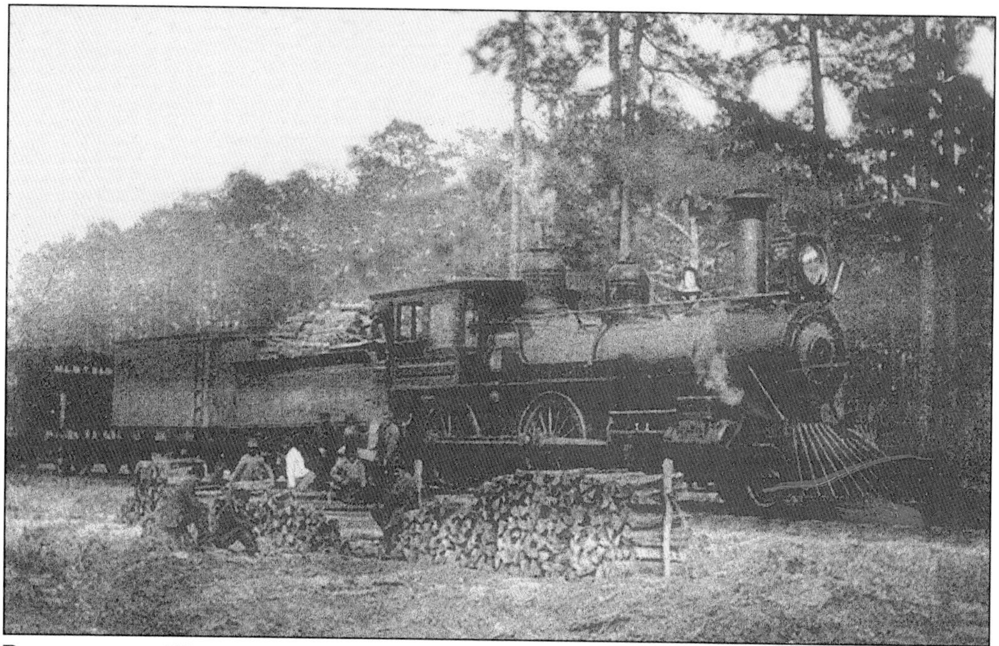

Pausing at a Woodpile. An early locomotive similar to the *Sabine* is seen taking on fuel in this 1880s photo. Locomotives like this one used wood for fuel, which was just right for service in old Calcasieu Parish, where wood was available in abundance. (Courtesy of Imperial Calcasieu Museum.)

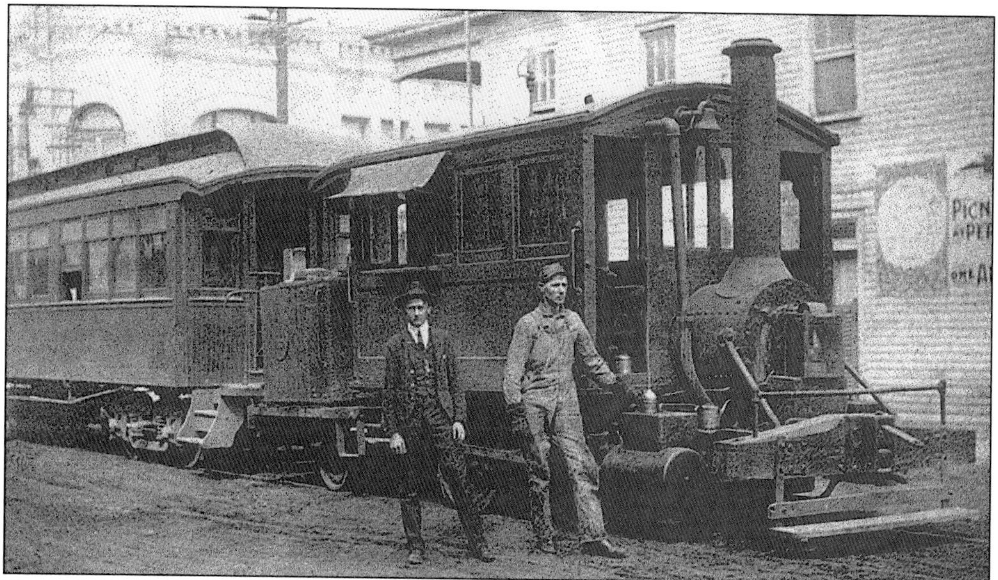

The Broad Street Railroad. Conductor Ed Knapp (left) and engineer Joe Roux stand beside the old Watkins "Dummy" locomotive at the corner of Broad and Ryan Streets in Lake Charles in this 1904 photograph. The Dummy was operated from 1891 to 1906 out Broad Street to Boulevard and then south in a circle on the prairie where land promoter J.B. Watkins proposed locating an urban development. The Dummy's speed was 8 miles per hour. Many of its passengers were Lake Charles High School students riding to and from school. (Courtesy of Imperial Calcasieu Museum.)

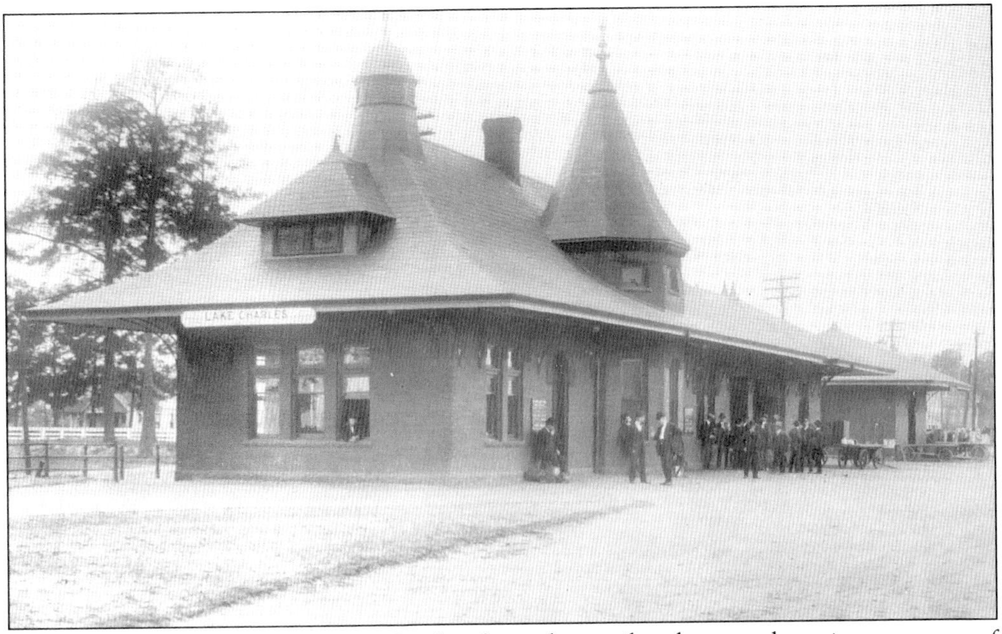

THE SOUTHERN PACIFIC STATION. In the days when railroads were the primary means of long-distance land transportation, every good-sized railroad town had a nice station. This photo was taken of the Southern Pacific station in Lake Charles in 1909. (Courtesy of Imperial Calcasieu Museum.)

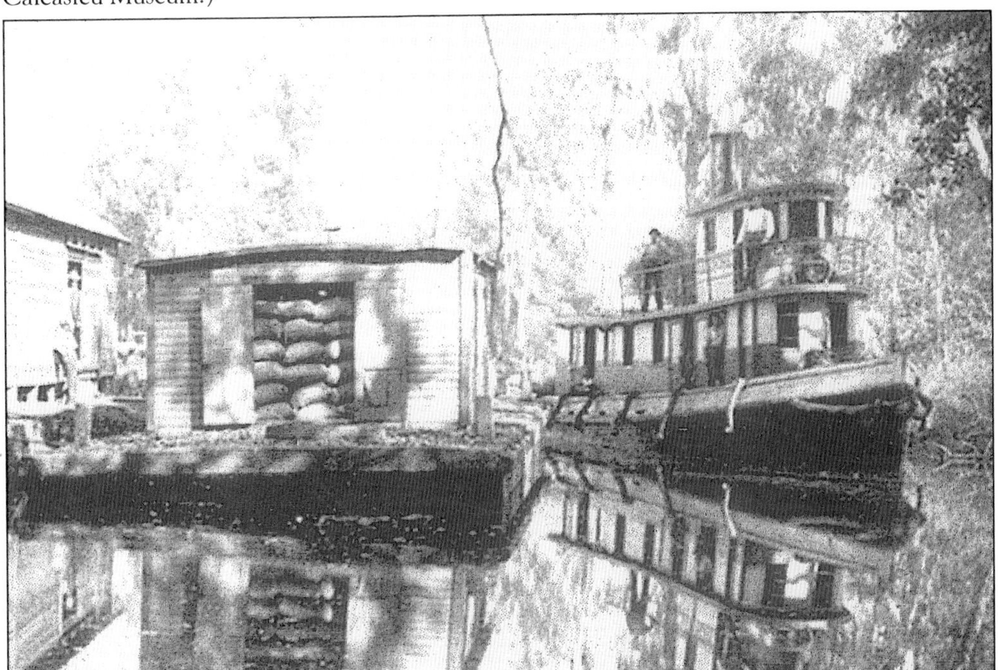

THE CHOUPIQUE BAYOU TUG. The steam tugboat *Elsinore* was working on Choupique Bayou in 1902 when this photo was taken. From the earliest times, the many bayous in the southern part of Imperial Calcasieu Parish provided routes over which heavy goods could be moved inexpensively. (Courtesy of Imperial Calcasieu Museum.)

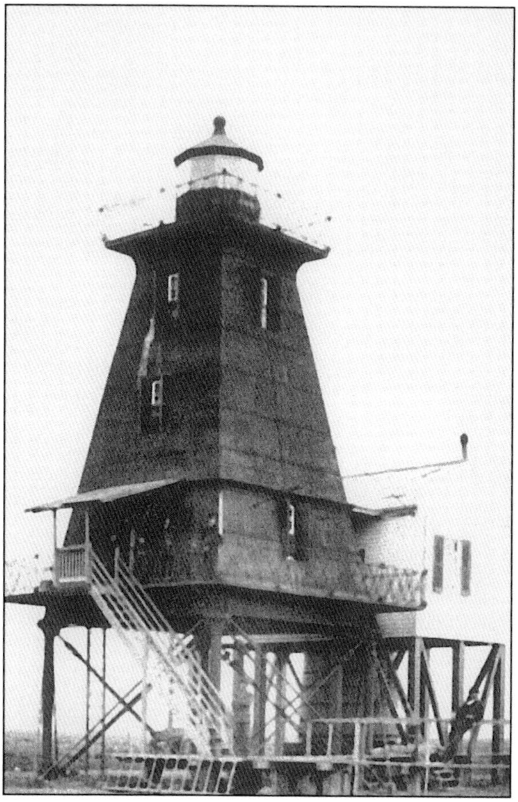

The Calcasieu River Lighthouse. In 1875 the federal government built this 60-foot-tall screw-pile lighthouse at the mouth of the Calcasieu River. The keeper and his family lived on the first two floors, and the attached building was used as a kitchen. Around 1939, the lighthouse was taken out of service. It was later dismantled, and the site was dredged for the Calcasieu-Cameron Ship Channel. (Courtesy of McNeese Archives.)

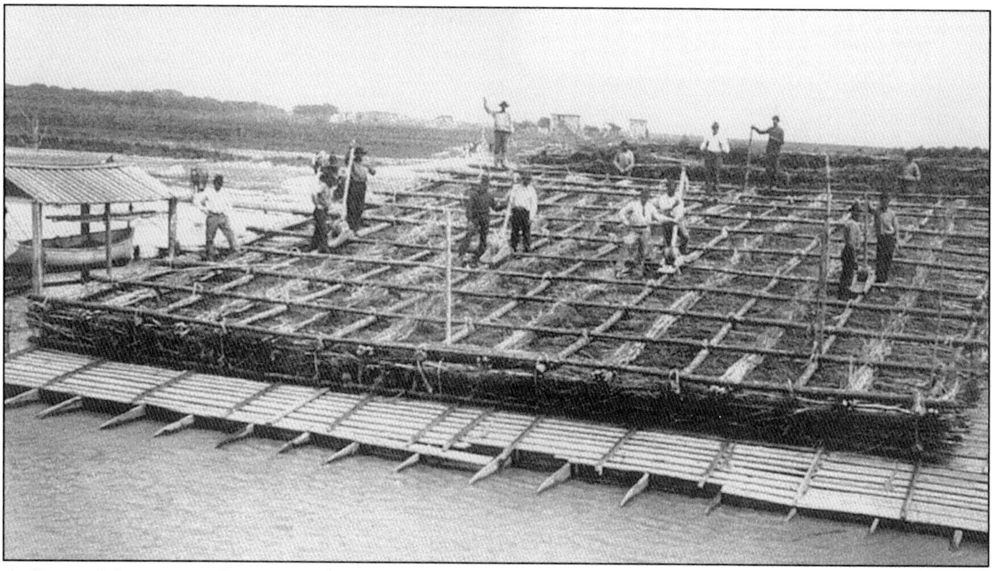

A Jetty Mattress. In 1893, these workmen were busy at the mouth of the Calcasieu River, binding willow tree branches into pads to be used as the foundation of jetties. Jetties were needed to relieve the problems vessels had been having for years with "crossing the bar," or getting across the shallow spot at the mouth of the river. The bar was caused by a buildup of silt as river water slowed down upon entering the Gulf of Mexico. (Courtesy of Imperial Calcasieu Museum.)

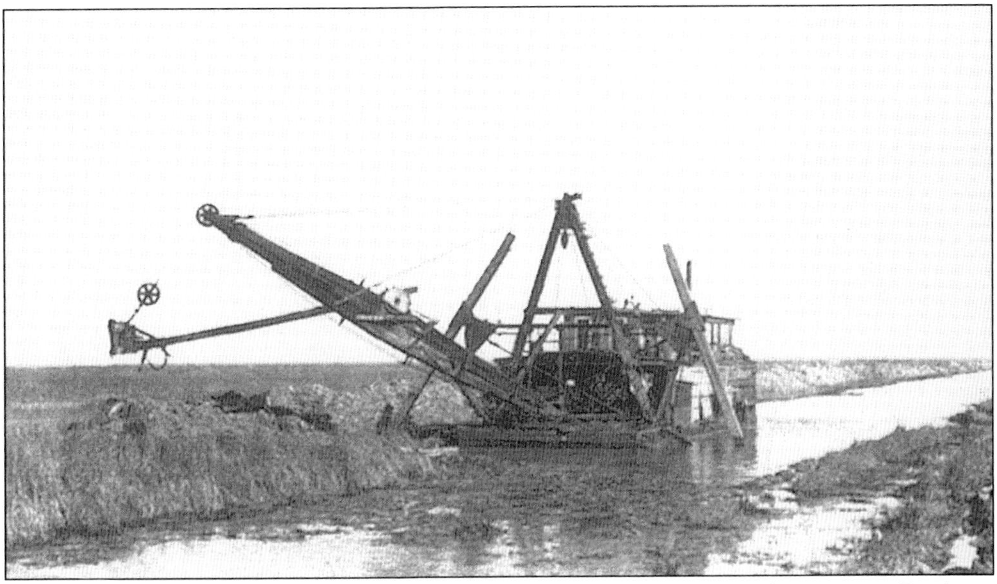

AN OLD-TIME DIPPER DREDGE. A dipper dredge boat belonging to the Streater Dredging Company of Lake Arthur is shown digging a canal across miles and miles of Southwest Louisiana marshland in this 1920s photo. Semon Benoit of Lake Charles was an operator of this dredge. Canals such as this one opened the "impenetrable" marshes to navigation, hunting, trapping, fishing, oil exploration, and other uses. (Courtesy of Charlsie Benoit.)

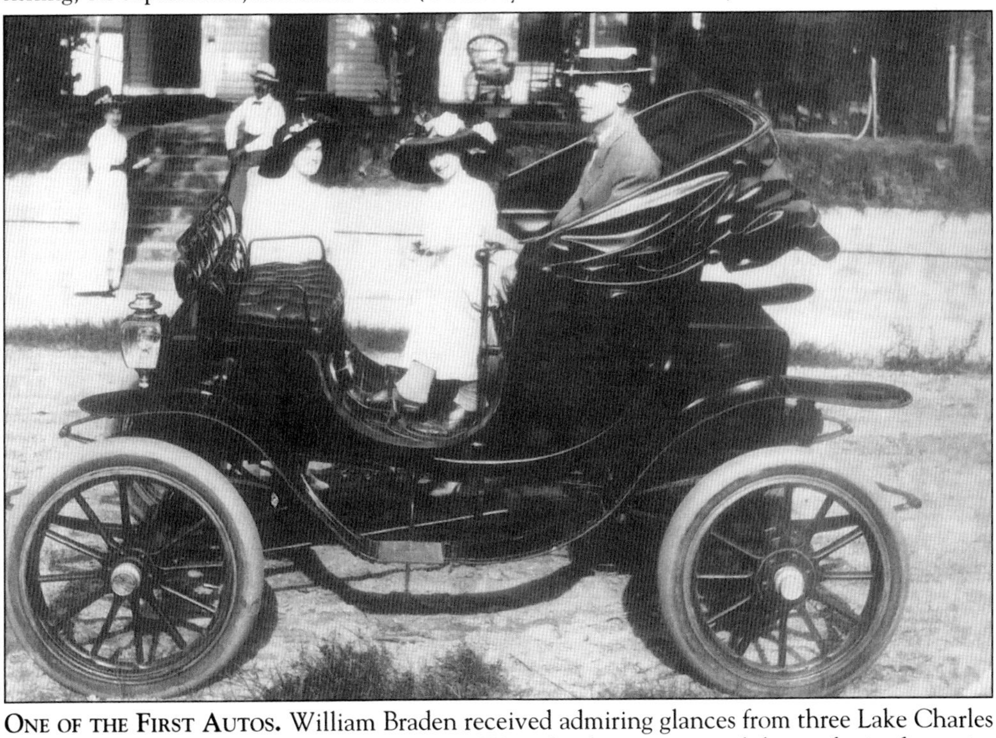

ONE OF THE FIRST AUTOS. William Braden received admiring glances from three Lake Charles young ladies when he took his father's 1910 Waverly electric automobile out for its first spin. Another very early automobile was purchased and brought into the area by Dr. J.H. Watkins, also of Lake Charles. (Courtesy of McNeese Archives.)

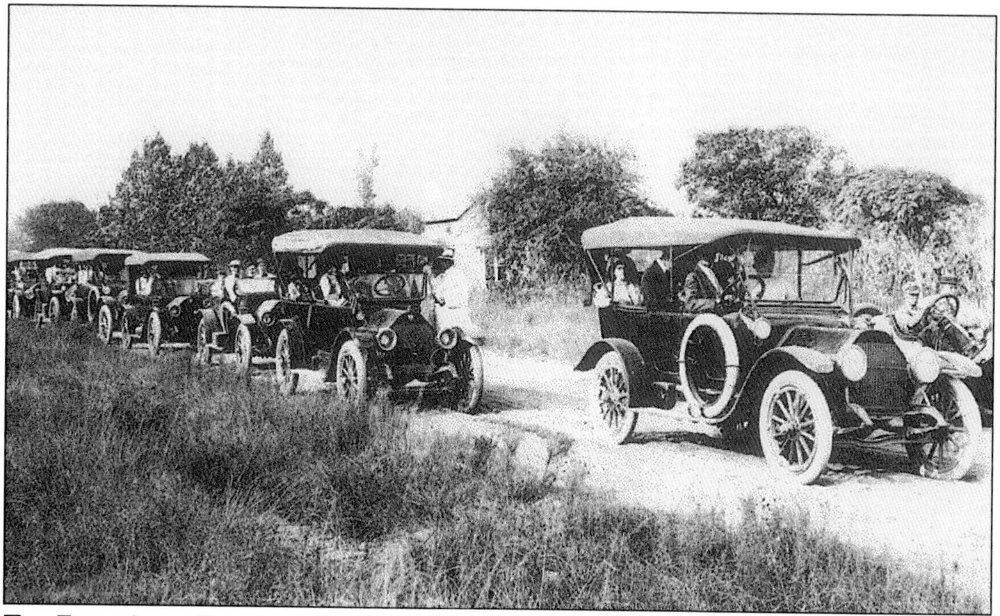

The First Auto Tourists. On September 5, 1913, the Pathfinders, an automobile touring group originating in the East, passed through Calcasieu Parish along the route that would later be called the Old Spanish Trail (U.S. Highway 90). At the time of the Pathfinders' journey, the entire route through Calcasieu Parish was dirt roads, and all of the rivers had to be crossed on ferries. The first "tourist camps" (motels) were not built in the parish until about 1924. (Courtesy of Imperial Calcasieu Museum.)

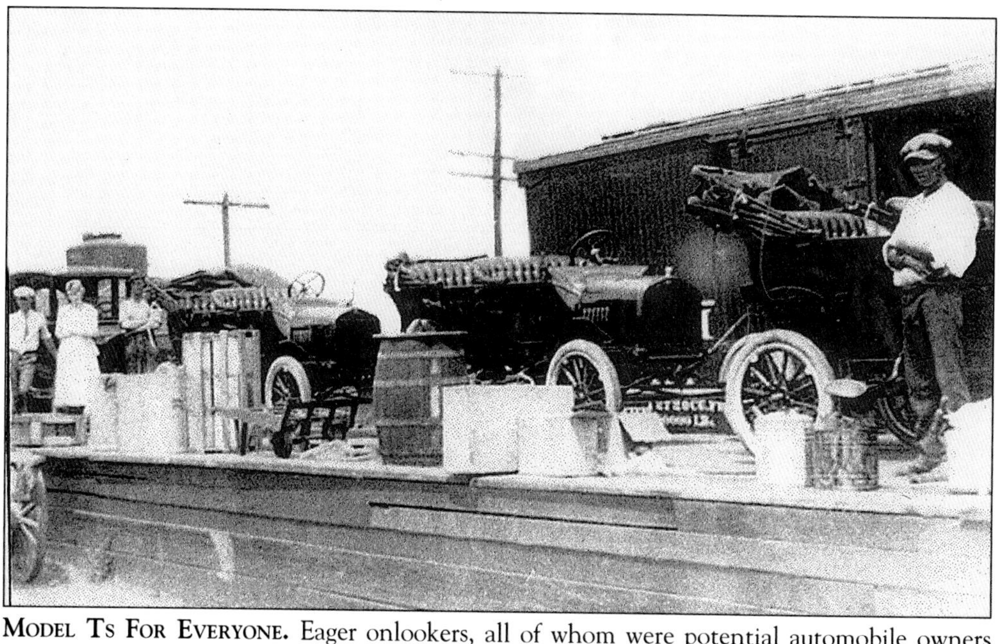

Model Ts For Everyone. Eager onlookers, all of whom were potential automobile owners thanks to Henry Ford, watch a string of Model Ts being unloaded at a railroad siding in Lake Charles just prior to World War I. This automobile shipment and many more like it ended the era of land transportation by horse and mule in Imperial Calcasieu. (Courtesy of Imperial Calcasieu Museum.)

Five

INDUSTRY

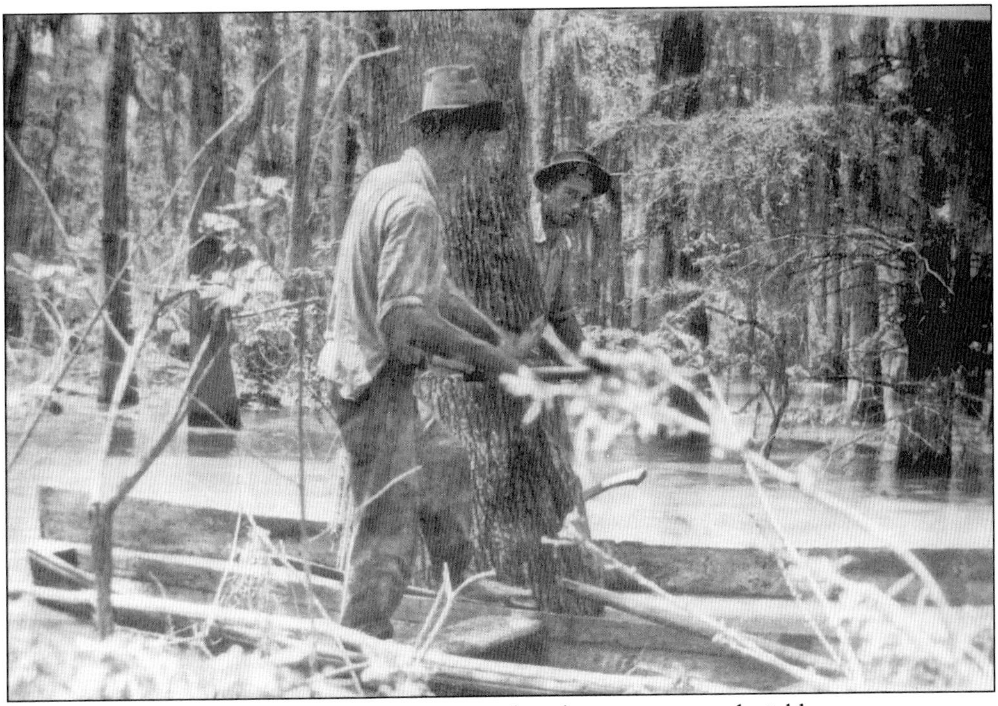

SWAMP LOGGERS. Two Calcasieu swampers stand in their pirogues and wield a cross-cut saw on a hardwood tree in this photo taken when the chief means of transporting logs to sawmills was by floating them down the river. After cutting down this tree, the swampers would mark the log so that it could be directed to the correct sawmill during its journey downstream. (Courtesy of McNeese Archives.)

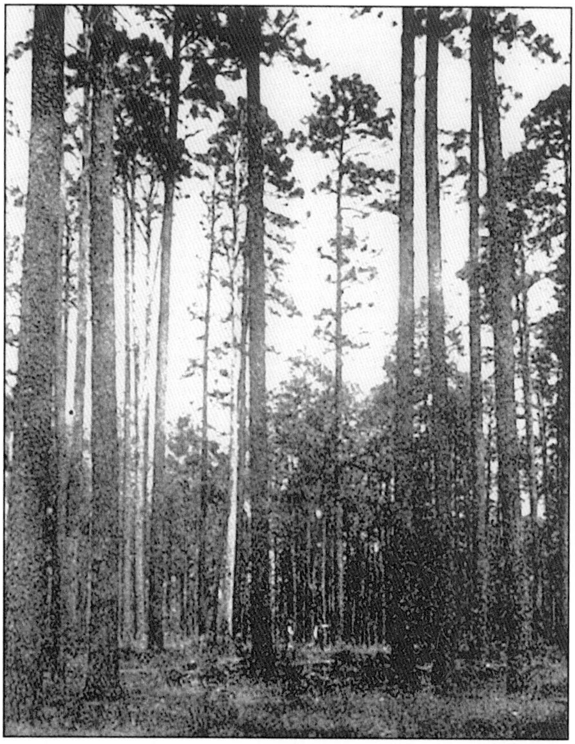

The Yellow Pine Forest. Two timber scouts are sizing up the prospects of the virgin longleaf yellow pine forest pictured here. Longleaf yellow pine was the basic raw material of the gigantic Imperial Calcasieu lumber industry. These forests had not been cut before the industry got started in the 1850s. By 1919, 46 mills were operating in the district, collectively cutting timber at the rate of a section, or 640 acres per day. By 1924, there were no longleaf yellow pines left. (Courtesy of McNeese Archives.)

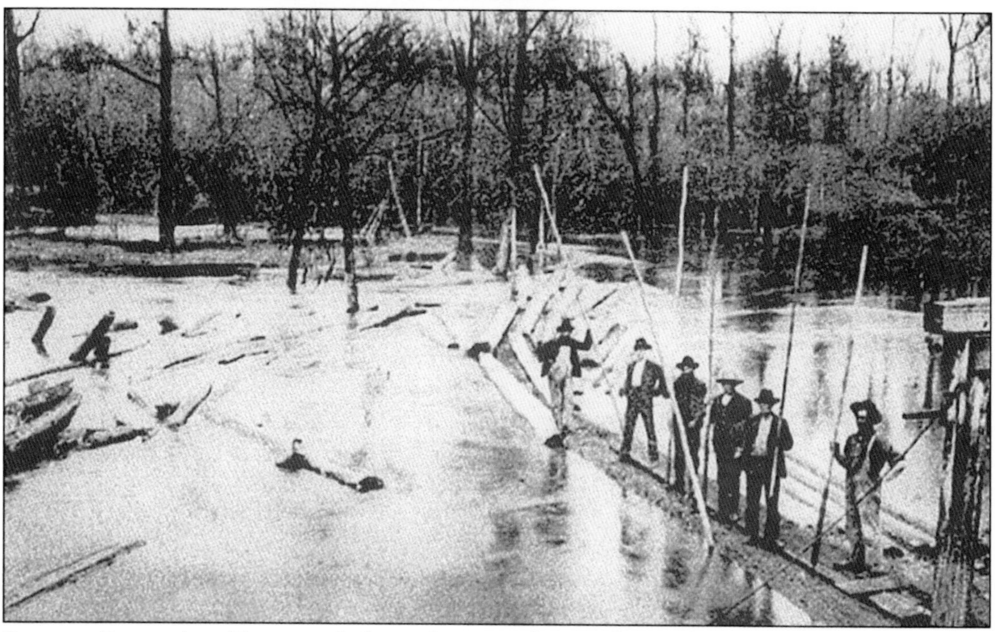

Rafting Logs. An old postcard photo shows workers gathering logs into "rafts," which they would then float to the appropriate mills. Some idea of the number of logs that came down the Calcasieu River each year may be gained from this story: in 1903, a log jam, estimated by mill owner J.A. Bel to be of more than 100,000 logs, was finally broken by the use of 100 sticks of dynamite. The jam had been building near the mouth of Ouiska (Whiskey) Chitto Creek for three years. (Courtesy of McNeese Archives.)

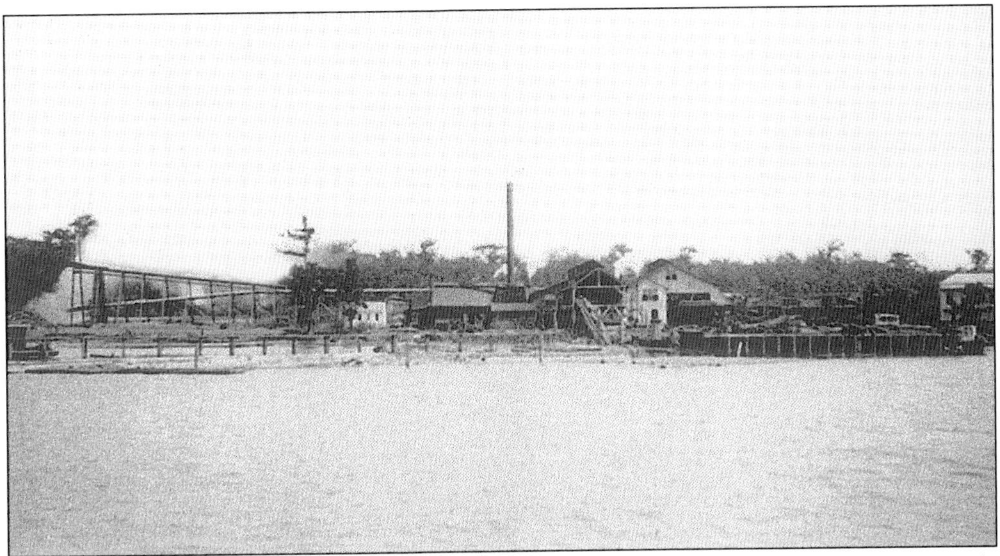

A Waterside Sawmill. Drew's Mill, shown here in 1893, is a typical example of a waterside sawmill. Incoming logs were pulled up the inclined ramp, near the picture's center, to be sawed by a huge circular or band saw. Sawdust from this operation was sent to the burn pile, far left, by means of a long inclined tube. Lumber—the finished product—was stacked in back until it could be shipped via schooner from the dock on the right or by a railroad spur running behind the mill. (Courtesy of Imperial Calcasieu Museum.)

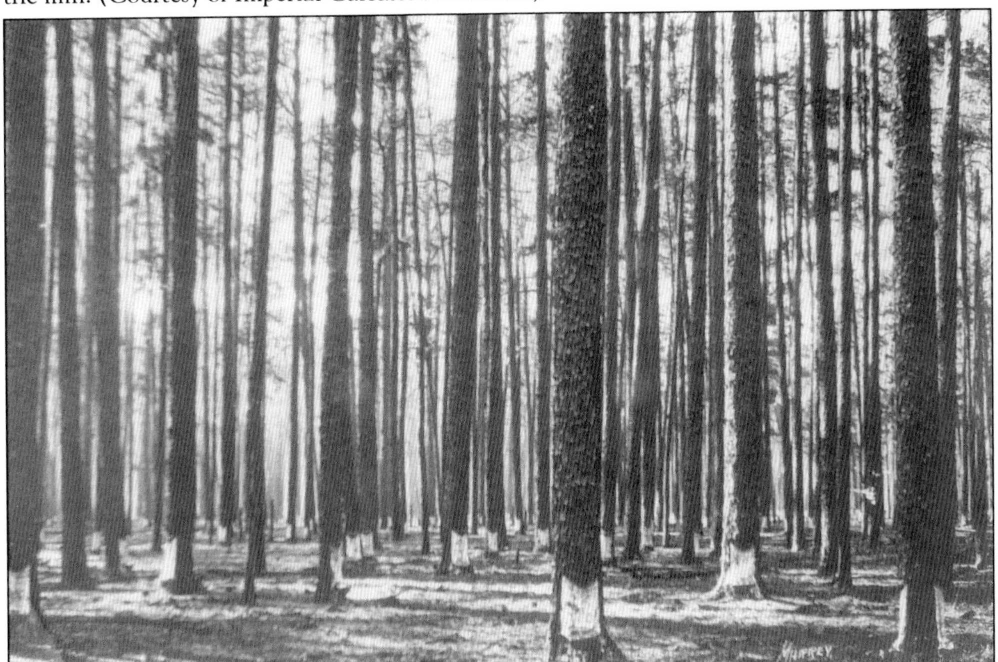

Making Them Bleed. Thousands of longleaf yellow pines in this forest in northern Imperial Calcasieu are being bled of their resin for distillation into turpentine. After about three years of bleeding, the trees were cut down. Each turpentine camp employed about 200 hackers who were noted for their haunting woods calls and their ability to hack about 2,000 to 3,000 trees each day. (Courtesy of McNeese Archives.)

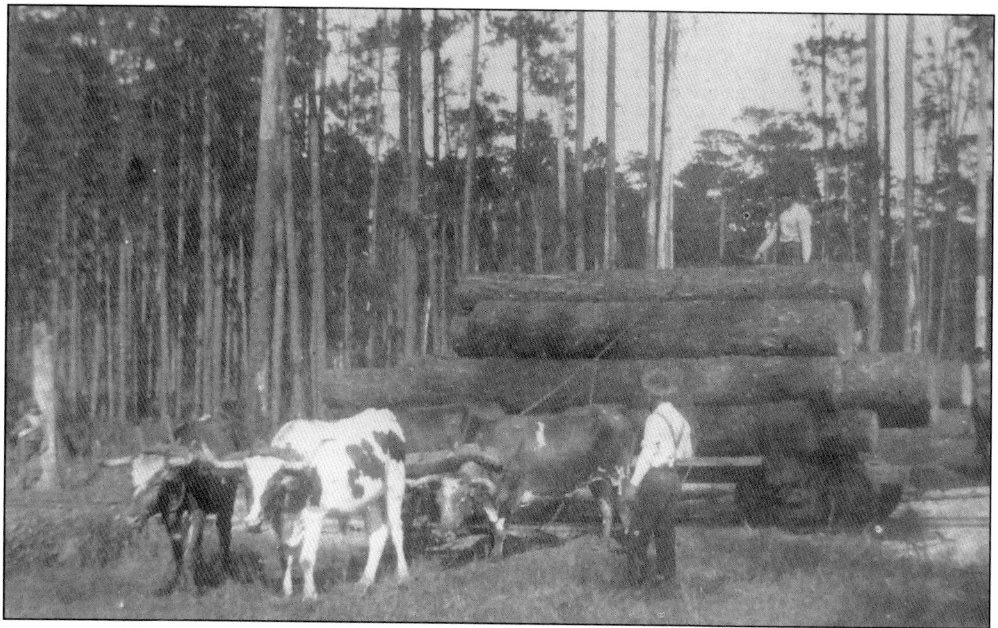

Loading a Flatcar. Oxen were still being used to load tram railway flatcars in the 1890s, as shown in this photograph taken near Lake Charles. The logs on the car were rolled up a ramp on the other side of the car. A few years after this photo was taken, most of the work once done by oxen was done by steam-powered equipment. (Courtesy of McNeese Archives.)

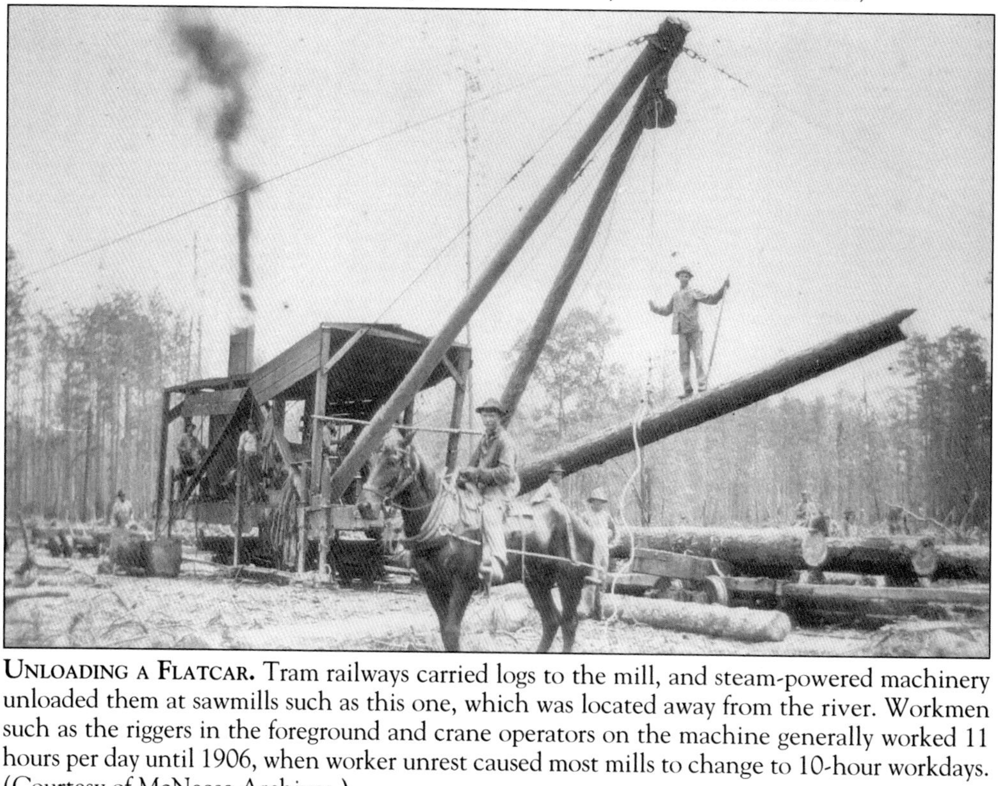

Unloading a Flatcar. Tram railways carried logs to the mill, and steam-powered machinery unloaded them at sawmills such as this one, which was located away from the river. Workmen such as the riggers in the foreground and crane operators on the machine generally worked 11 hours per day until 1906, when worker unrest caused most mills to change to 10-hour workdays. (Courtesy of McNeese Archives.)

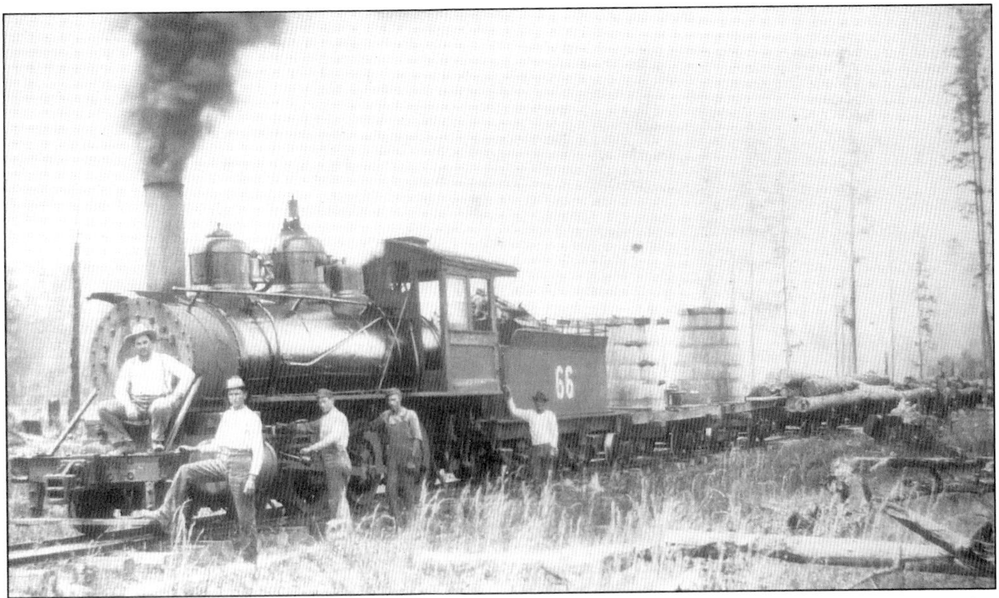

The DeQuincy Tram Railroad. The engineer and crew of this narrow-gauge train in the DeQuincy area were on their way back to the mill when they stopped to have their photograph taken around 1920. This was one of many tram railroads used to haul logs to sawmills in Calcasieu Parish. The first of these were put in by the Edgewood Land and Logging Company (between Westlake and DeQuincy) and the Bradley-Ramsey Company (north of Lake Charles). (Courtesy of McNeese Archives.)

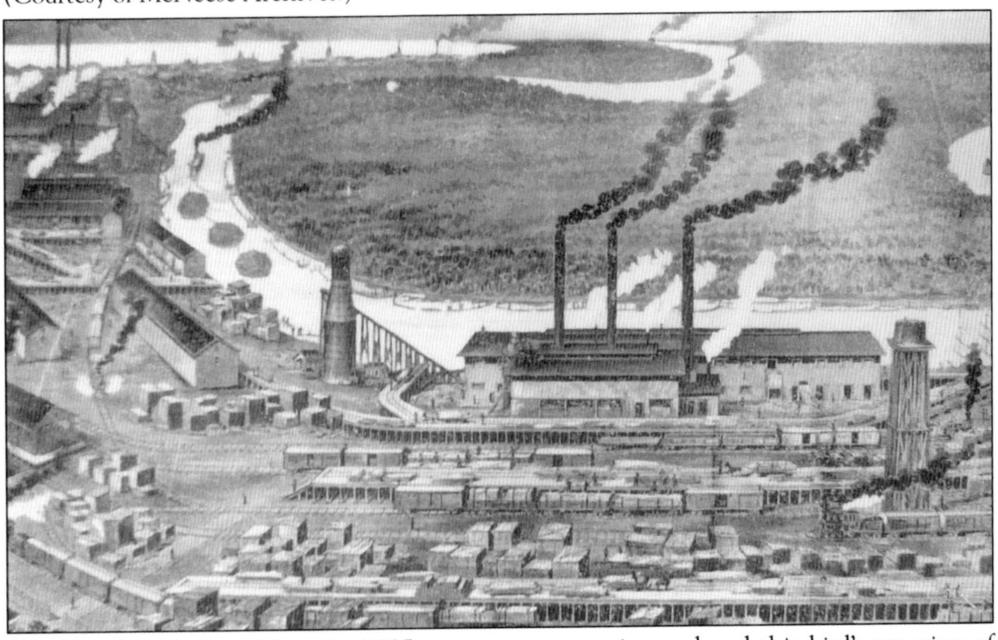

The Bradley-Ramsey Mill. In 1905 an anonymous artist produced this bird's-eye view of the Bradley-Ramsey Lumber Company's operation north of Lake Charles. The river curving off to the left is the Calcasieu as it flows into Lake Charles where other mills are in operation. During 1905, Bradley-Ramsey produced 60 million board feet of lumber. (Courtesy of McNeese Archives.)

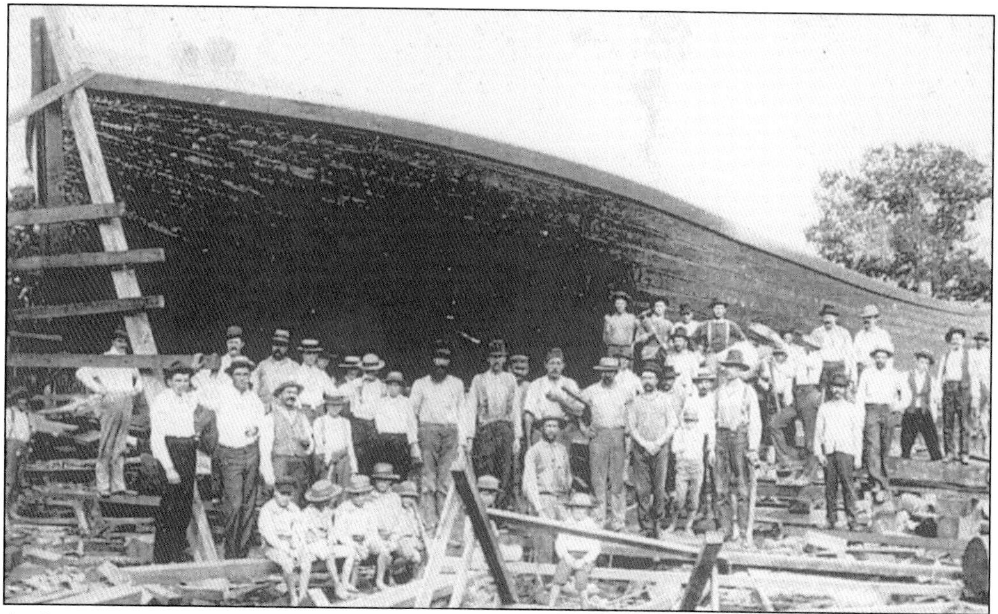

A Calcasieu Shipyard. Shipbuilding was already an established Calcasieu River industry when this photo was taken at the J.A. Bel mill in the early 1900s. The workmen shown here are building an ocean-going barge with Calcasieu pine and hardwood. Crews like this, working under the guidance of former Nordic sailors, built most of the several hundred schooners used in the Calcasieu lumber trade, plus other vessels such as steamboats, tugs, and huge barges. (Courtesy of McNeese Archives.)

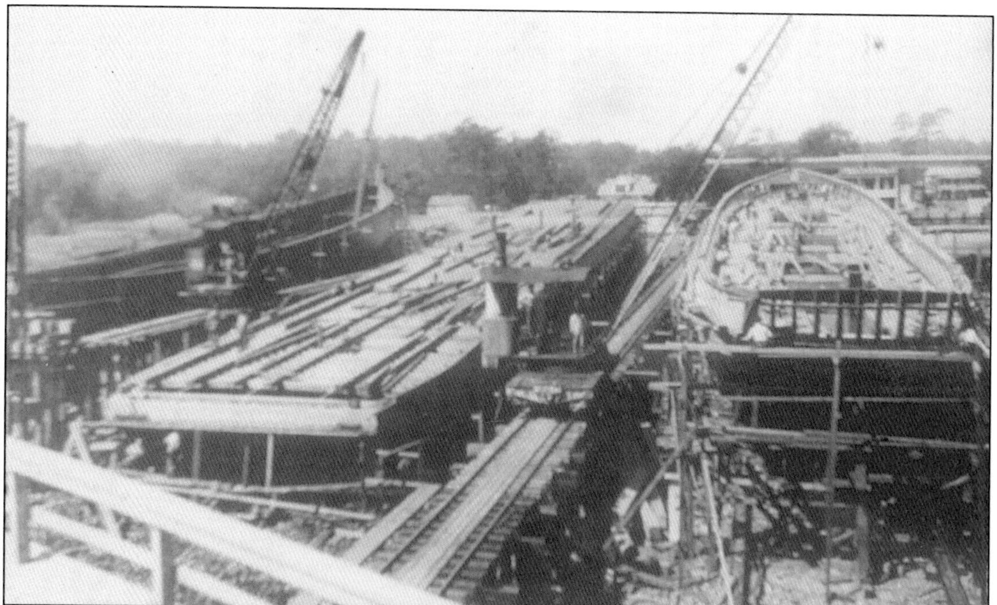

Schooners on the Ways. The hulls of two large, wooden schooners are taking shape on the ways at Clooney's Construction and Towing Company shipyard west of Lake Charles in this c. 1918 photo. In 1918, Clooney's had been in business for 12 years, during which time it had constructed over 300 large wooden vessels using Southwest Louisiana lumber. (Courtesy of Imperial Calcasieu Museum.)

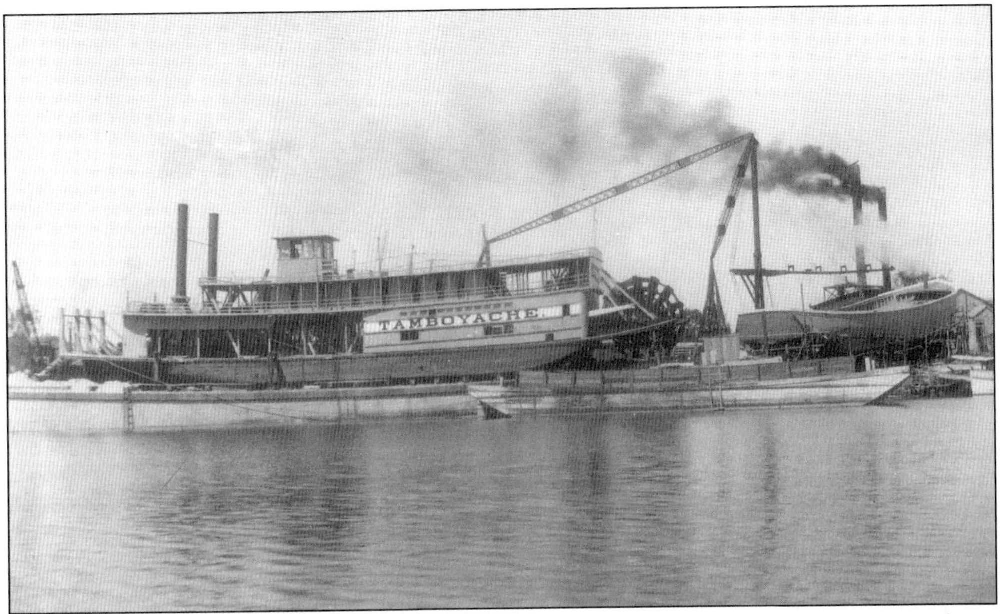

A New Stern-wheeler. Clooney's shipyard built the stern-wheeler *Tamboyache*, seen here, and many much larger craft during the heyday of longleaf yellow pine in Southwest Louisiana. In 1919, a year after this photo was taken, this shipyard constructed an ocean-going barge that was 260 feet long and capable of holding 30,000 barrels of oil. The barge required 1.2 million board feet of lumber in its construction. (Courtesy of Imperial Calcasieu Museum.)

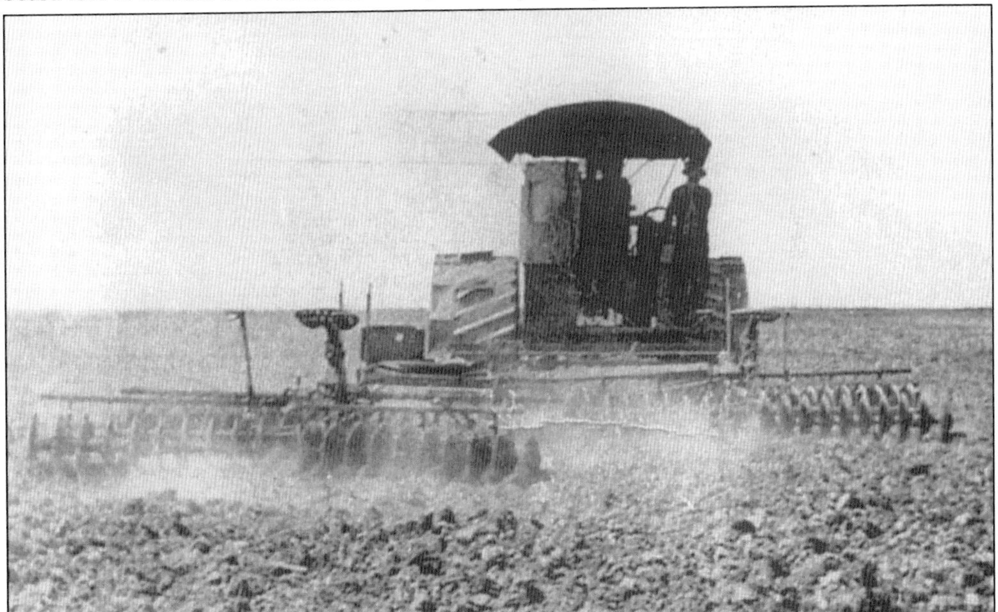

The Rice Industry. A large field is being disked by an expensive, steam-powered tractor in this photo, taken about 1910. Steam tractors and long irrigation canals dramatically increased rice acreage and production in the early 1900s. During these years, many businessmen invested in land and canal companies, which purchased and used tractors such as this. (Courtesy of Helen Kendall Collection.)

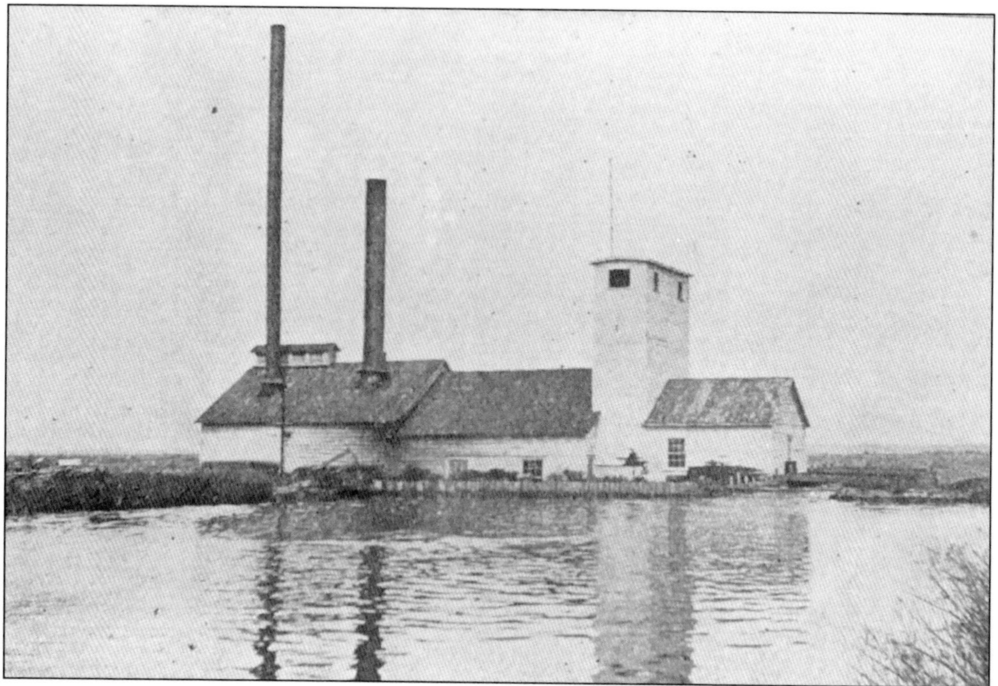

AN IRRIGATION CANAL PLANT. This 1905 photograph shows one of the pumping plants owned by the Farmers' Canal Company. The water in the foreground was pumped out of English Bayou, northeast of Lake Charles, and was sent through a system of canals and pumping stations to thousands of acres of rice in fields many miles away. (Courtesy of McNeese Archives.)

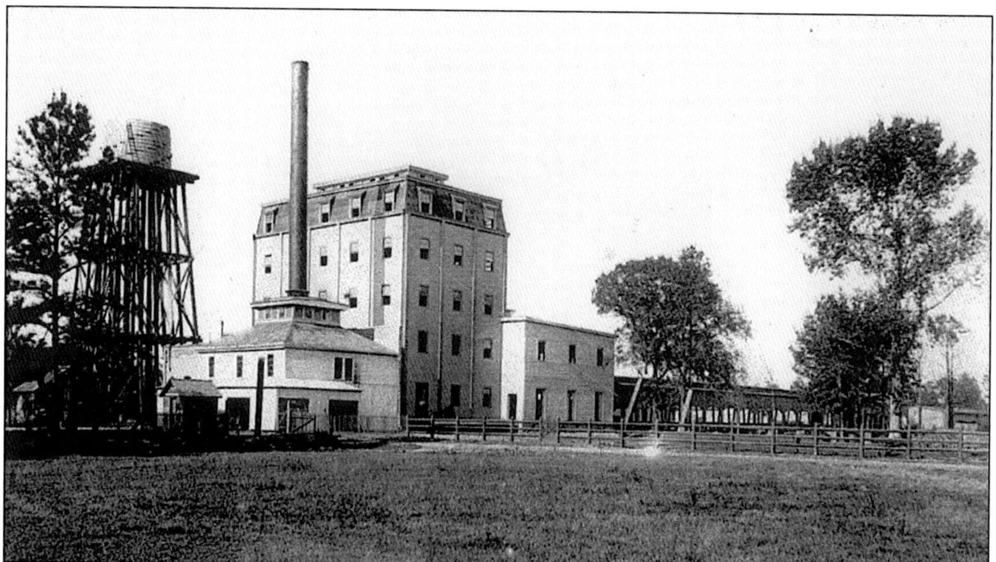

A LARGE RICE MILL. The Lake Charles Rice Milling Company plant, shown here in 1893, was located on the Calcasieu River north of Lake Charles. The plant provided milling, packaging, and marketing for locally grown rice. The first rice ever shipped from Lake Charles was sent to Galveston, TX, in 1879, according to the *Lake Charles Echo*. The rice had been processed in the Ryan & Sons mill. (Courtesy of Imperial Calcasieu Museum.)

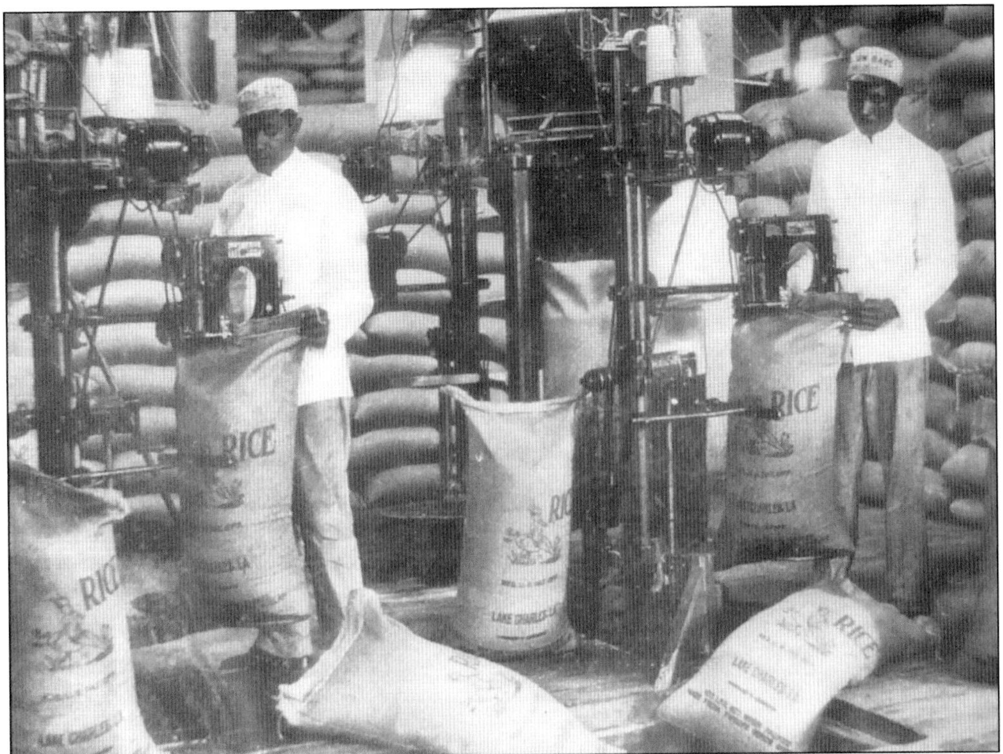

BAGGING RICE. Workmen inside the Lake Charles Rice Mill are shown here using bagging machines to fill and close 100-pound sacks of milled and polished rice. This mill grew in size as the industry expanded until it became what many people said was "the largest rice mill in the world." Another important local rice mill was established in 1898 on Front Street in Lake Charles by W.C., Walton, and Charles Wall. (Courtesy of McNeese Archives.)

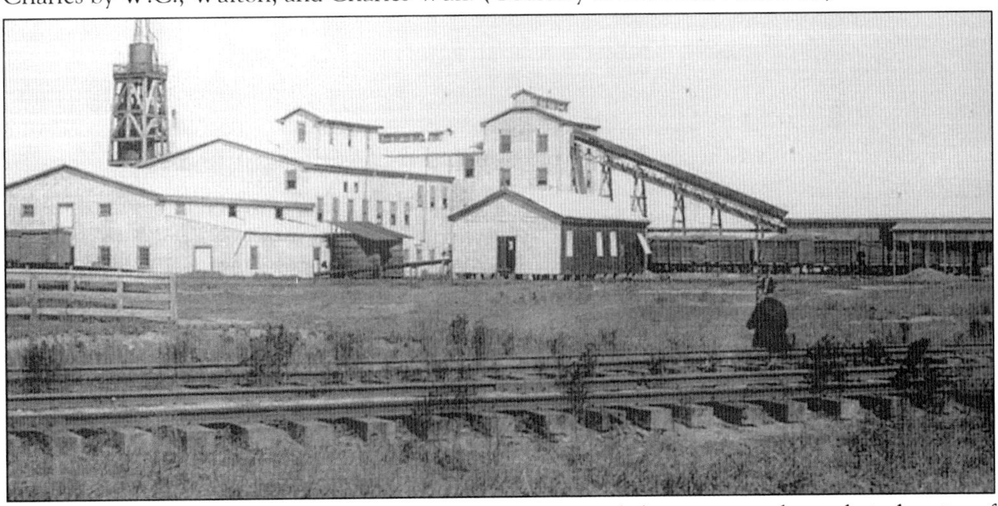

THE OLD SUGAR REFINERY. One of the most conspicuous failures among the early industries of Imperial Calcasieu is represented in this 1893 photo of the old Lake Charles Sugar Refinery. This refinery was built by the North American Land and Timber Company, an English investment firm affiliated with J.B. Watkins, as part of its promotion of an early 1880s investment in nearly a million acres of Southwest Louisiana land. (Courtesy of Imperial Calcasieu Museum.)

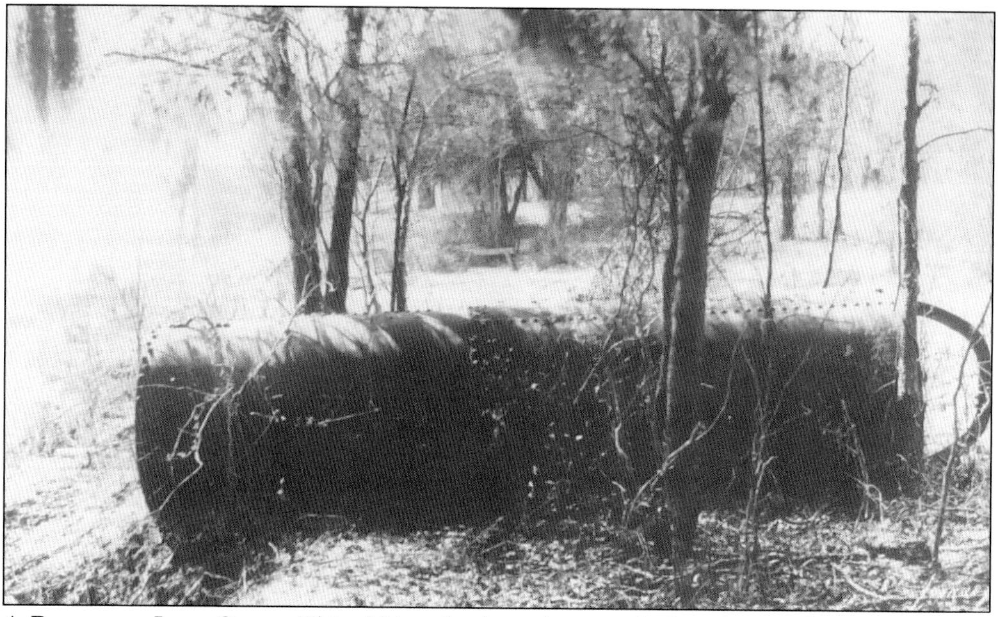

A Relic of a Lost Cause. This old iron bucket, photographed in the woods near Rose Bluff along the Calcasieu River south of Sulphur, was built in the early 1870s to be lowered into a mine shaft and filled with sulphur. The project failed because of problems with water, quicksand, and poisonous gases, and the bucket was never put to its intended use. (Courtesy of McNeese Archives).

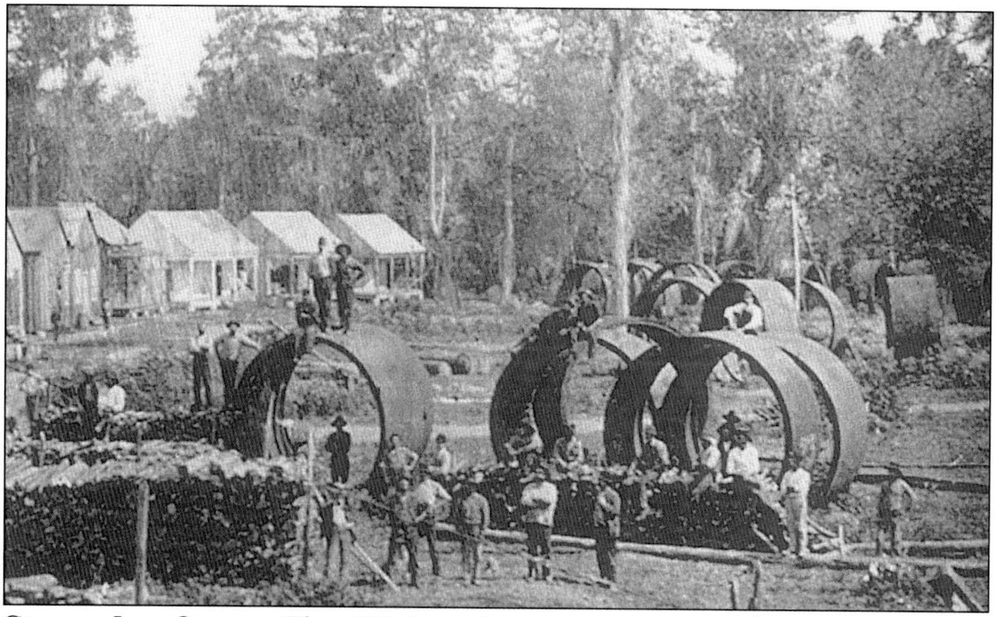

Gigantic Iron Caissons. This 1871 photo shows workmen at a French firm's mine near the present-day town of Sulphur. The men proudly display the huge iron cylinders, or caissons, they had recently rolled to the site from the Calcasieu River. Manufactured in France, the caissons were 11 feet in diameter and 5 feet long, and they weighed 7.5 tons each. The firm's engineers hoped to use the caissons to seal the walls of the 450-foot vertical mine shaft they planned to dig to a deposit of pure sulphur. (Courtesy of Imperial Calcasieu Museum.)

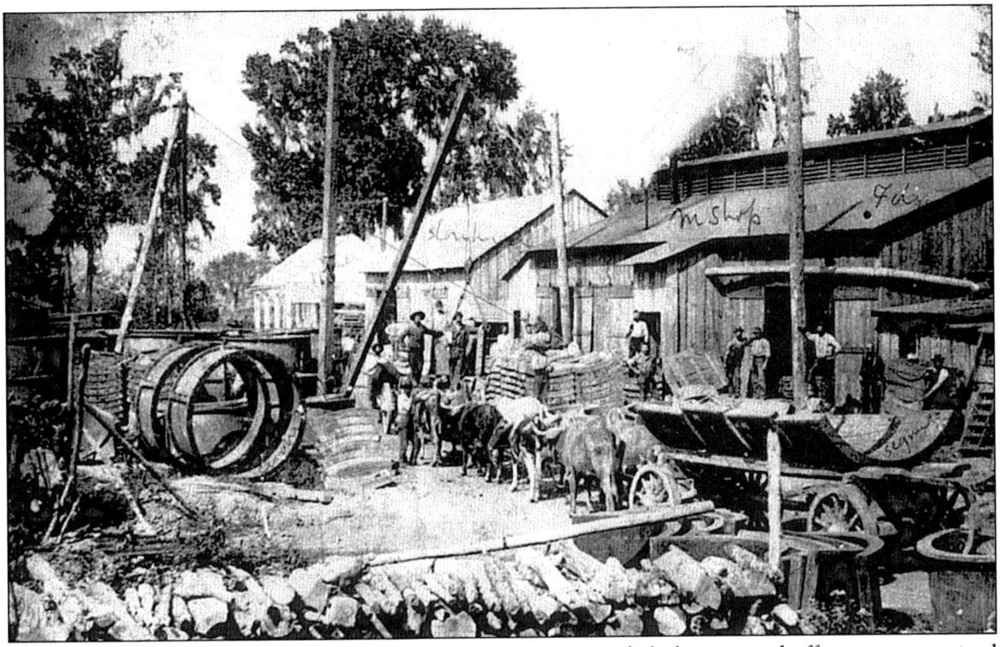

Another Try for Sulphur. After the first sulphur mine failed, a second effort was organized to attempt to dig a mine using lighter, more easily managed iron segments. These segments, which were also manufactured in Europe, are shown arriving in a wagon pulled by a team of eight oxen in this 1873 or 1874 photo. The crane on the extreme left may have been the one used to lower these caissons into the mine. (Courtesy of Imperial Calcasieu Museum.)

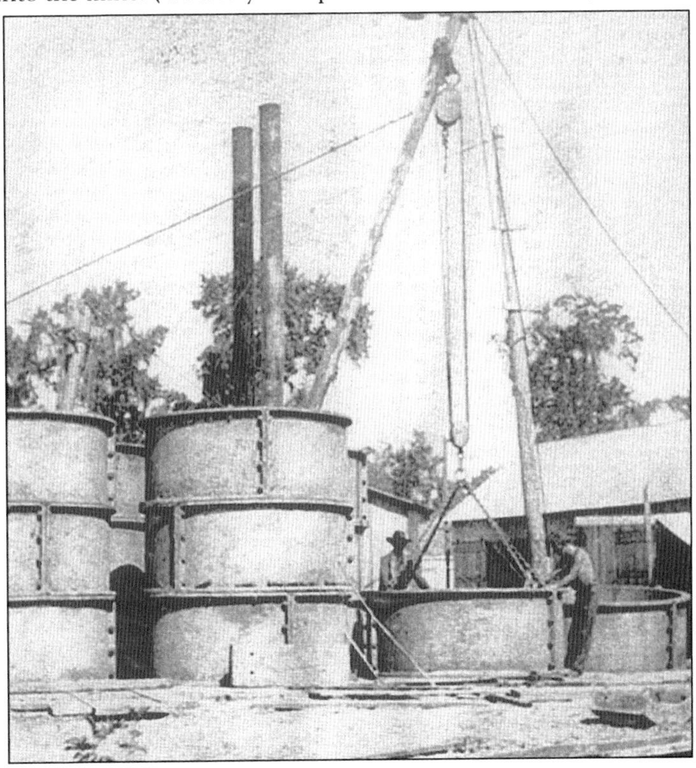

A Horrible Mining Disaster. Stacks of assembled cast-iron caissons and two workmen using a crane to lift them are shown in this photo also taken in 1873 or 1874 at the West Calcasieu sulphur mine. The attempt to dig two parallel shafts failed when five miners died from drowning and hydrogen sulfide gas poisoning about 180 feet below the surface. In 1876, the land and equipment in this million-dollar investment were auctioned off in a sheriff's sale for nonpayment of taxes. (Courtesy of Imperial Calcasieu Museum.)

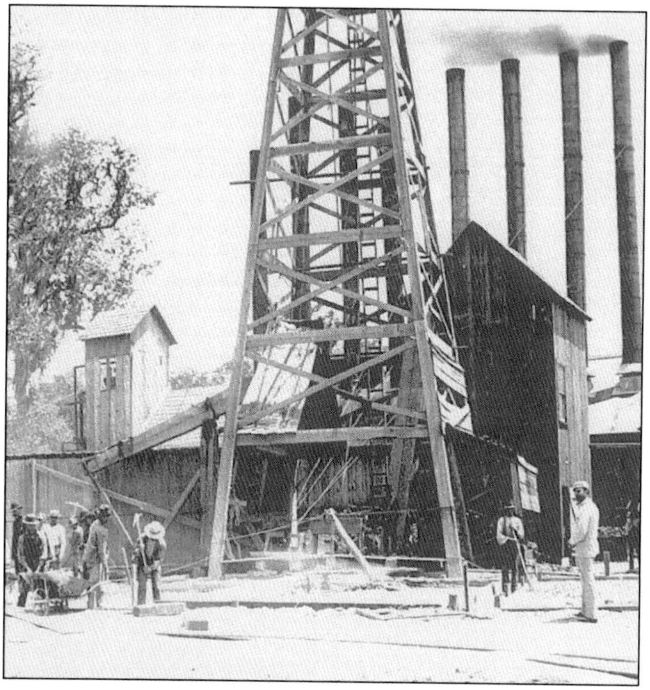

Molten Sulphur. Herman Frasch, a former Standard Oil Company chemist, began working in 1890 at the old Sulphur mine on a revolutionary new mining process. This photo, taken on Christmas Eve, 1894, shows the success of Frasch's efforts when liquefied sulphur began spewing out of a pipe onto the ground (under the derrick). The workmen on the left are scurrying to build additional forms to contain the sulphur. Frasch's first steam plant is in the background. (Courtesy of Imperial Calcasieu Museum.)

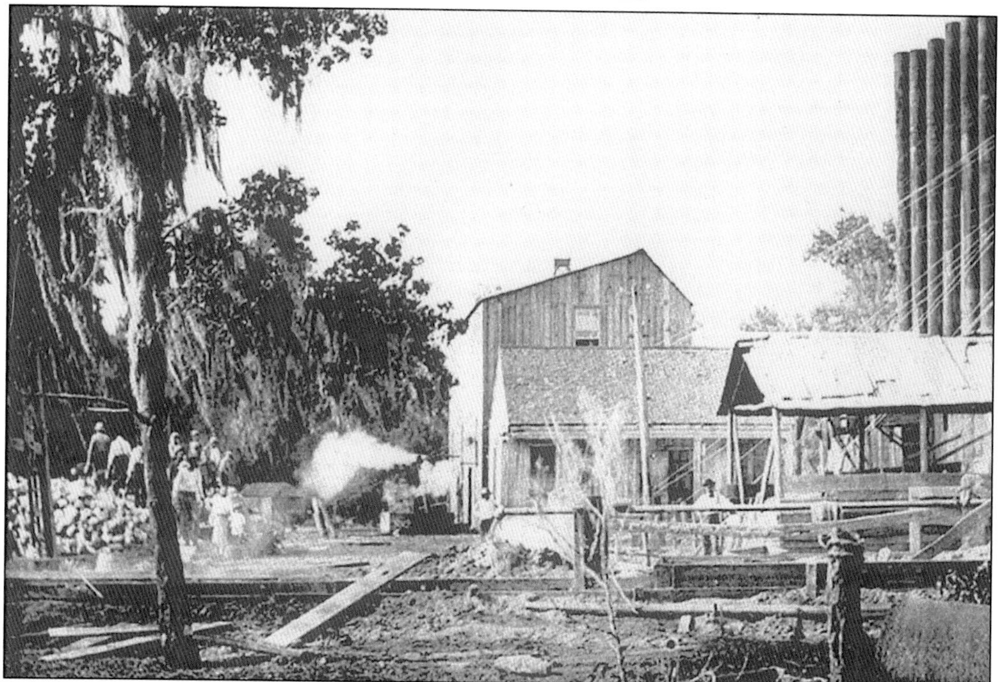

Frasch at a Distance. Herman Frasch stands, hands on his hips, near a shed on the right side of this late 1894 or early 1895 photograph. The men on the far left are using wheelbarrows to move pieces of newly dried sulphur into a pile. After discovering how to bring sulphur to the surface from a depth of over 400 feet, Frasch and his employees spent the next seven years perfecting his extraction process and the methods of drilling wells that would not quickly cave in. (Courtesy of Imperial Calcasieu Museum.)

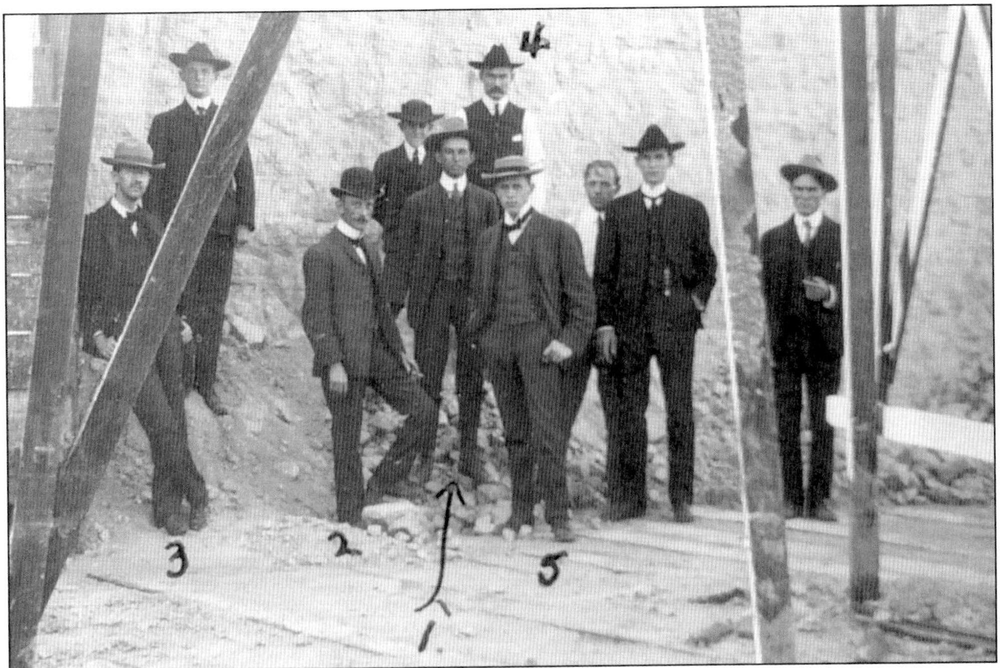

UNION SULPHUR OFFICIALS. Plant officers of Frasch's Union Sulphur Company gathered for this casual group photo sometime in the early 1900s. The numbered officers are as follows: (1) John L. Henning, plant manager; (2) Hugo Spitzer, chief chemist; (3) Sam W. Shancocil, office manager; (4) Daniel O'Brien, office manager; and (5) ? Eileisgaard, engineer. By this time, Frasch had moved to New York City, where he and his wife lived in the Royal Suite of the brand new St. Regis Hotel. (Courtesy of Imperial Calcasieu Museum.)

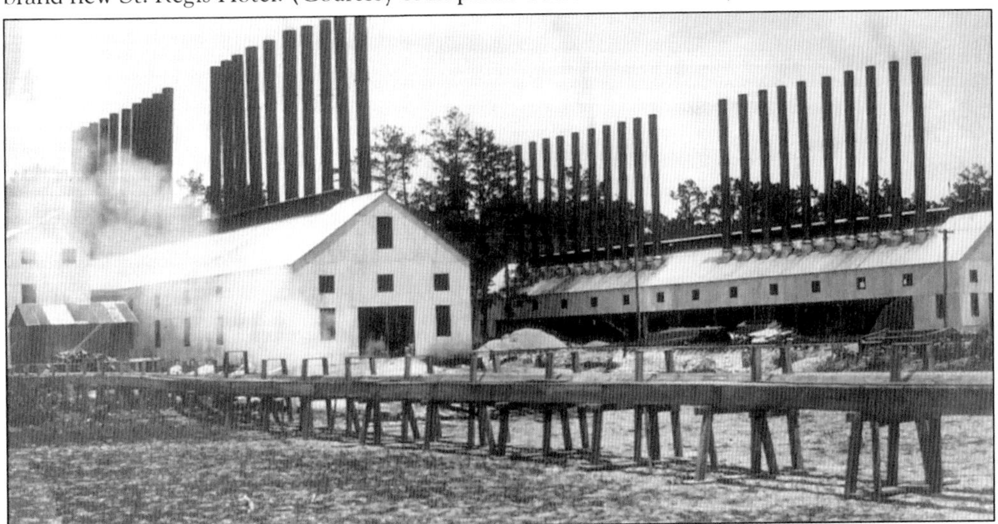

HUGE POWER PLANTS. By 1906, the Union Sulphur Company was operating in Calcasieu Parish what was believed to be the largest collection of steam-generating plants in the world. The stacks in this photo represent only a few of the 140 boilers then in use, a number that was still not considered sufficient to meet production demands. The mines had an output of 400 to 600 tons of sulphur per day. The trestle system in the foreground held pipes that carried steam and hot water to the wells. (Courtesy of Imperial Calcasieu Museum.)

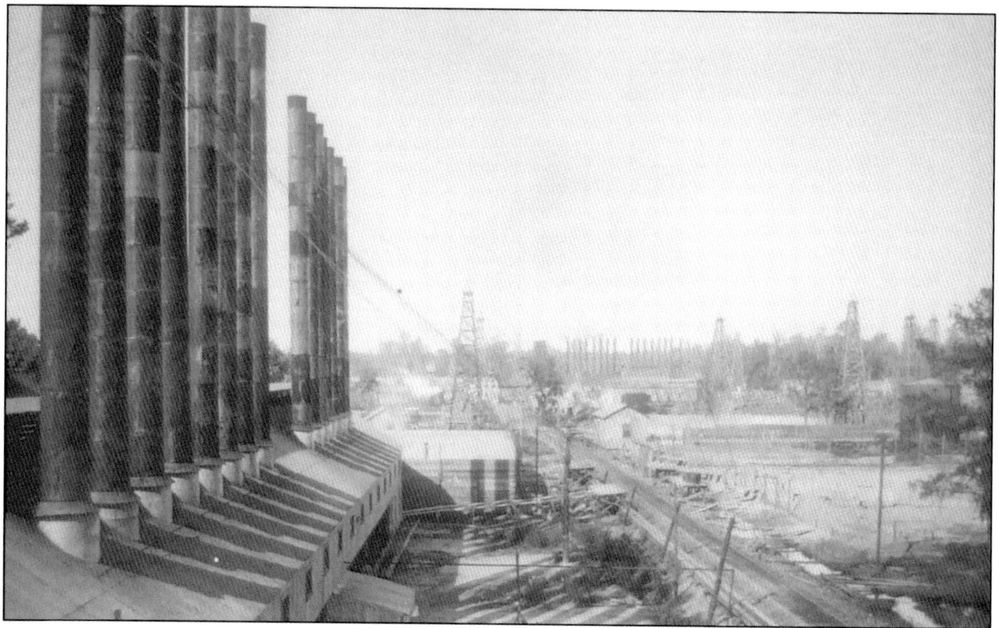

A SULPHUR MINES SCENE. Some idea of the extent of development at Union Sulphur's mines in western Calcasieu Parish during the early 1900s can be gained from this photograph. The smoke stacks of various power plants can be seen in the left foreground and far center. Sulphur wells are represented in this photo by the derricks that are strewn across the scene. Steam and hot water lines move diagonally across the landscape from the power plants to the wells. (Courtesy of Imperial Calcasieu Museum.)

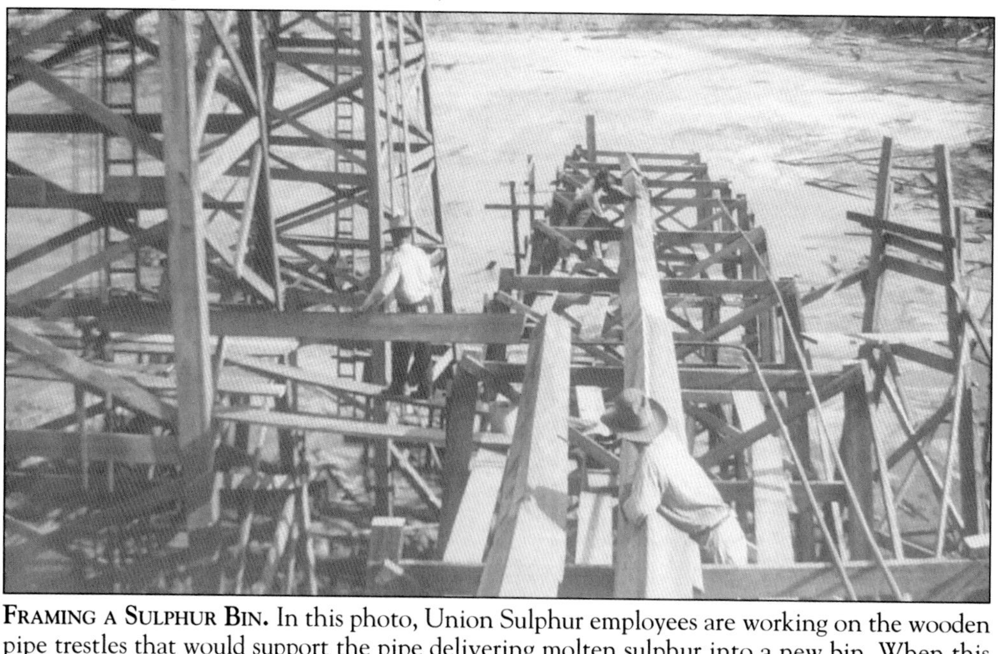

FRAMING A SULPHUR BIN. In this photo, Union Sulphur employees are working on the wooden pipe trestles that would support the pipe delivering molten sulphur into a new bin. When this bin was completed, it would hold thousands of tons of cooling sulphur as it solidified into one gigantic yellow cake. Sulphur bins occupied the area of a city block and were topped off at 50 feet. (Courtesy of Imperial Calcasieu Museum.)

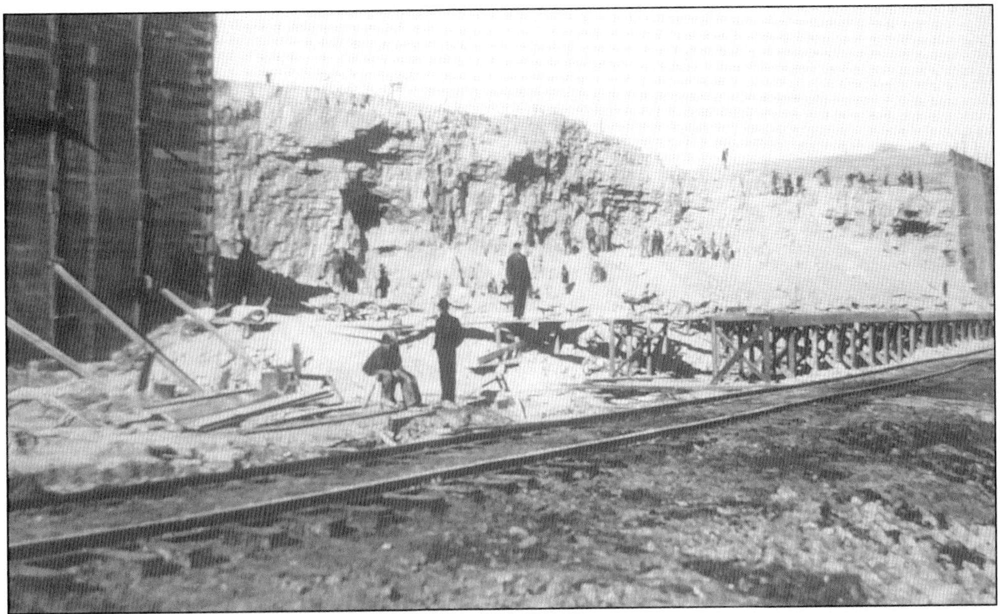

A MOUNTAIN OF SULPHUR. The mountain in this early 1900s photo is pure sulphur. The pile of rubble in the center is sulphur that was dynamited so that it could be loaded on railroad cars. The size of the workmen, who appear as dark spots in the upper far right, gives an idea of the immensity of this mound. The boards and framing have not yet been removed on the extreme left and right. (Courtesy of Imperial Calcasieu Museum.)

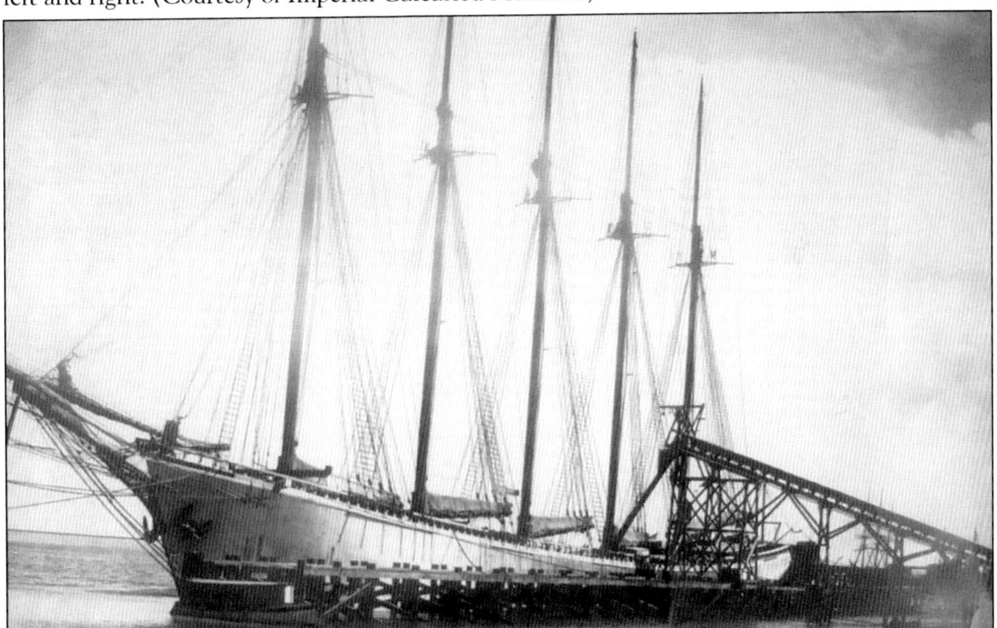

A SABINE RIVER DOCK. Sulphur is being loaded into a cargo ship in this photo taken around the time of World War I at Union Sulphur's dock on the west side of the Sabine River. Shipments from this dock continued from 1908 to about 1927. The company ceased mining operations in 1924 when its supply of sulphur was considered depleted, but it continued shipping from stockpiles for several more years. (Courtesy of Imperial Calcasieu Museum.)

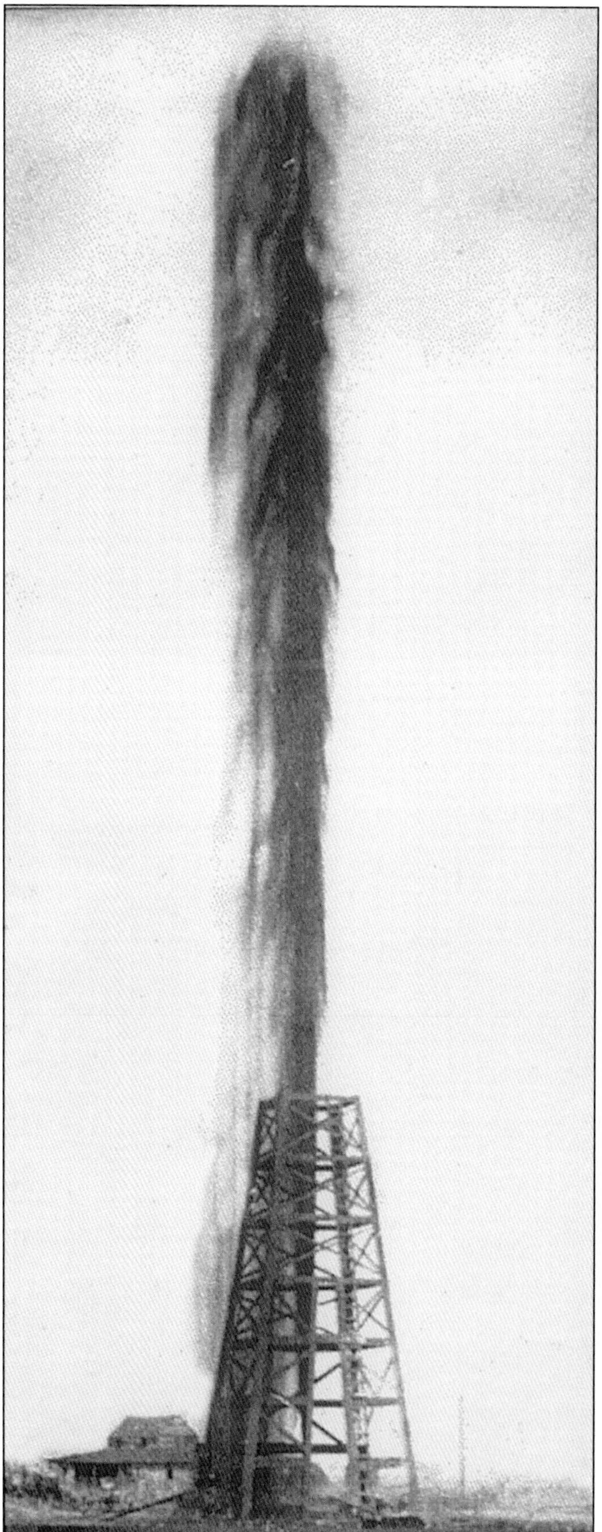

Gusher! In 1901 the first oil discovery in the South at Spindletop near Beaumont, TX, set off an epidemic of oil fever that spread instantly to Louisiana. The first oil in Louisiana was discovered by the Heywood Brothers in the summer of that same year near Jennings, just a few miles east of the Calcasieu Parish line. This photograph shows a Jennings oil field gusher spouting oil to an amazing height. In the following months, the Jennings field produced strike after strike, which kept oil fever high in neighboring Imperial Calcasieu until this parish's first oil gusher was brought in 3 miles west of Welsh in August 1902. In the summer of 1910, a few miles south of Vinton in western Calcasieu, the very productive Vinton oil field was "gushered" in. This field attracted drillers and oil speculators from all over the country. John Geddings Gray, the owner of all the land and mineral rights in the area, leased drilling sites to dozens of companies, and many of them struck oil. To accommodate the men working at the Vinton oil field, workers and businessmen put up a boom town of tents and unpainted frame houses, which they named Ged in honor of John Geddings Gray. (Courtesy of McNeese Archives.)

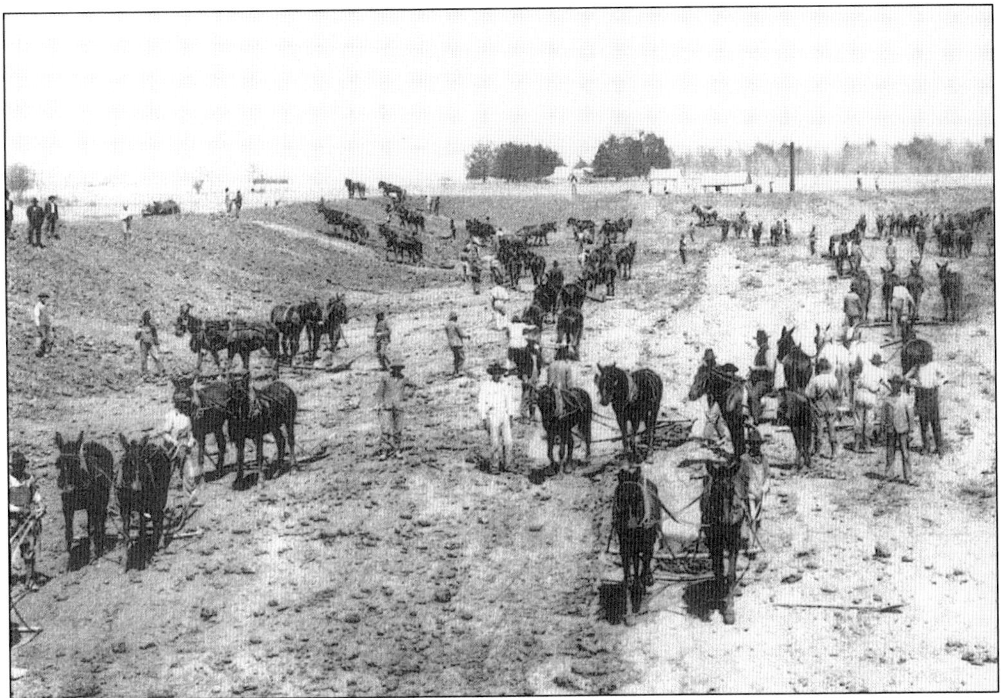

Digging an Oil Pit. A huge oil pit is being dug by scores of mule drivers in this photo taken at the Jennings oil field shortly after its discovery. Drillers built a few steel storage tanks, but open pits such as this were commonly used. In 1905, when the open pits filled up, the drillers began allowing their oil to run off into nearby Bayou Nezpique, which flowed into the Mermentau River and continued all the way to the Gulf of Mexico, a distance of about 80 miles by water. (Courtesy of McNeese Archives.)

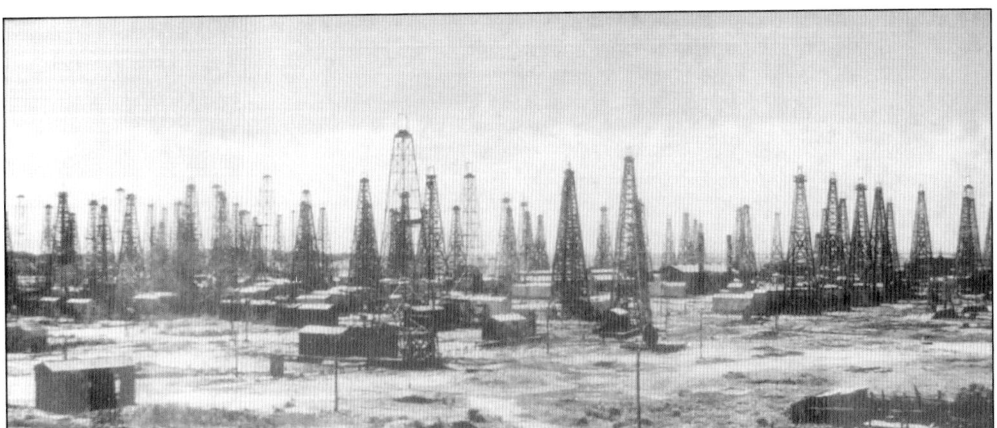

The Vinton Oil Field. Within a couple of years of the original oil strike near Vinton, drillers practically filled a 160-acre area with derricks. With wells allowed as close as 50 feet apart, new strikes encouraged the drilling of new wells nearby. When the new wells struck oil, they took production away from the original well. All of this drilling was done by about 1,500 workers, most of whom lived in tents and hastily built shacks in the boom town of Ged. The oil was hauled to the Southern Pacific Railroad in wagons until pipe lines were built. (Courtesy of McNeese Archives.)

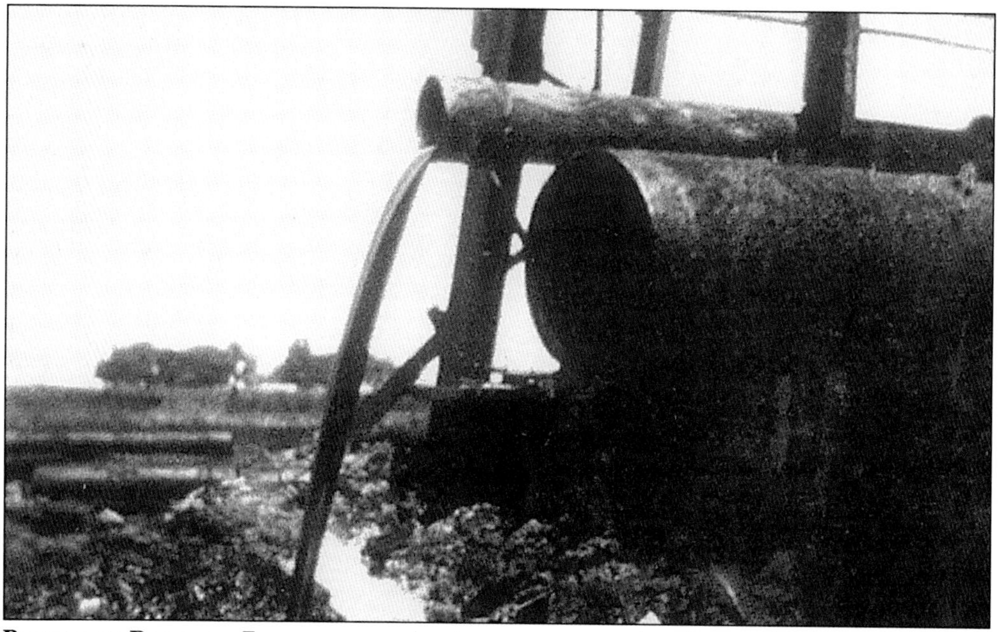

Pollution Problem. For many months there was so much oil pouring out of the ground in the Vinton oil field that all of the storage tanks became filled and the excess oil was directed into large, open ponds, one of which was said to be the size of a small lake. Eventually, however, most drillers learned to contain their oil. In 1917, the Vinton oil field produced 1.63 million barrels, and nearby Edgerly Field produced 1.01 million barrels. (Courtesy of McNeese Archives.)

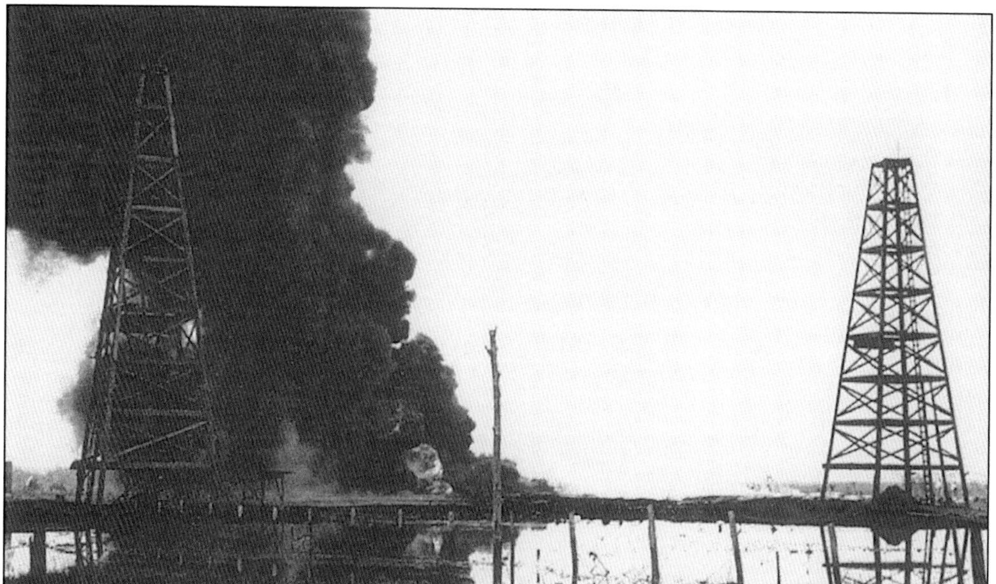

Oil Field Fires. Flames of 50 to 100 feet and plumes of black smoke that could be seen for miles were not unusual in early Southwest Louisiana oil fields. Fires, such as this one at the Jennings oil field shortly after its discovery, often completely destroyed derricks, machinery, and storage tanks and ignited the thick layer of oil that covered the ground around most of the wells. (Courtesy of McNeese Archives.)

Six

Churches, Schools, and Clubs

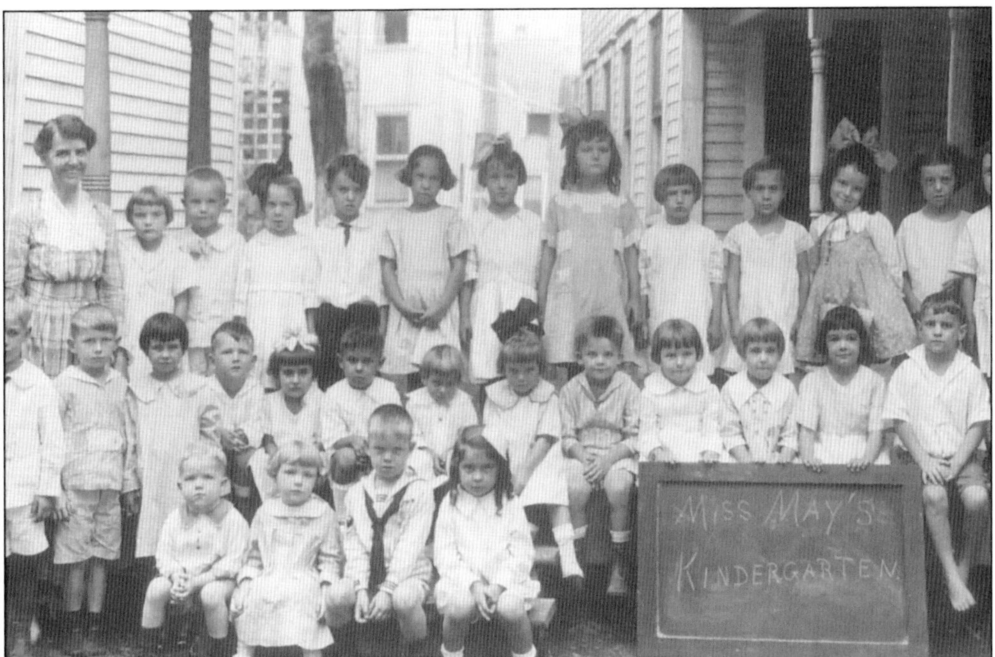

Perfect Little Angels. Miss May Breazele's kindergarten class in Lake Charles shows all of the innocence and charm that children of this age can muster in this photograph taken on October 29, 1919. By this time, the importance of education was more fully realized throughout the parishes of Southwest Louisiana, thanks to the pioneering work of teachers like Thomas Rigmaiden, Mrs. J.W. Bryan, and John McNeese. (Courtesy of Imperial Calcasieu Museum.)

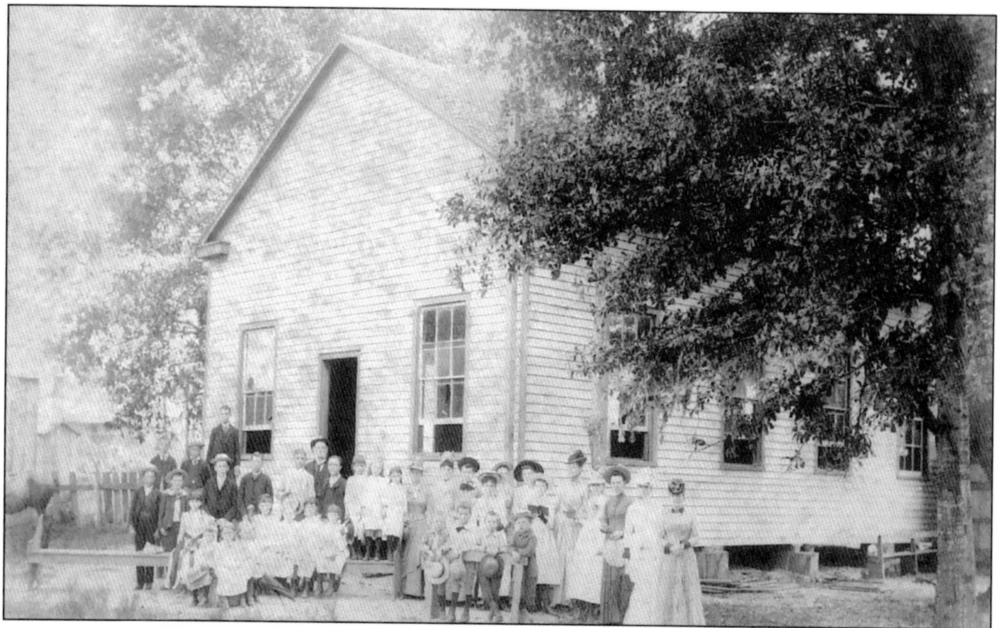

AN EARLY ONE-ROOM SCHOOL. Mrs. J.W. Bryan taught Lake Charles children in this school on Ryan Street in the 1870s. She met her future husband when he gave her a job teaching children in the rooms over his Ryan Street store shortly after the Civil War. They were married in 1869, and Mrs. Bryan continued her teaching, moving down the street to this building. The Bryans had eight children. (Courtesy of Imperial Calcasieu Museum.)

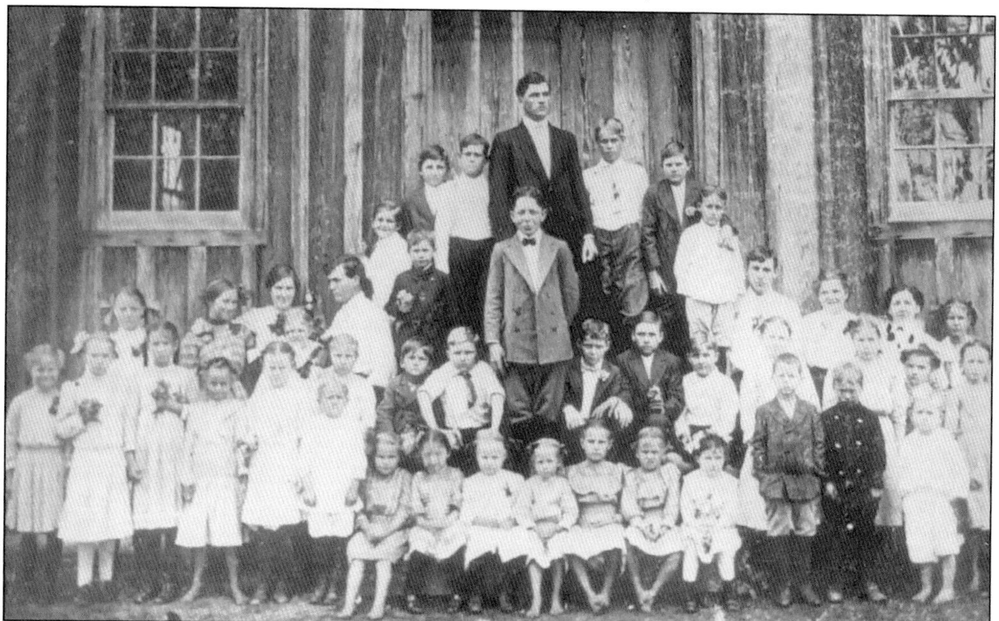

AN EARLY COUNTRY SCHOOL. In 1911, the teacher and students of Dry Branch School in the Sugartown area of old Calcasieu Parish posed for this group photo beside their school. By this time, the reforms School Superintendent John McNeese had championed for 23 years in the small schools of the parish were turning them into models for schools throughout the state. (Courtesy of McNeese Archives.)

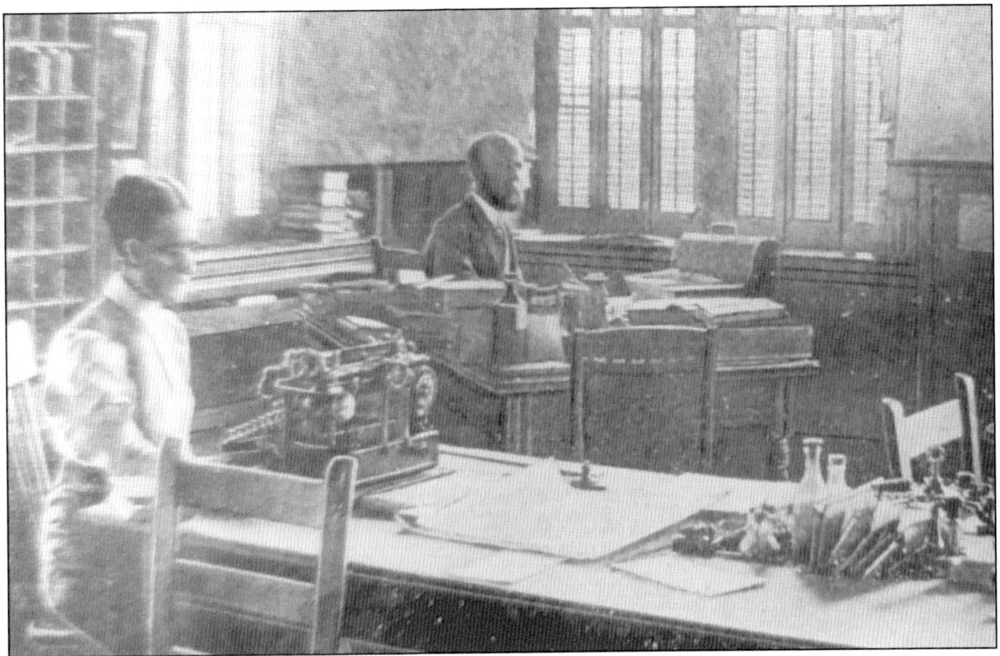

Superintendent McNeese. John McNeese (seen here working in his office in 1900 with his daughter and secretary, Emma McNeese Squires) officially served as superintendent of the schools of Imperial Calcasieu Parish from 1888 until his retirement in 1913. McNeese State University was named for him because of the remarkable leadership he provided for the early schools of Calcasieu Parish. (Courtesy of McNeese Archives.)

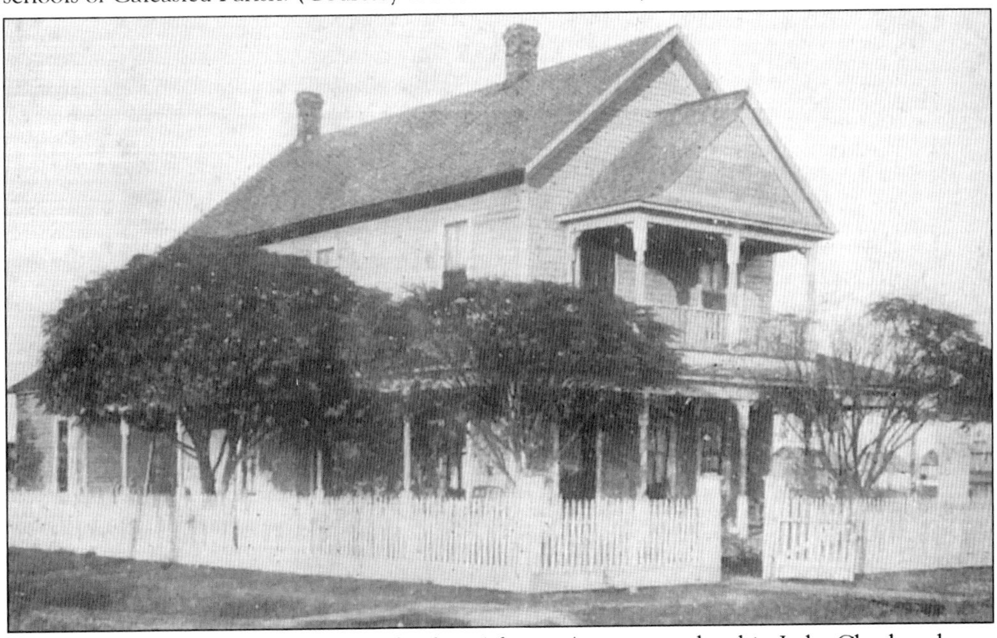

An early Lake Charles School. The first African-American school in Lake Charles, shown here, was originally built as an African-American lodge hall. Professor W.O. Boston, a noted leader in early schools, taught in this building, located on Broad Street near Louisiana Avenue. (Courtesy of McNeese Archives.)

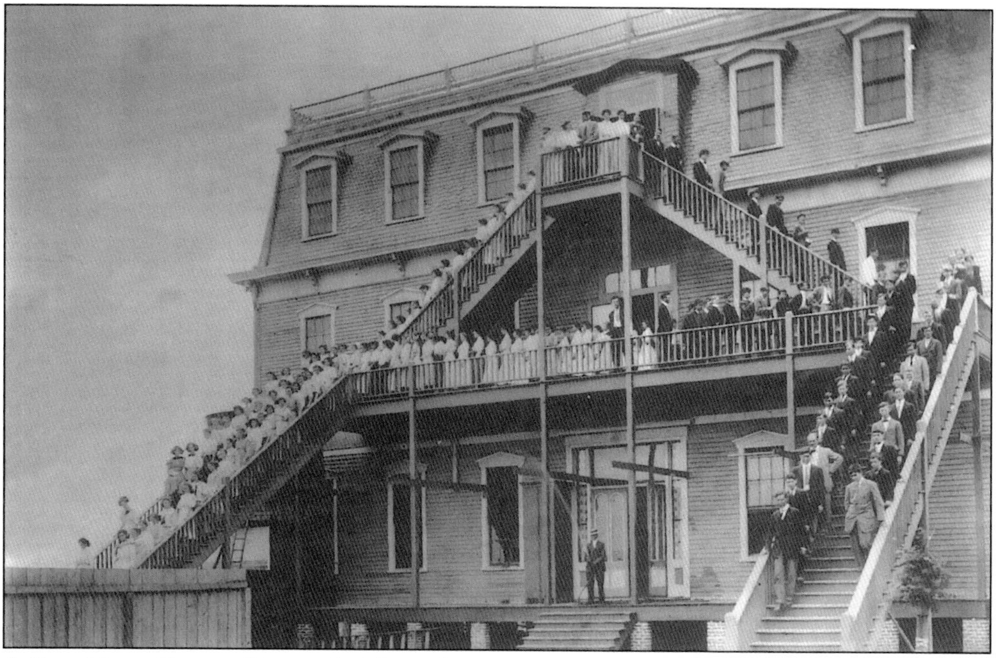

A Fire Drill Photo. Boys and girls used separate entrances and exits in early Lake Charles schools, as is shown in this 1910 photograph. Here they posed during a fire drill at the old Lake Charles High School on Boulevard, east of town. This building was constructed in 1889 by the Congregationalists of New England as Lake Charles College and was later purchased by the school board at the urging of Superintendent John McNeese. This photo shows the back side of the building. (Courtesy of McNeese Archives.)

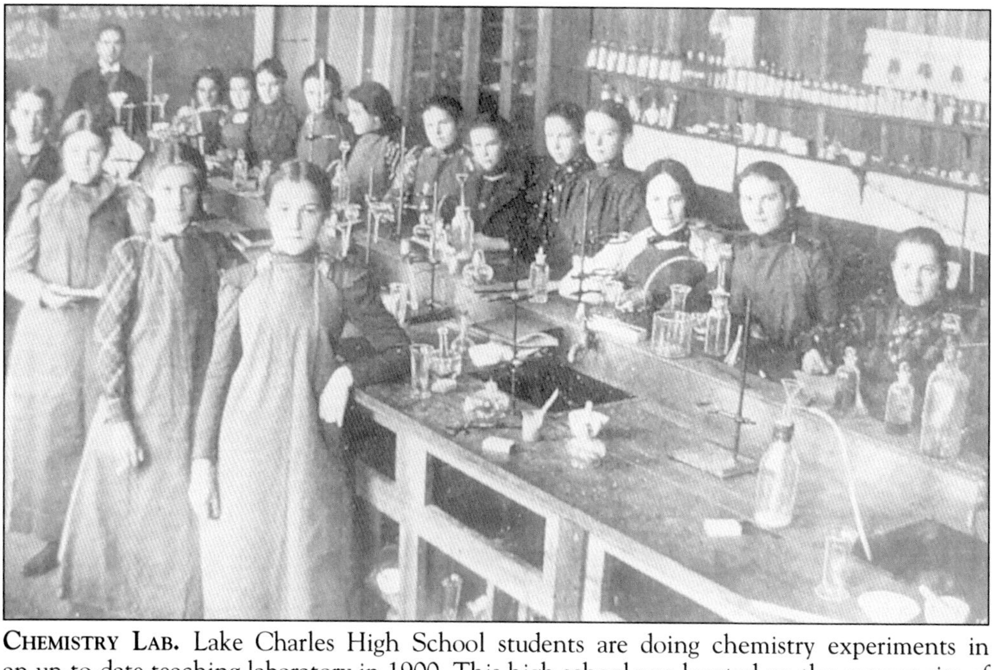

Chemistry Lab. Lake Charles High School students are doing chemistry experiments in an up-to-date teaching laboratory in 1900. This high school was located on the present site of the old Central School but in an earlier building. (Courtesy of McNeese Archives.)

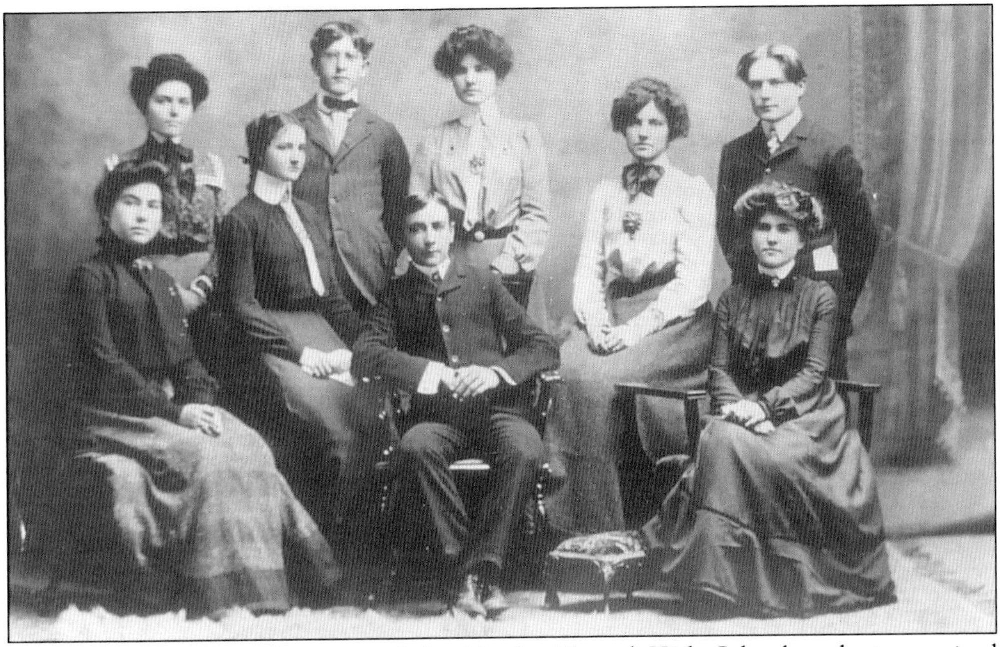

The Class of 1902. These nine Lake Charles Central High School graduates received their educations in the town's first permanent public school, which was located at the site now known as Central School. This school opened its doors in 1890 with Prof. O.S. Dolby as principal at a location that was then considered open prairie and too far out of town. (Courtesy of McNeese Archives.)

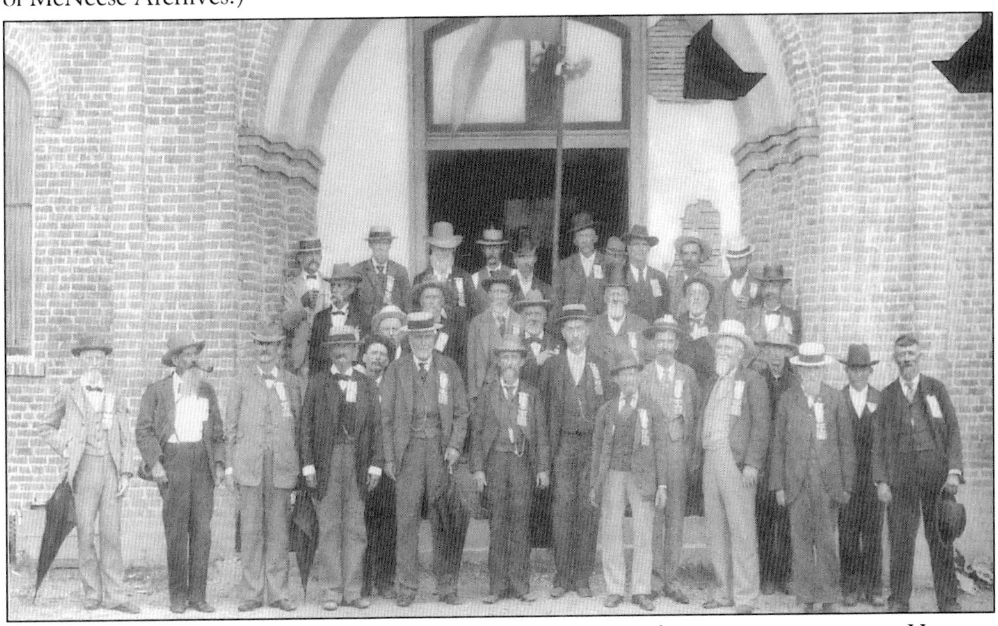

Old Veterans. These United Confederate Veterans were on their way to a reunion in Houston when they assembled on May 22, 1895, for this photograph. They are standing at the front entrance of the old Calcasieu Parish Courthouse. The years had taken their toll since 1888, when an earlier photo of this organization showed over 50 men in attendance. (Courtesy of Imperial Calcasieu Museum.)

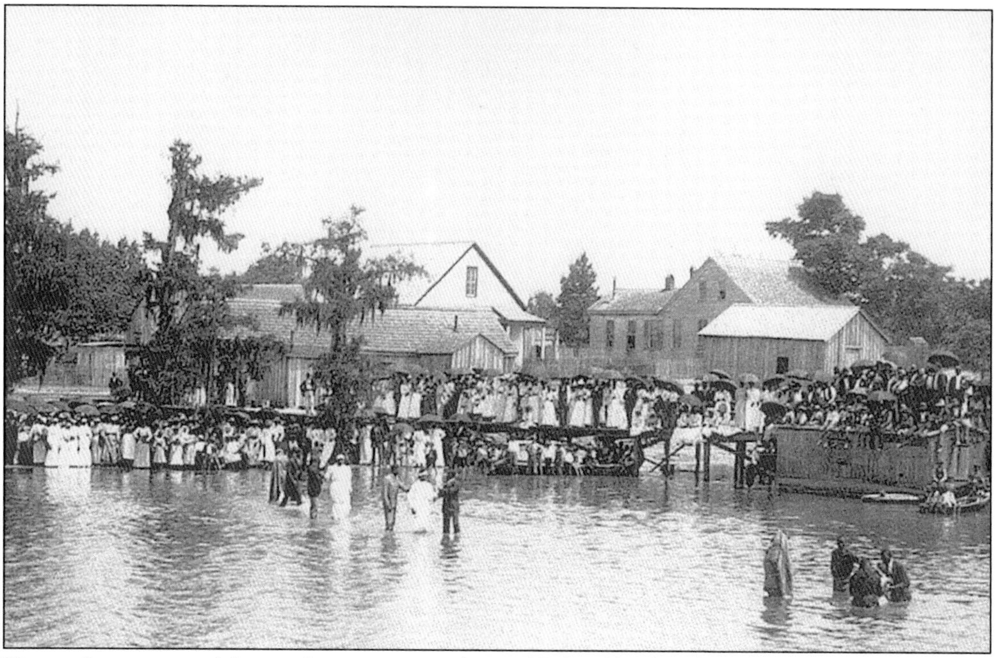

Total Immersion. African-American members of Lake Charles churches frequently gathered at the river for a baptismal ceremony. Here two ministers assist a newly baptized person, lower right, as other candidates, dressed in white, wade out for their turns. This photograph is one of the "Sturdevant's Views" series taken at various Imperial Calcasieu locations in 1893. (Courtesy of Imperial Calcasieu Museum.)

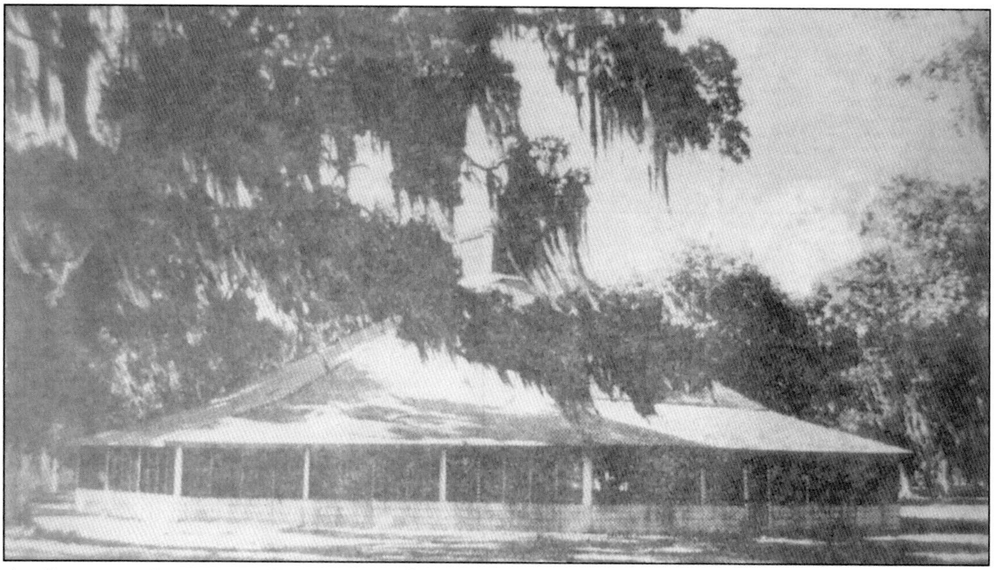

A Summer Spiritual Retreat. The Lake Arthur Camp Meeting, the oldest non-denominational gathering place in Southwest Louisiana, was organized on the east shore of beautiful Lake Arthur in 1897 and is still in service. The Tabernacle Building, shown here on an old postcard, is still surrounded by camps and dormitories. In the summer, when guest ministers hold services in this building, many camp-goers reside in the surrounding park. (Courtesy of Imperial Calcasieu Museum.)

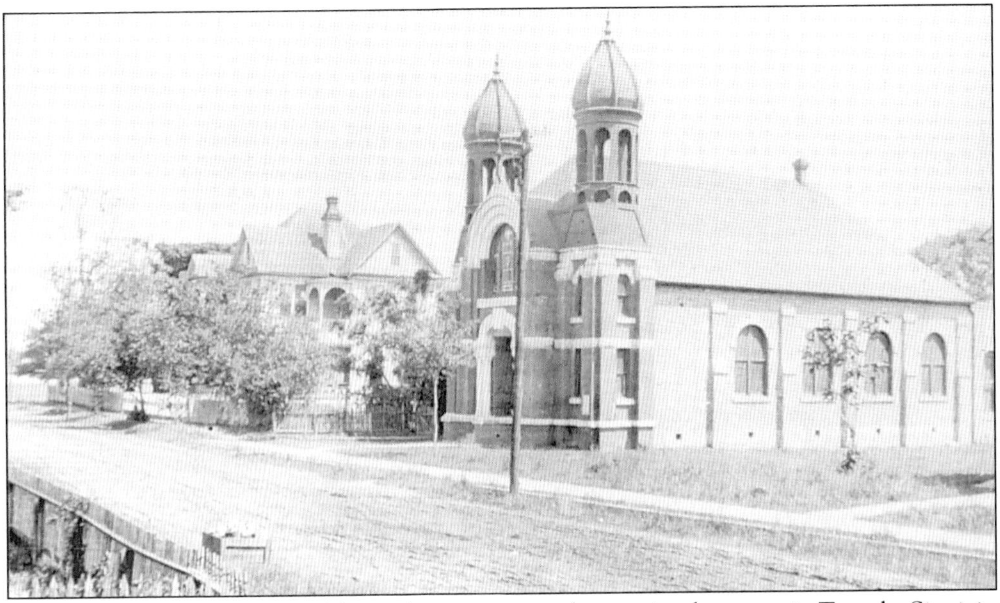

TEMPLE SINAI. One of the oldest religious meetinghouses in the state is Temple Sinai in Lake Charles. The temple is shown here as it looked before its twin towers were destroyed in the hurricane of 1918 and paving was applied to Hodges Street. (Courtesy of Helen Kendall Collection.)

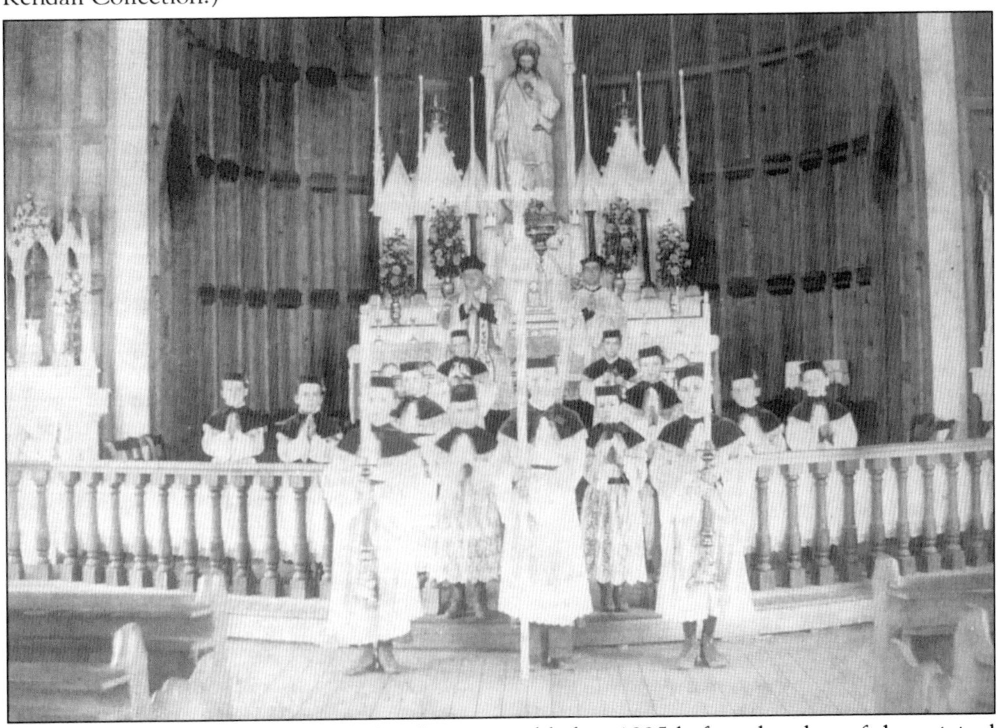

A CATHOLIC ALTAR. Priests and altar boys assembled in 1895 before the altar of the original Immaculate Conception Catholic Church in Lake Charles. This church burned in the great Lake Charles fire of 1910 and was replaced by the present structure, now known as Immaculate Conception Cathedral. (Courtesy of Imperial Calcasieu Museum.)

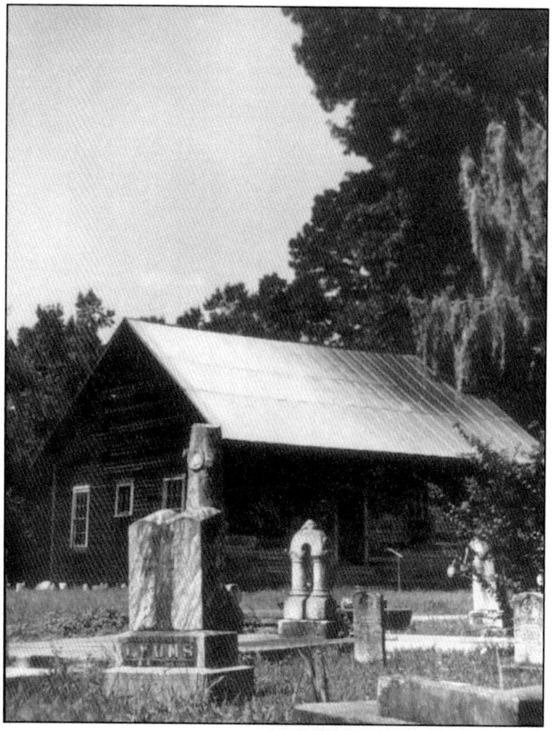

Big Woods Baptist Church. Small Protestant churches, such as the Antioch Primitive Baptist Church (shown here), were built in the timberlands of northern Imperial Calcasieu by Anglo-American immigrants from southeastern states. This church, commonly called Big Woods Baptist because it was moved to the Big Woods Community ten years after its founding in 1828, was the oldest Baptist church west of the Mississippi River in Louisiana, until recently, when it burned. (Courtesy of Imperial Calcasieu Museum.)

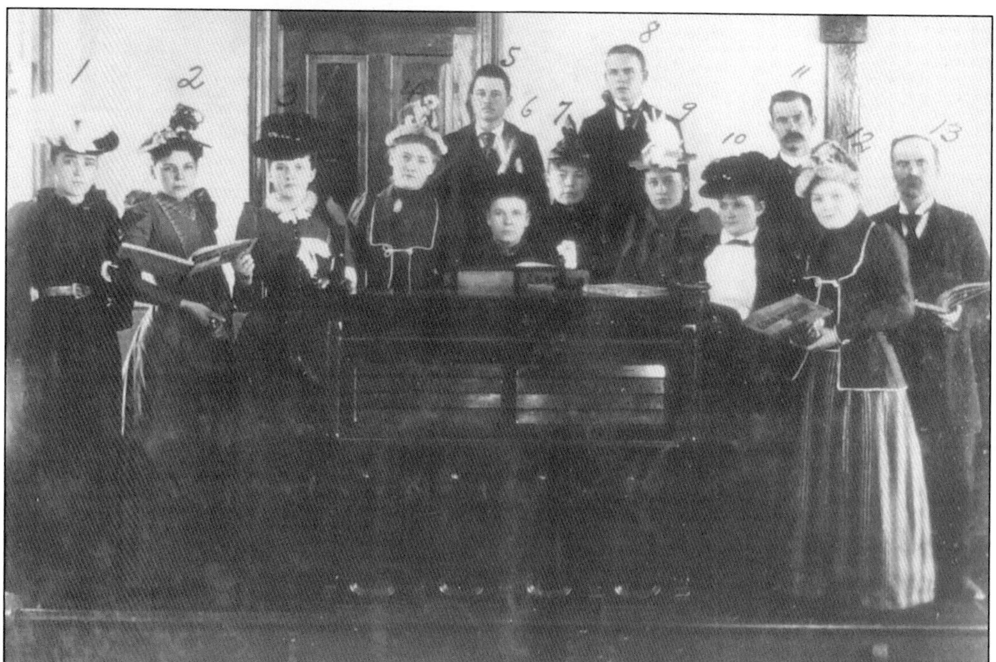

A Baptist Church Choir. The choir of the Baptist Church in Lake Charles gathered around a small, pedal organ in the 1890s. Choir members are as follows: (1) Nellie Davis, (2) Estelle Bulloch, (3) Clara Davis, (4) Myrtle McClelland, (5) Albert Hawkings, (6) Lee Bryan (organist), (7) Jeffie Gould, (8) Jim Bryan, (9) Lillie Knapp, (10) Mrs. ? Reed, (11) Mr. ? Alford, (12) Maxie McClelland, and (13) Briggs Mead. (Courtesy of McNeese Archives.)

HER FIRST COMMUNION. Beulah Blanche Boudreaux was ten years old when she took her first communion on July 29, 1915, in the Catholic Church at Mermentau. Land for the church in which she took communion was donated to the church by her grandfather, Jean Castex, the founder of the town. The connection between the Catholic Church and Southwest Louisiana dates all the way back to the original explorers and French settlers. (Courtesy of Lynn and Eva Bourdier.)

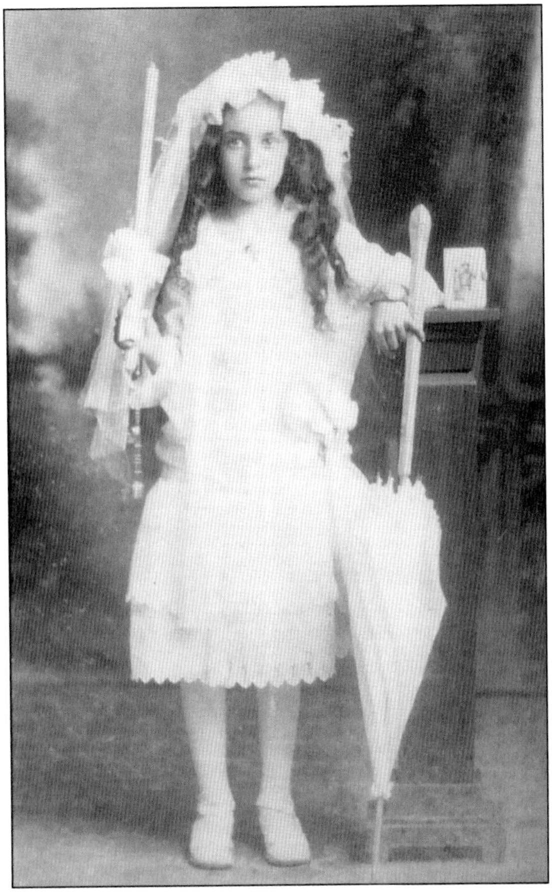

A FIRST COMMUNION CLASS. The "new" Immaculate Conception Catholic church looms large in this photograph, taken on April 2, 1920, of a large class of first communicants. The boys and girls in this photo represent only about one-fourth of the total number in the original panoramic photograph. This church structure was built after the original was destroyed in the great fire of 1910.

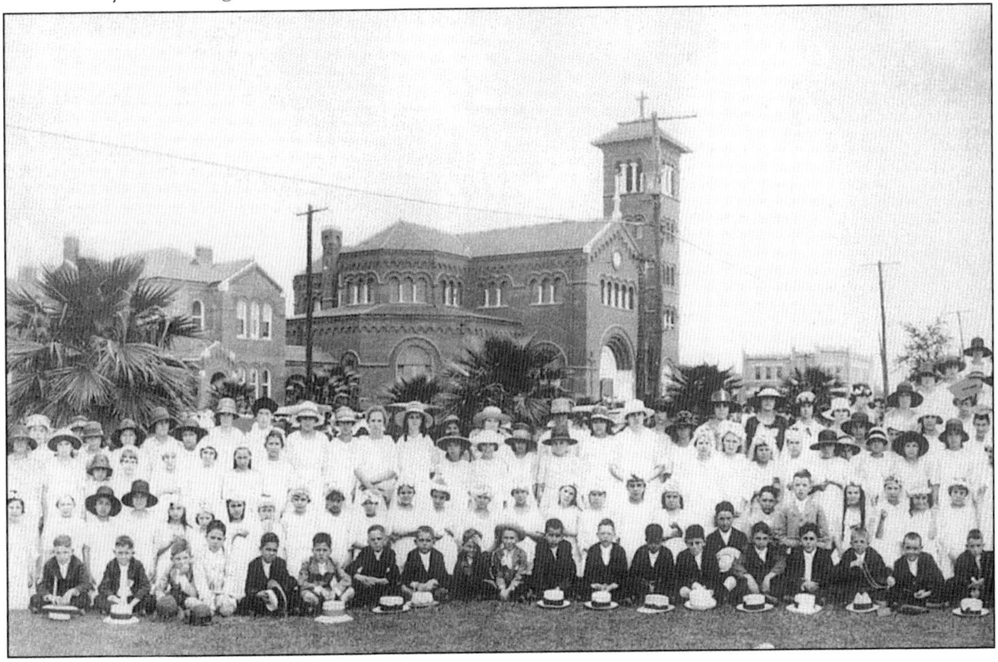

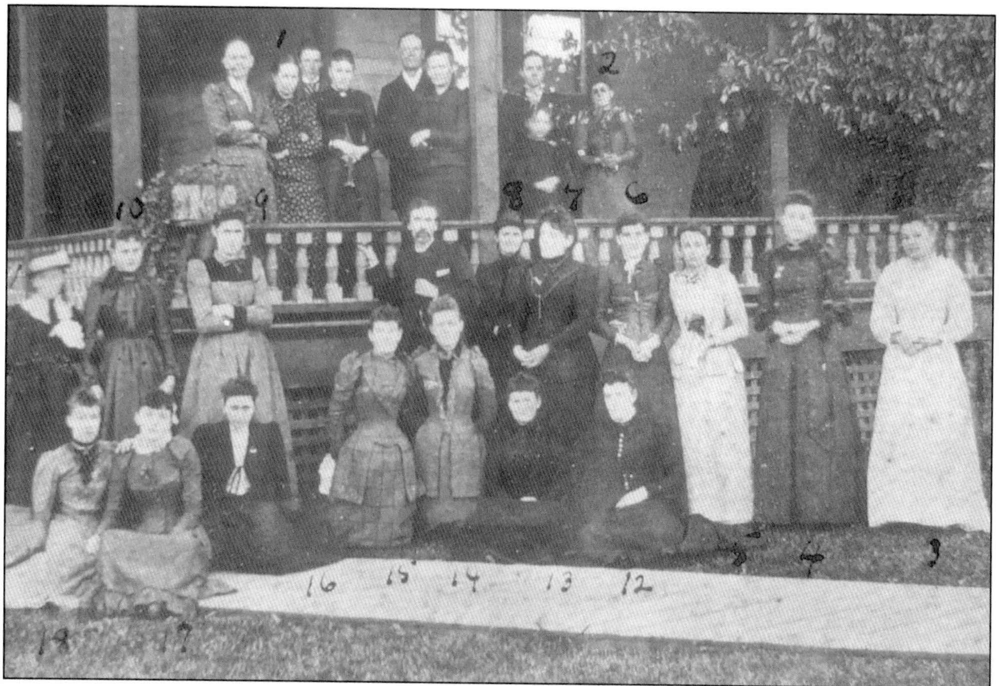

Young W.C.T.U. Activists. The Young Women's Christian Temperance Union was part of a movement for the abolishment of saloons that became very active in Imperial Calcasieu beginning about 1890. This photograph was taken on New Year's Day, 1892, at a reception given in honor of visiting activist Dr. ? Clay (with hand on rail), a New Orleans Methodist minister. He was the first president of the state's Society for the Prevention of Cruelty to Children. (Courtesy of McNeese Archives.)

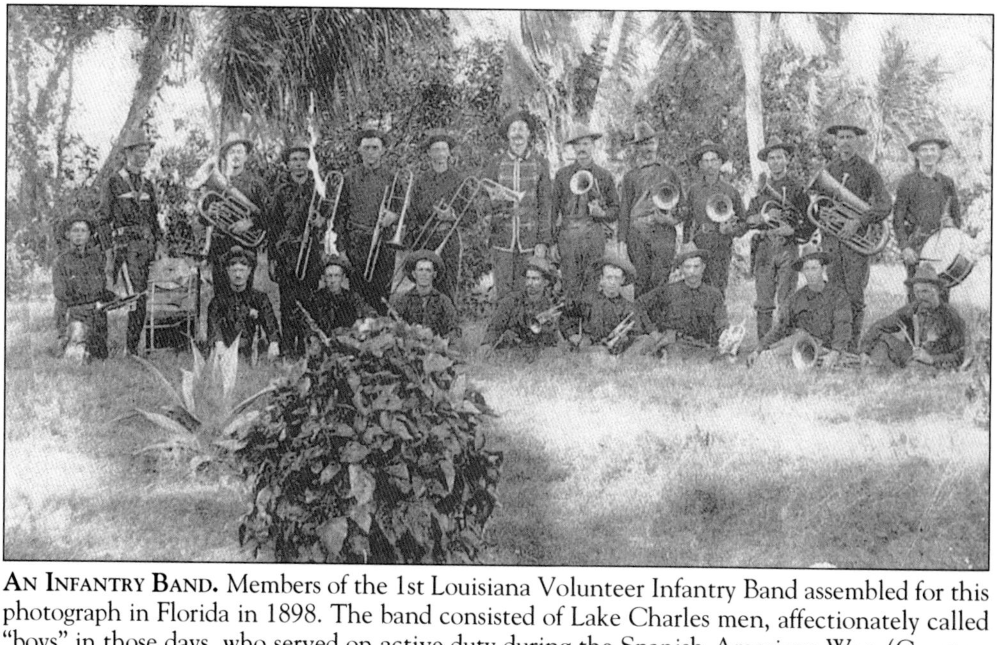

An Infantry Band. Members of the 1st Louisiana Volunteer Infantry Band assembled for this photograph in Florida in 1898. The band consisted of Lake Charles men, affectionately called "boys" in those days, who served on active duty during the Spanish-American War. (Courtesy of McNeese Archives.)

Seven

LEISURE

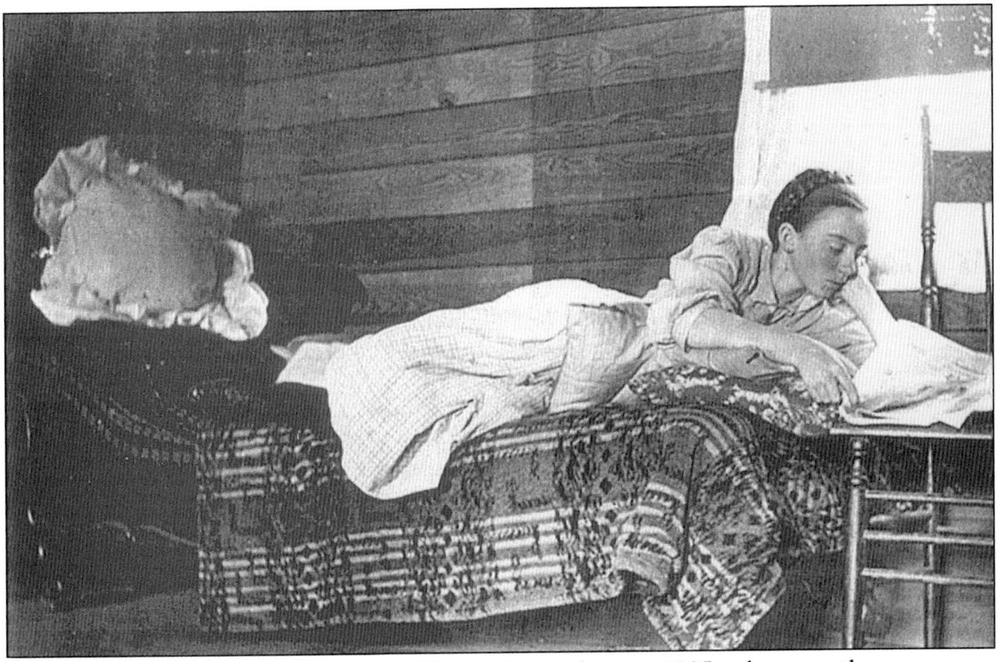

THE WEEKLY NEWSPAPER. Helen Bland Davies is seen here, c. 1905, relaxing with a newspaper in the home of her parents, David and Mary Davies, both college graduates, who taught her how to read. Calcasieu newspapers available by mail at that time included the *Lake Charles Daily/Weekly American* and the *Lake Charles Daily/ Weekly Press*. (Courtesy of Helen Kendall Collection.)

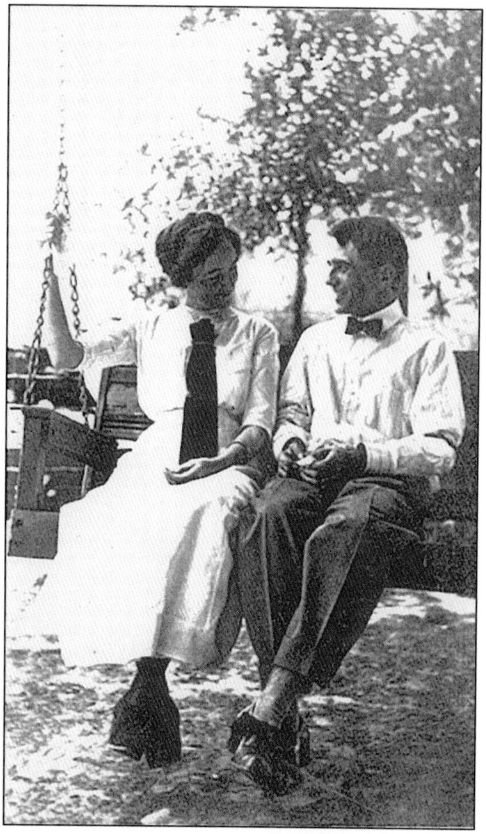

A Sunday Afternoon Visit. In the early 1900s many Imperial Calcasieu folk dressed up and went buggy riding or visiting on Sunday afternoons. The unidentified young man in this photo spent part of a 1912 Sunday afternoon calling upon Emma Davies at the farm home of her parents in southeast Calcasieu Parish. (Courtesy of Helen Kendall Collection.)

Sunday Sightseeing. Two couples out for a Sunday afternoon sightseeing ride have met in this dim photo at what is believed to be one end of a new bridge being built across Contraband Bayou. The bayou is located a few miles southwest of Lake Charles. Taking photographs during Sunday excursions was another popular pastime of the early 1900s for those who could afford cameras and darkrooms. (Courtesy of Helen Kendall Collection.)

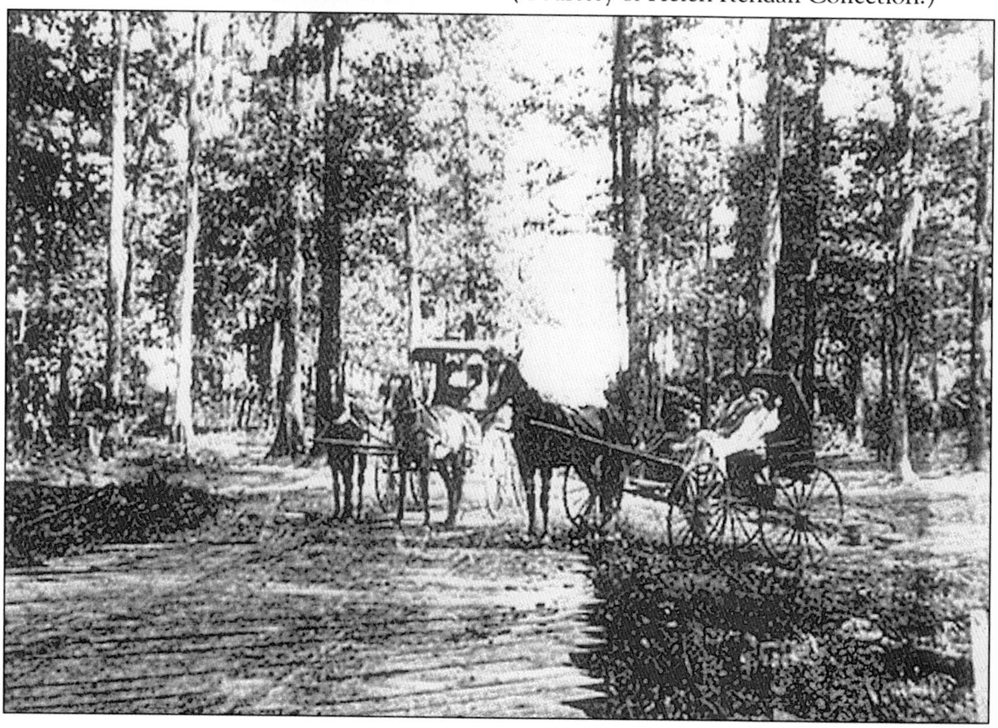

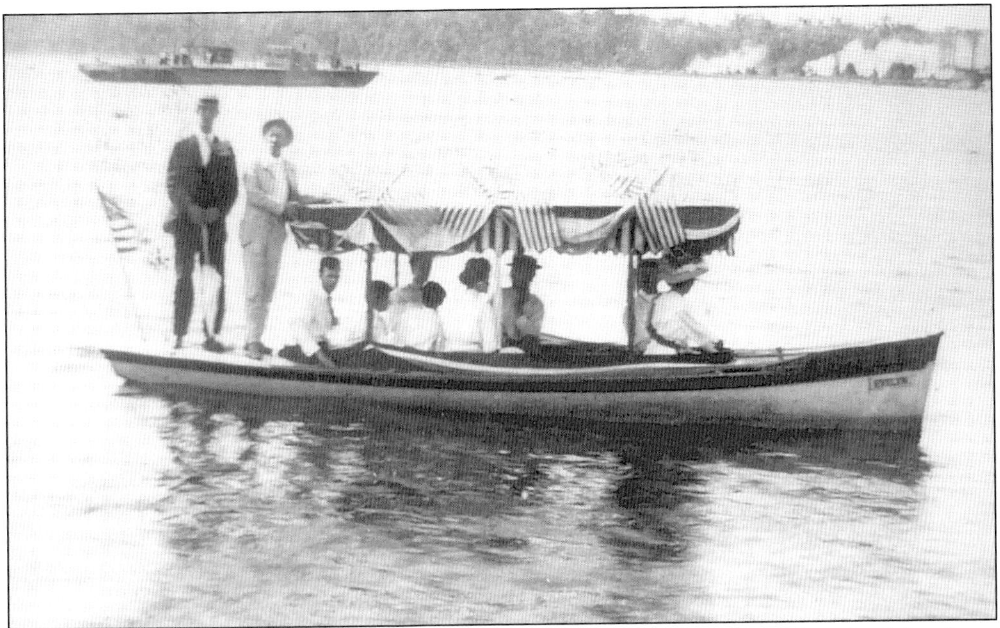

Boating on the Fourth. American flags decorate the pleasure craft *Levelin*, which has been taken out for a cruise on July 4, 1909. Note the neckties, jackets, and elaborate hats of the passengers. The smoke in the far distance is from the burn pile of a sawmill on Lake Charles. (Courtesy of Imperial Calcasieu Museum.)

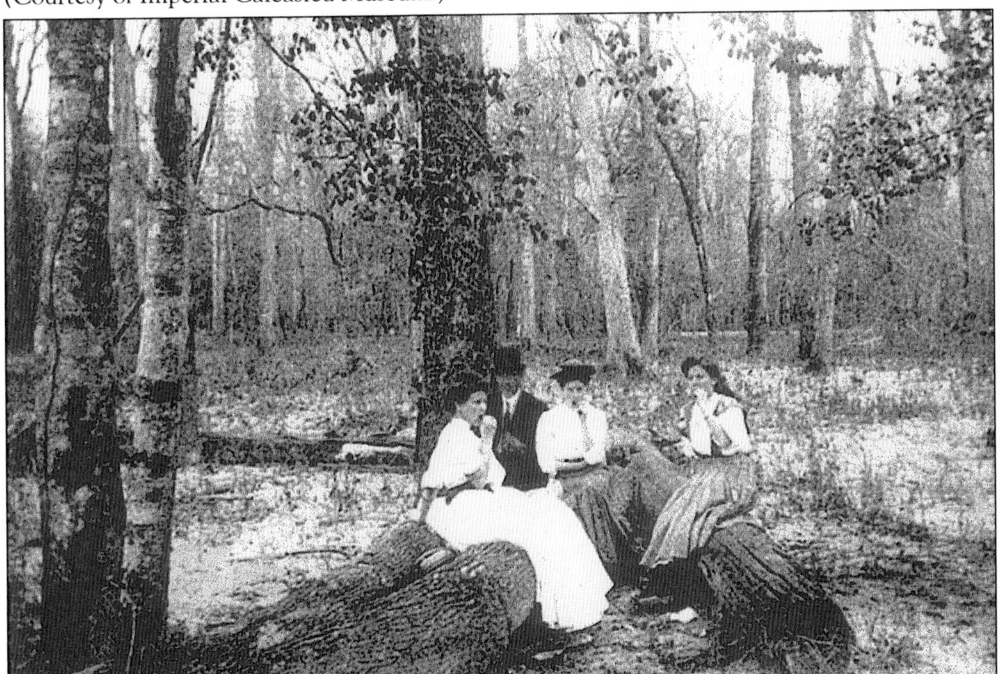

Picnicking with Friends. Taking along a picnic lunch on a Sunday excursion was popular and necessary in Imperial Calcasieu in the early 1900s. At that time, there were some cafes in the towns, but travel by buggy was very slow and the grocery stores were closed on Sundays. (Courtesy of Imperial Calcasieu Museum.)

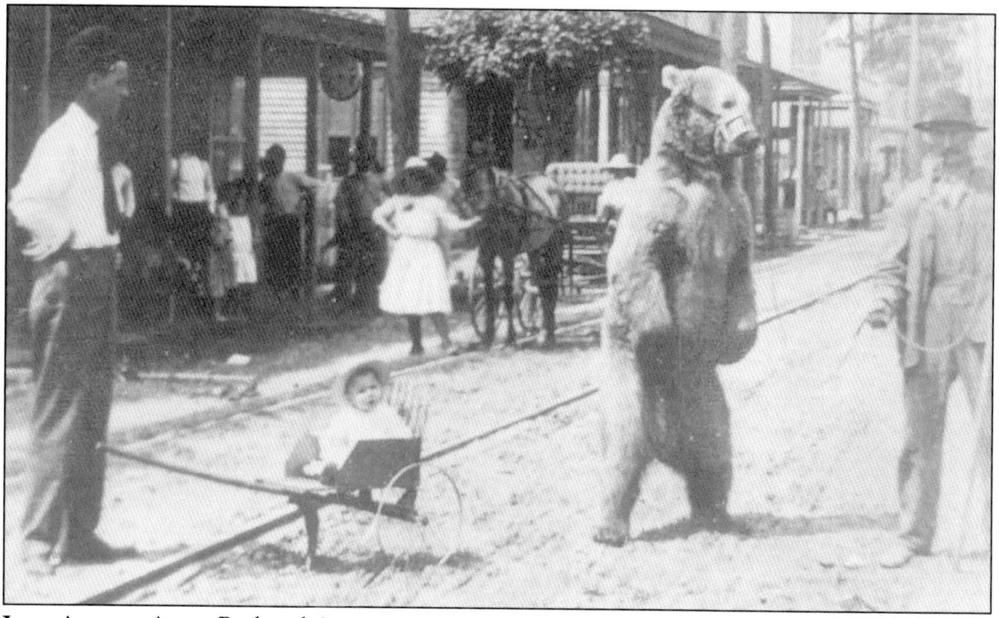

Live Animal Acts. Railroad Avenue in north Lake Charles was the scene of an animal act in this c. 1910 photograph. At that time, laws pertaining to cruelty to animals and protection of children from exposure to danger were either nonexistent or seldom enforced, as can be verified by this photo. (Courtesy of Imperial Calcasieu Museum.)

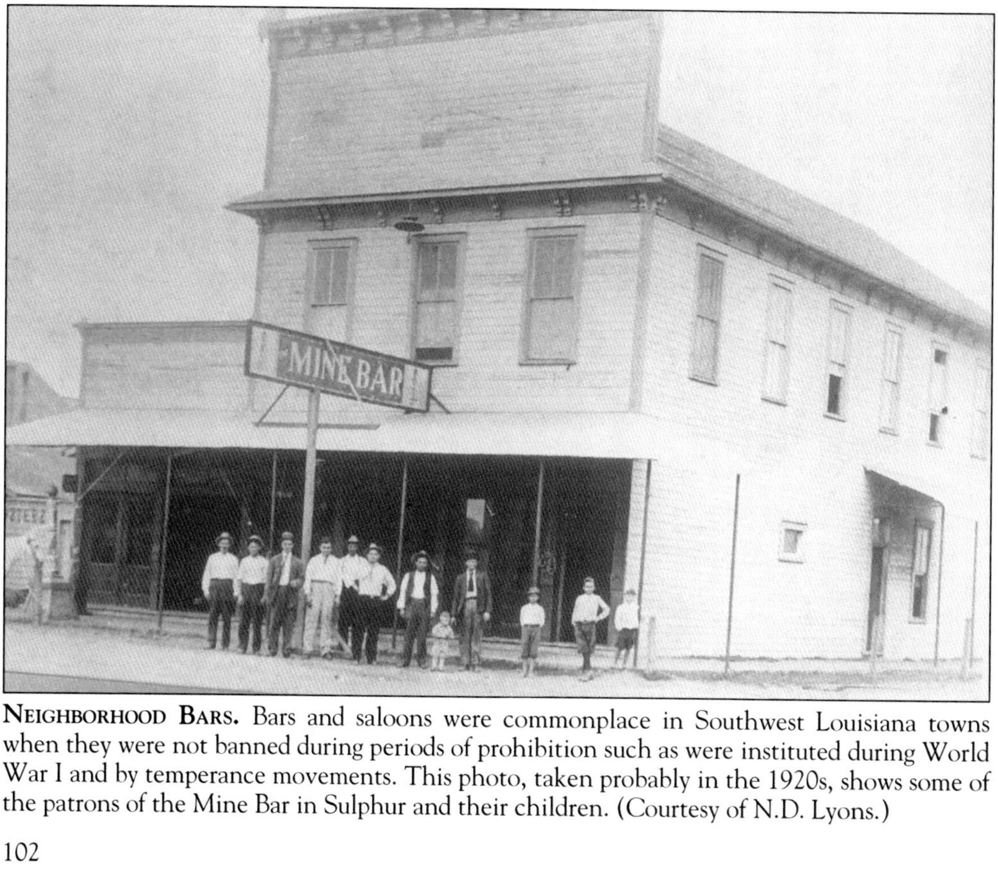

Neighborhood Bars. Bars and saloons were commonplace in Southwest Louisiana towns when they were not banned during periods of prohibition such as were instituted during World War I and by temperance movements. This photo, taken probably in the 1920s, shows some of the patrons of the Mine Bar in Sulphur and their children. (Courtesy of N.D. Lyons.)

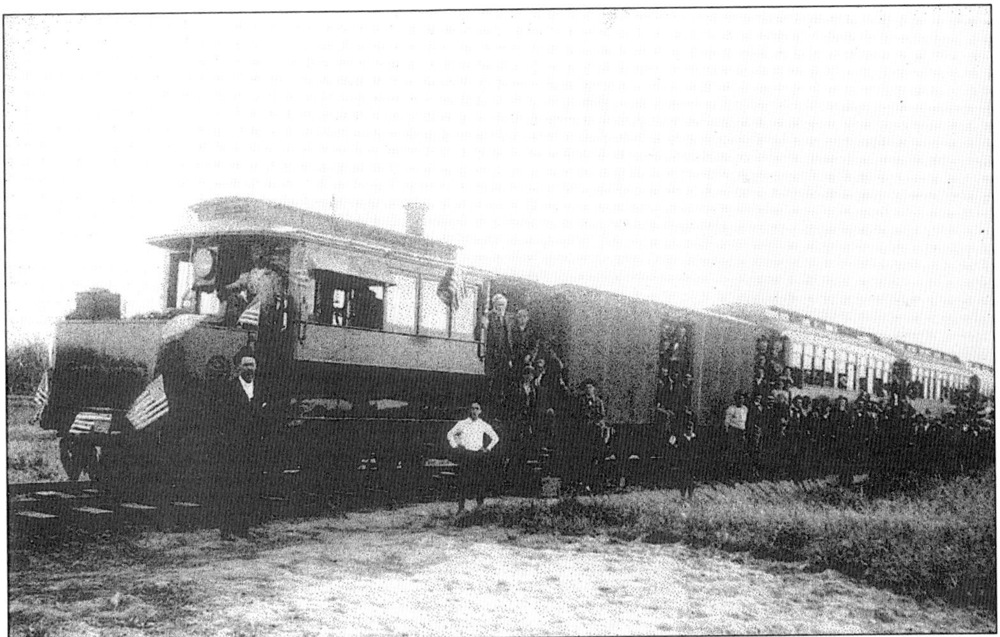

A RAILROAD EXCURSION. Weekend railroad excursions to nearby towns were popular after the coming of the railroads in 1880. This 1893 excursion train picked up passengers all along the line and allowed them a couple of hours for visiting their destination town, such as Orange, Beaumont, and Lake Charles, before returning them to their hometowns. In May 1911, over 2,000 people from as far away as Morgan City came to Lake Charles in 12 excursion railroad cars. (Courtesy of Imperial Calcasieu Museum.)

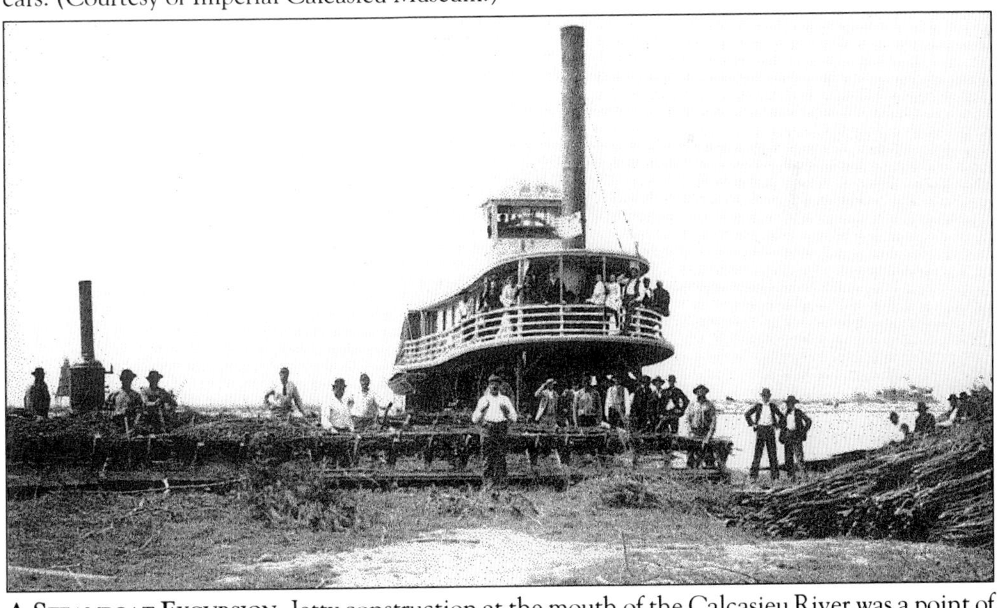

A STEAMBOAT EXCURSION. Jetty construction at the mouth of the Calcasieu River was a point of interest for the passengers on this 1893 weekend excursion aboard the steamer *Hazel.* A similar trip in 1911 aboard the *Rex* included meals and music by the First Regiment Band and stops at Leesburg (Cameron), the Gulf Hotel, the beach, and the lighthouse. (Courtesy of Imperial Calcasieu Museum.)

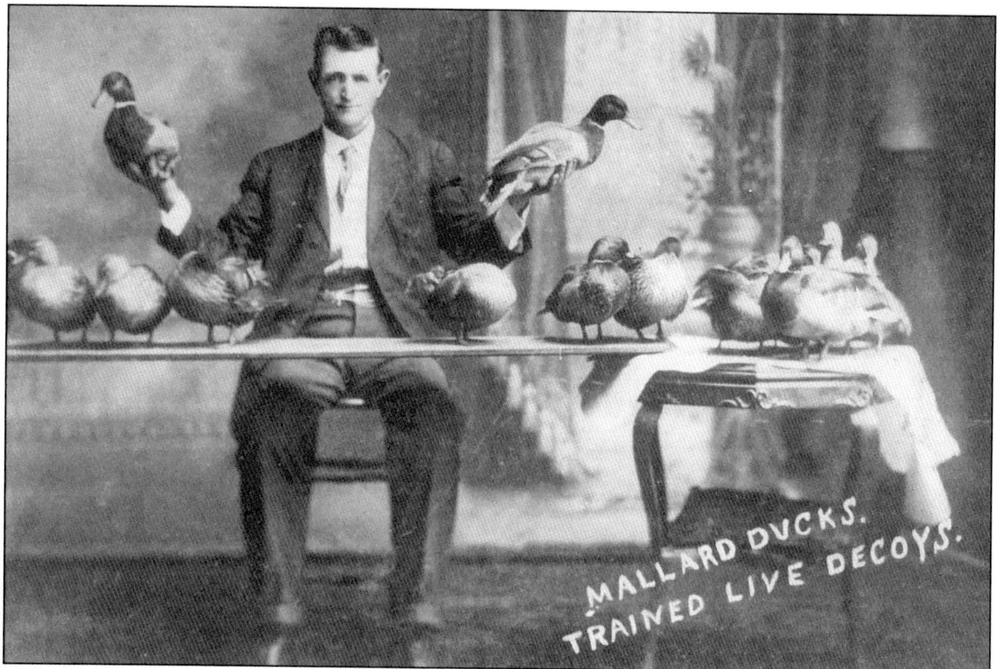

TRAINED DECOYS. Trained, live decoys are being offered to duck hunters in this old photo taken in Lake Charles. The use of live decoys is now prohibited, along with other practices once popular, such as baiting ponds, shooting with "duck cannons," and hunting all day. The millions of wild ducks and geese that spend their winters in Southwest Louisiana and are now hunted for recreation were once a major food source for many residents. (Courtesy of Jennie Reichley.)

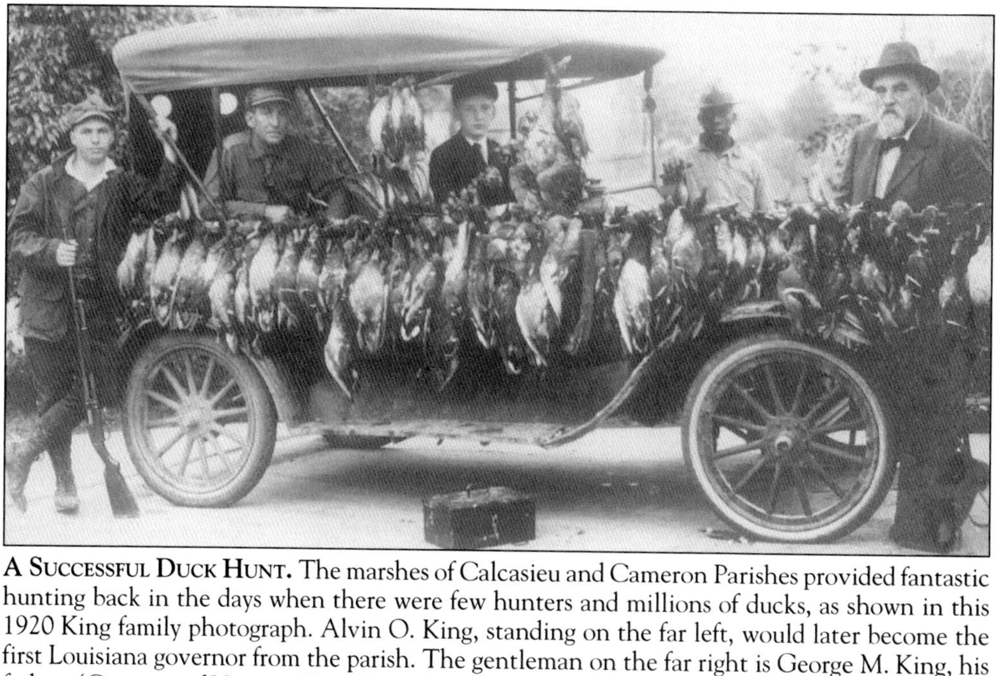

A SUCCESSFUL DUCK HUNT. The marshes of Calcasieu and Cameron Parishes provided fantastic hunting back in the days when there were few hunters and millions of ducks, as shown in this 1920 King family photograph. Alvin O. King, standing on the far left, would later become the first Louisiana governor from the parish. The gentleman on the far right is George M. King, his father. (Courtesy of Virginia King Pruitt.)

A Calcasieu Turkey. Turkeys and large animals such as deer, wolves, and bears were common in Imperial Calcasieu when this photo was taken about 100 years ago. Hunting trips in search of these animals were the favorite winter pastime of many male Calcasieu residents. Another animal that was present at that time but is seldom seen today is the rattlesnake. (Courtesy of McNeese Archives.)

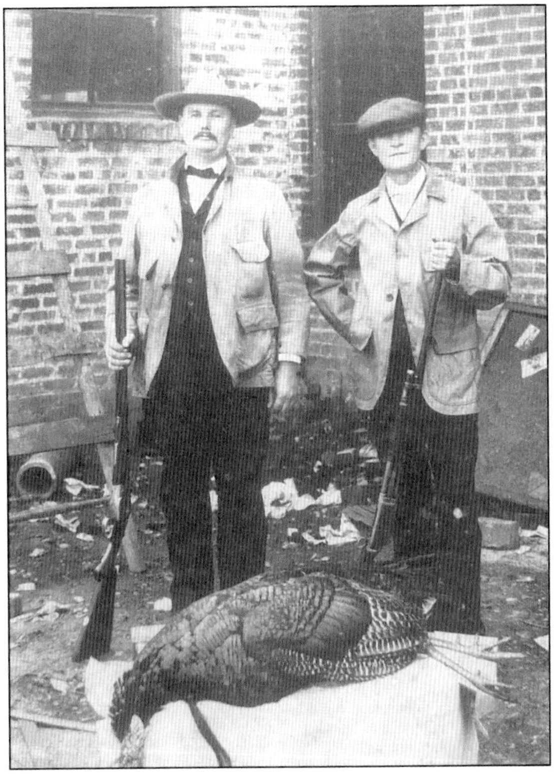

Good Day, Dangerous Marsh. Ben Collins of Lake Charles, far right, and his friends had a successful hunt around the year 1900. Collins and others often hunted in the big, almost impenetrable marsh west of Big (Calcasieu) Lake near Hackberry. Beginning December 16, 1900, Collins and many others spent days searching for Capt. Tom Kaough, a friend, who became lost in this marsh. Kaough's bones were not found until April 21, 1901. (Courtesy of Zelma Jones and Blanche Suydam Collection.)

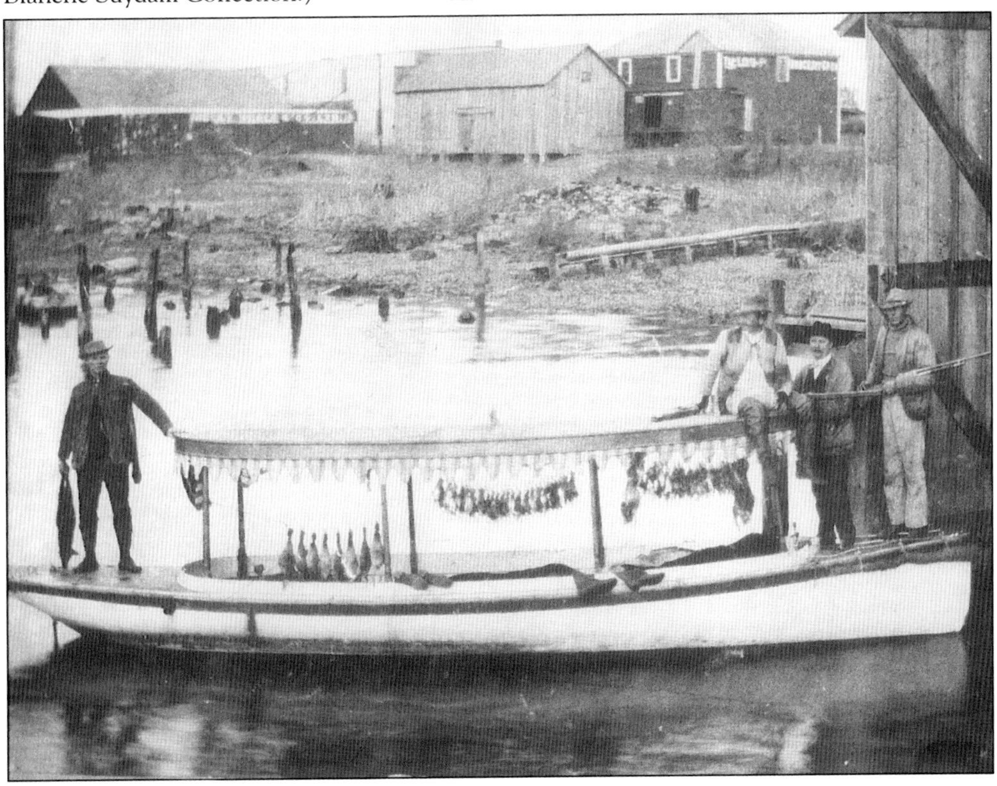

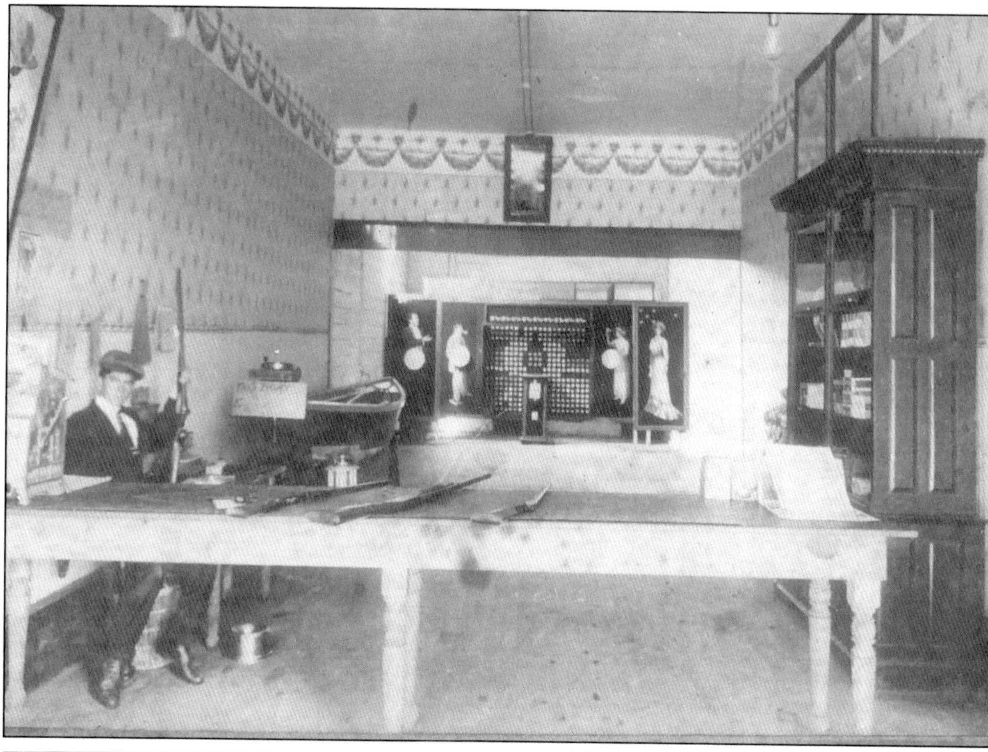

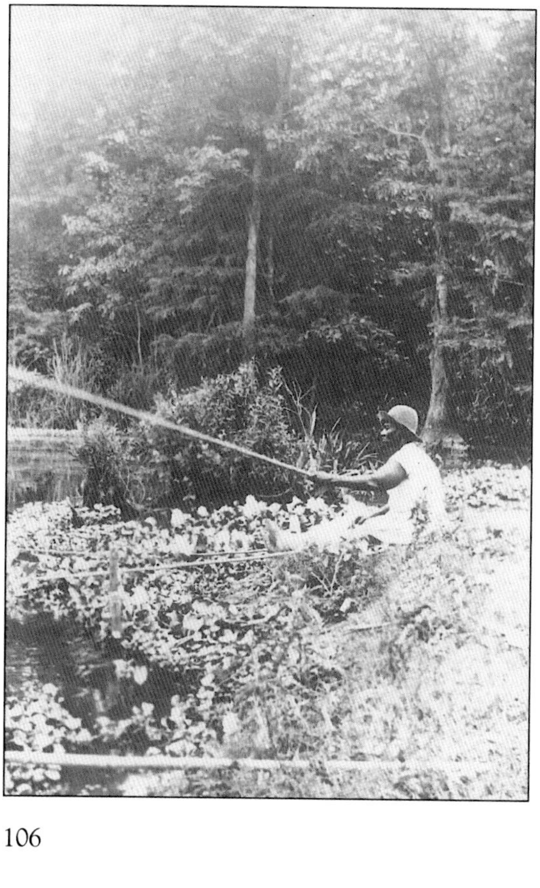

A Downtown Shooting Gallery. In an age when guns were considered a necessity for hunting and protection, finding a .22 caliber-rifle shooting gallery on Ryan Street in downtown Lake Charles probably did not seem very unusual. In the 1880s, 1890s, and early 1900s, many men commonly carried guns to town despite laws providing fines for this practice. (Courtesy of Jennie Reichley.)

A Quiet Afternoon. The many bayous, rivers, lakes, creeks, coulees, and marshes of Imperial Calcasieu were loaded with perch, bass, and catfish in the days before salt water intrusion, pollution, and over-fishing. For many early Imperial Calcasieu residents, spending a quiet afternoon fishing from a river bank was the height of pleasurable entertainment. (Courtesy of McNeese Archives.)

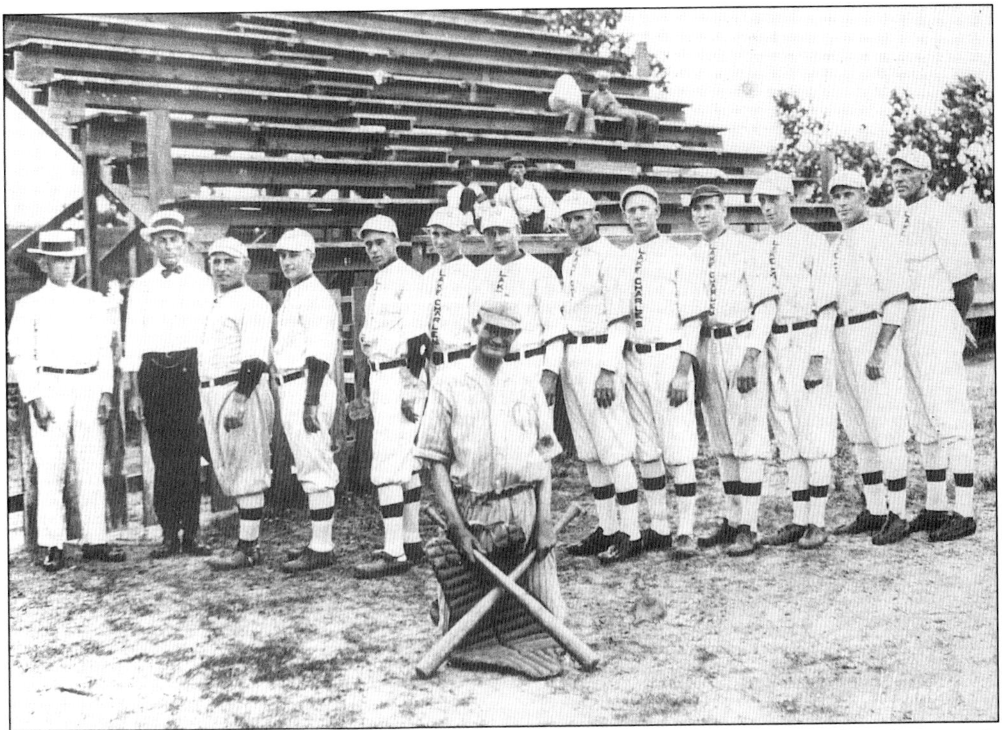

Baseball and Other Sports. The Lake Charles baseball team lined up for this photograph before a game in the early 1900s. In 1902, the *Weekly American* reported that 1,500 people watched a game between Lake Charles and Crowley. During these years, nearly every town had a baseball team and some, such as Bon Ami, south of DeRidder, even had a three-story YMCA equipped with a basketball gym, bowling alleys, and dressing rooms. (Courtesy of Zelma Jones and Blanche Suydam Collection.)

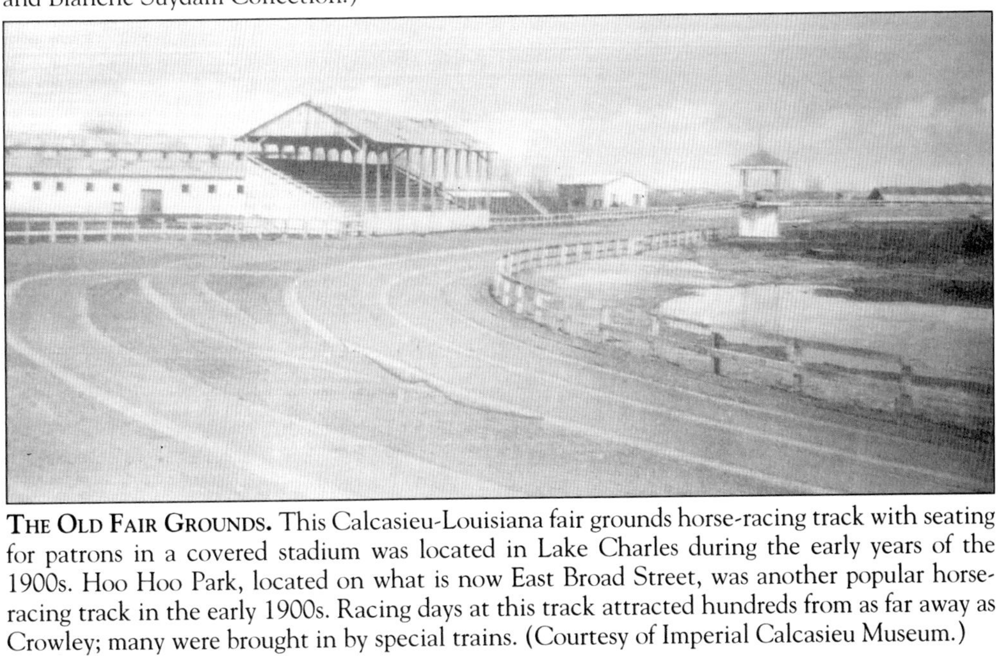

The Old Fair Grounds. This Calcasieu-Louisiana fair grounds horse-racing track with seating for patrons in a covered stadium was located in Lake Charles during the early years of the 1900s. Hoo Hoo Park, located on what is now East Broad Street, was another popular horse-racing track in the early 1900s. Racing days at this track attracted hundreds from as far away as Crowley; many were brought in by special trains. (Courtesy of Imperial Calcasieu Museum.)

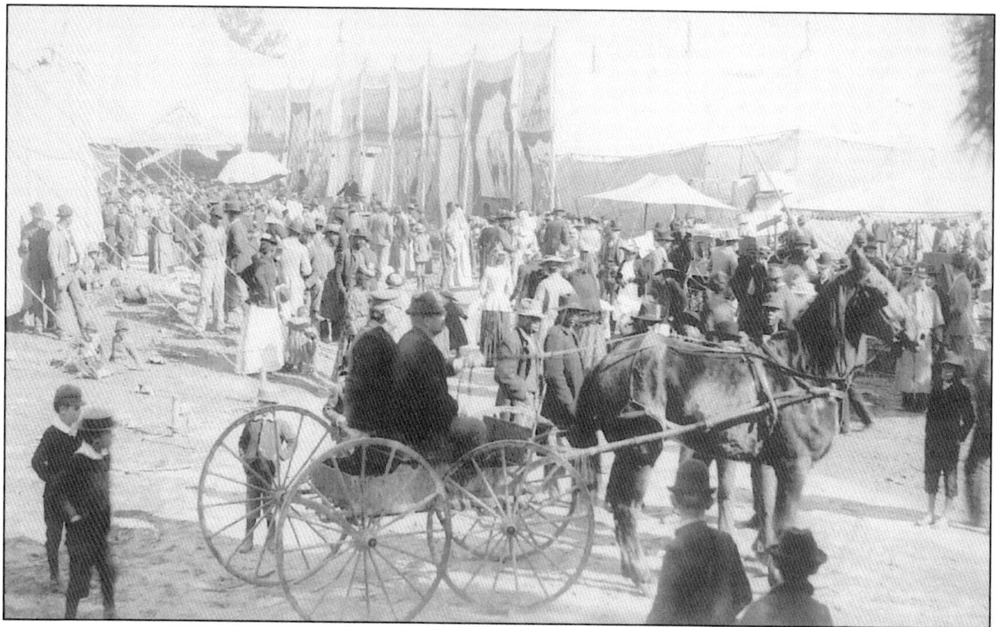

A Circus Comes to Town. When a circus came to town, as it did in this 1893 photograph taken in Lake Charles, country folk by the hundreds also came to town seeking entertainment. Weeks before the show's arrival, advance men would put up billboards all over town. Then, on circus day, the entertainers would stage one or more parades down the main street to bring in the crowd. (Courtesy of Imperial Calcasieu Museum.)

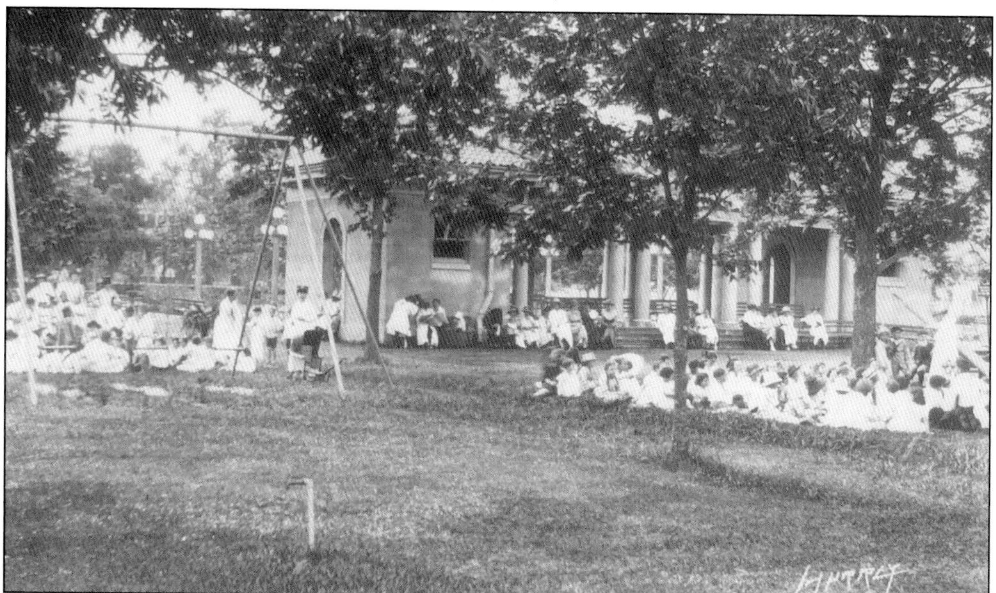

A Pretty Park. Lock Park in Lake Charles was only two years old when, on May 22, 1922, the town's recreation committee put on the "Story-Telling Time" shown here. At the time of the park's founding, two nearby trolley lines and the park's nearness to business and residential districts made its location seem ideal for a town park. Lock Park was donated to the town by the wife of the late Captain George Lock in memory of her husband. (Courtesy of McNeese Archives.)

Heavy Swimwear. These Calcasieu folk and many others sought summertime recreation on the Gulf beaches of Texas and Louisiana. Prior to 1920, it was not considered proper to expose very much of one's body at a beach or while swimming, no matter how difficult the heavy clothing made trying to stay afloat. (Courtesy of Susan Simmons.)

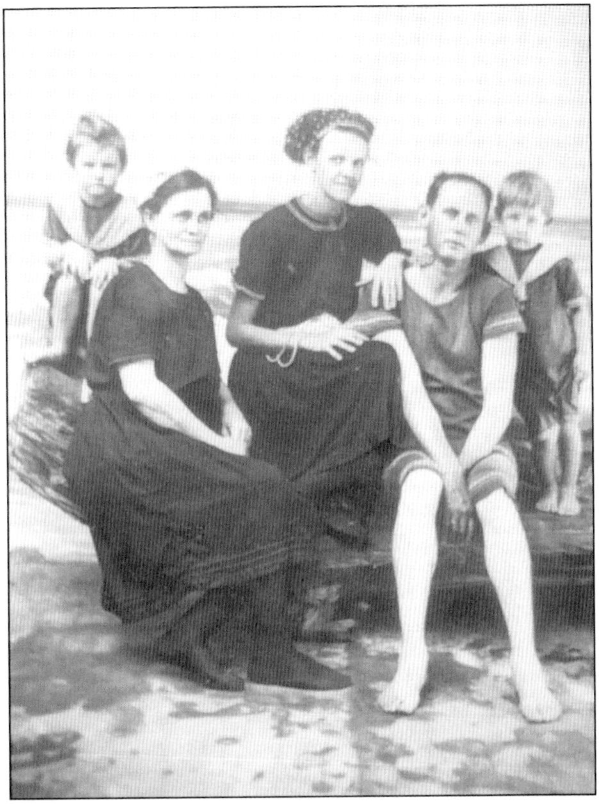

Beautiful Lake Arthur. A beautiful live oak, a long wharf, a boathouse, Spanish moss, a lake breeze, and a water slide are some of the attractions visible in this 1890s photograph taken at Lake Arthur. This lake and its namesake town have remained popular with summer vacationers throughout the years. Another popular summer spot for people of Calcasieu Parish was located on Big Lake. (Courtesy of Imperial Calcasieu Museum.)

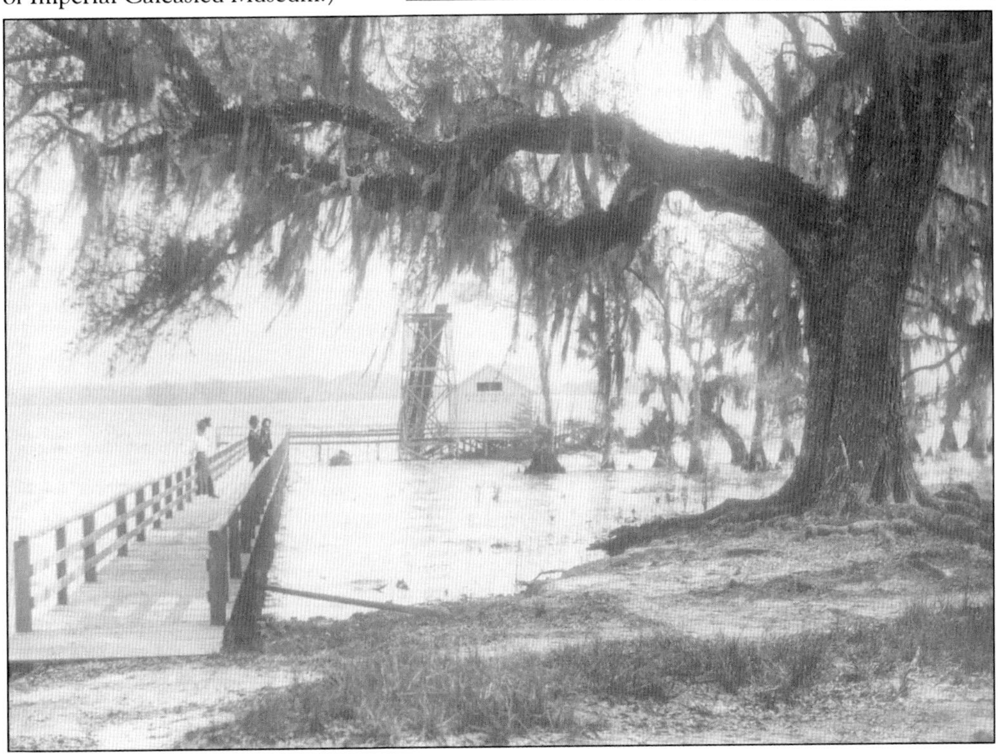

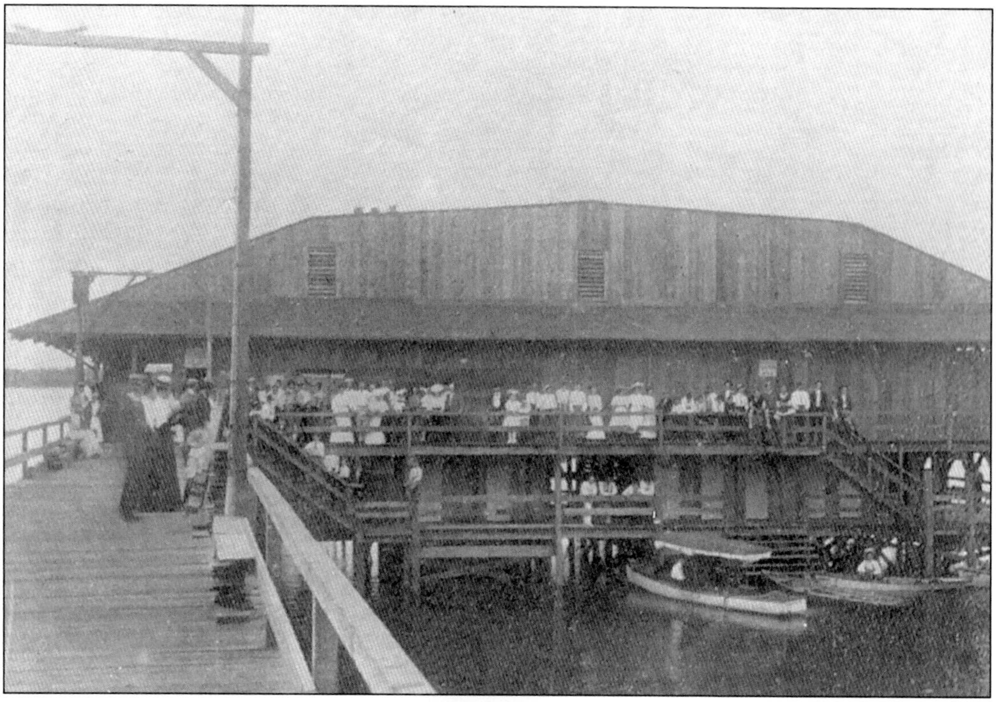

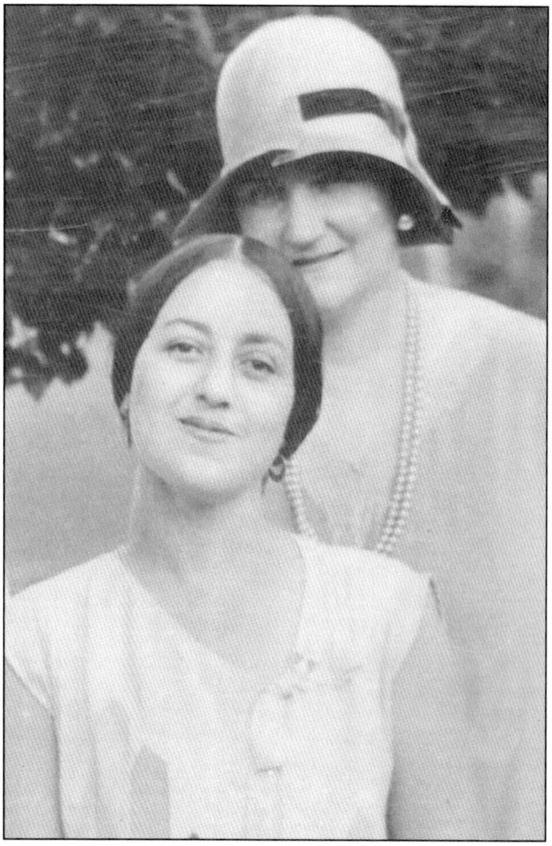

A GATHERING AT PLEASURE PIER. Theatergoers are gathering at the Pleasure Pier on Lake Charles (also called the Shell Beach Casino) in this 1907 photo. This large, multi-purpose building was used for theatrical productions, dances, roller skating, lectures, and the first Chautauqua held in the area. This structure was destroyed in the hurricane of 1918. (Courtesy of McNeese Archives.)

QUEENS OF ENTERTAINMENT. Rosa Hart, front, and Mrs. Emma Calvert Michie, both of Lake Charles, posed for this photo about 1920. In the coming years Miss Hart would become famous as the founder and director for 30 years of the Lake Charles Little Theater. Mrs. Michie would become famous for her high standards of management of the Majestic Hotel, a family business, and her long-standing friendships with the notable and famous people who visited Southwest Louisiana. (Courtesy of Imperial Calcasieu Museum.)

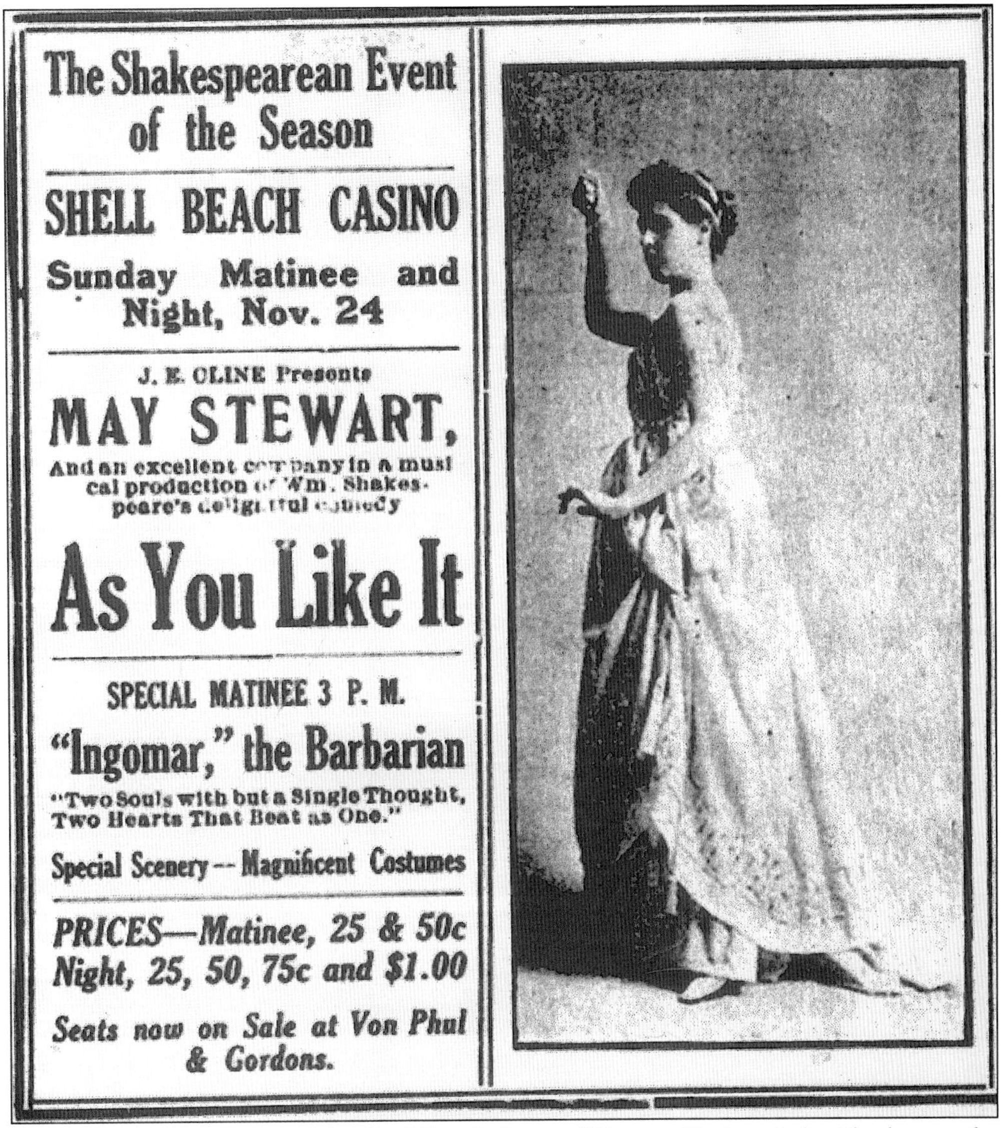

SHAKESPEARE ON THE LAKE. The Shell Beach Casino (Pleasure Pier) on Lake Charles was the site of many traveling shows in the early 1900s. The production of Shakespeare's *As You Like It*, advertised here, appeared at the Casino in 1907. In addition to shows of this type, the Casino also hosted light entertainments like "Billy Kersand's Minstrels," "Donnelly & Hatfield's Magnificent Minstrels," and plays such as *The Slow Poke*, which was billed as "a western play of heart interest." Among its more thoughtful entertainments, the Casino hosted William Jennings Bryan, the eloquent, populist Democrat, in January 1908, in an appearance that drew nearly 2,000 people. During this talk, according to a newspaper report, Bryan said someone had asked him how much money a man could have and still be considered a Democrat. "I replied," said Bryan, "there was no limit so long as he had the money, . . . but when the money had him, he'd have to get out." Other old-time showplaces in Lake Charles included the Williams Opera House, the "show grounds" opposite the Majestic Hotel, the Lyric Theater, the Peoples' Theater, and the Baseball Park. (Courtesy of McNeese Archives.)

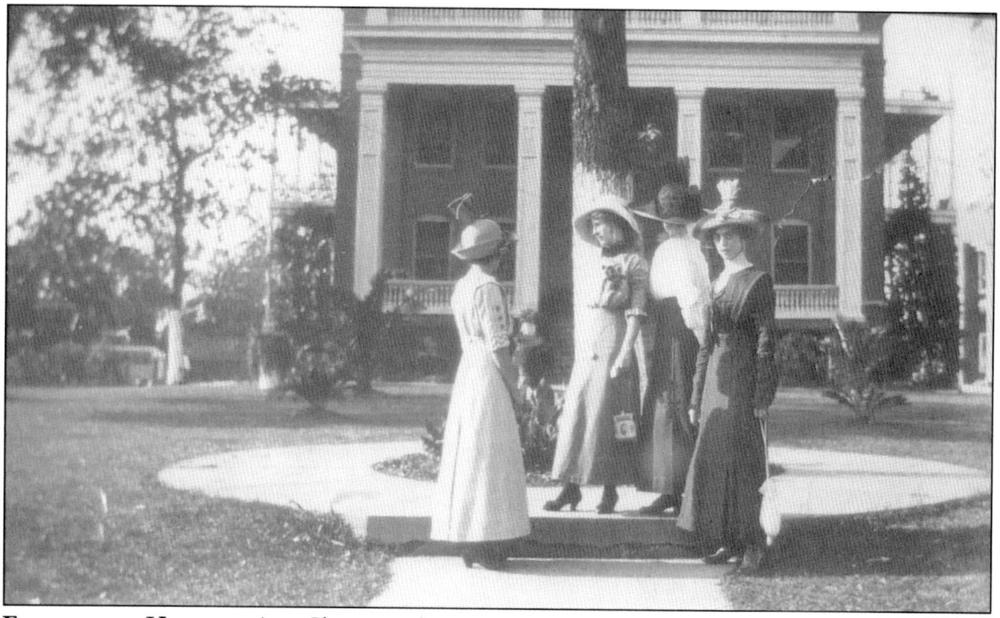

FASHIONABLE HATS FOR ALL. Shopping for pretty dresses or making them oneself from materials available in local shops were important pastimes for the ladies of Imperial Calcasieu. Here four ladies model the latest styles of around 1915 in front of St. Patrick Sanitarium (now Christus St. Patrick Hospital) in Lake Charles before new buildings were constructed in front of the original structure. (Courtesy of N.D. Lyons.)

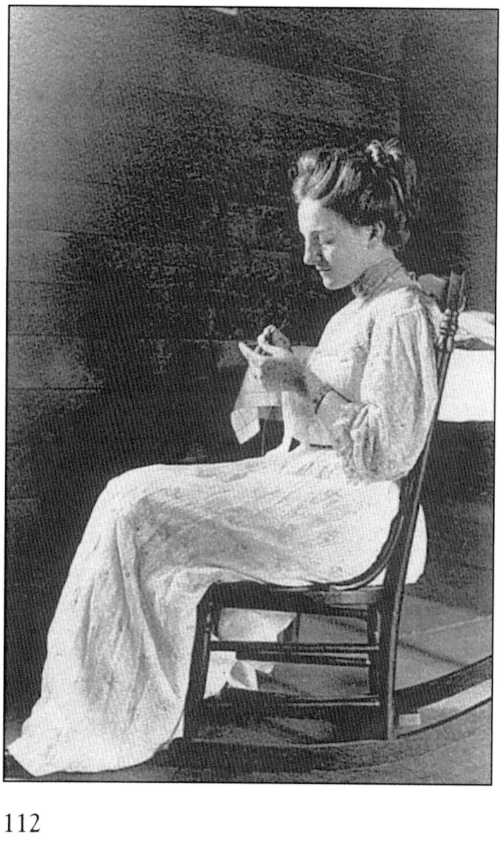

OR STAY HOME AND CROCHET. On Sunday afternoons when the weather was bad or plans just did not work out, Helen Davies Kendall liked to stay at home and either read or crochet. Many years after this photo was taken around 1910, she recalled the time she walked up to the corner of Ryan and Broad Streets in Lake Charles and decided that the mud in the street was just too deep for her to go across. Perhaps this was one of those muddy days. (Courtesy of Helen Kendall Collection.)

Eight

Memorable Events

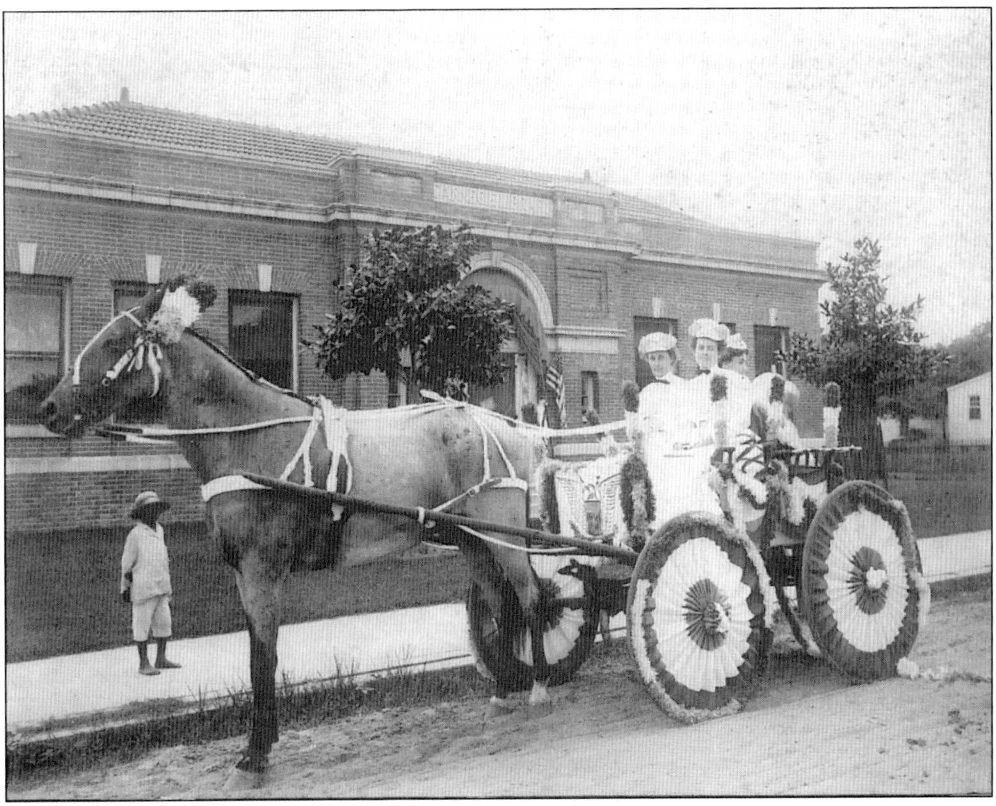

Celebrating the Fourth. Parades, picnics, fireworks, and speeches were especially important when Imperial Calcasieu residents celebrated the Fourth of July back in the days of horses and buggies. On July 4, 1909, Mrs. C.M. Richard (left) and Mrs. Margaret Allison (with the reins) paused in front of the Carnegie Library in Lake Charles to have their colorful vehicle admired and photographed before entering it in the parade being held that day on Ryan Street. (Courtesy of Imperial Calcasieu Museum.)

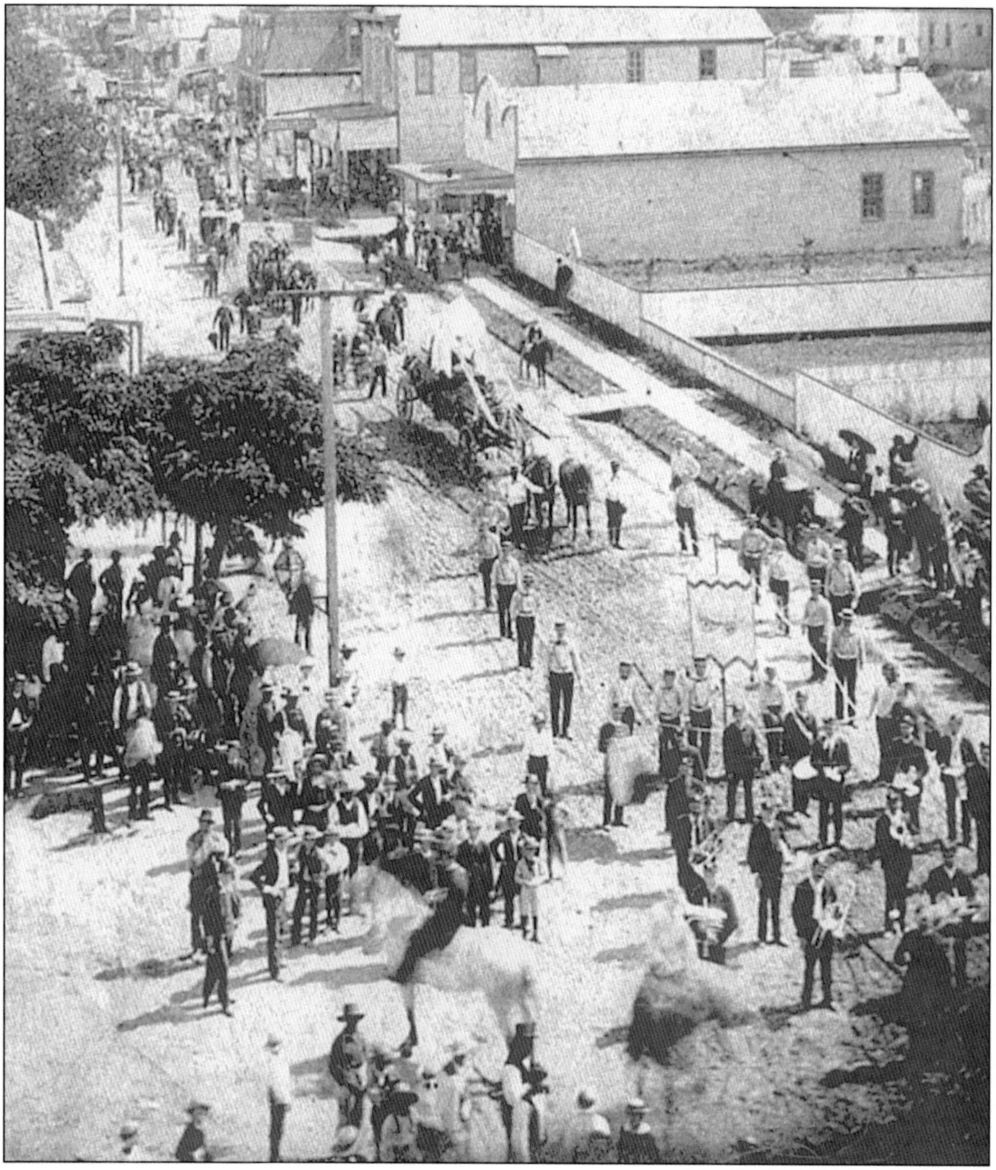

The Grand Fire Parade. On July 4, 1889, young Maude Reid, daughter of Calcasieu Parish sheriff Kinney Reid, was the queen of this parade put on by the volunteer fire companies of Lake Charles. She rode on the hook-and-ladder wagon, in the center of the photo, under the light-colored drapery. The lead unit (right foreground) was the Eureka Brass Band of the Phoenix Volunteer Fire Company. This photo was taken looking north along Ryan Street from the upper floor of the old Calcasieu Courthouse. In later years, Miss Reid spent countless hours collecting and recording historical memorabilia of Lake Charles. Concerning this photograph, which was copied from one of her many scrapbooks, she wrote that Bryan's Store was located on the west side of Ryan Street behind the chinaberry trees in the left foreground. (The space in front of the man on the white horse is the beginning of North Court Street.) According to Miss Reid, on the right side of Ryan Street, past the fenced yards, were located, from right to left, Croom's Bakery, Sol Bloch's Store (two stories), and Dr. Knapp's Drugstore. (Courtesy of McNeese Archives.)

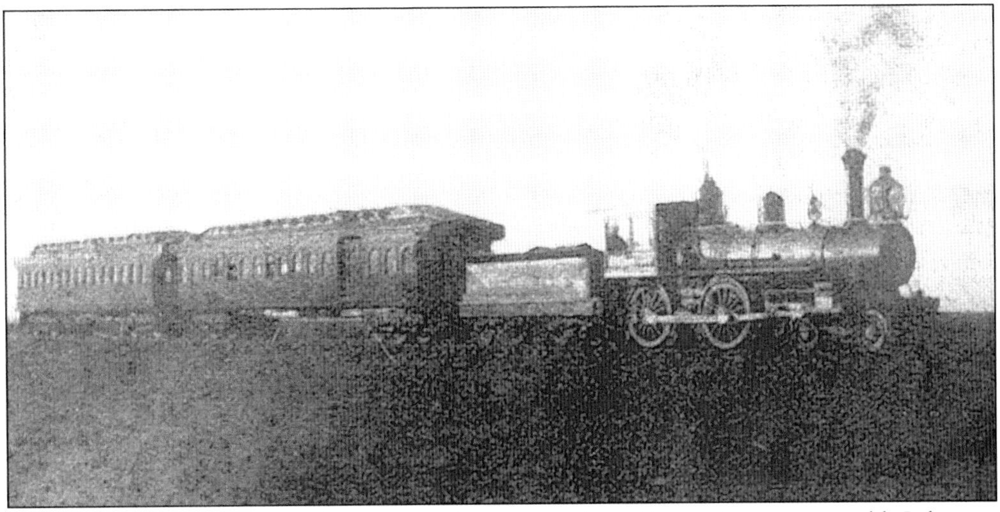

THE FIRST RAILROAD. This photograph shows one of the first trains to serve old Calcasieu Parish upon the completion of the east-west Louisiana & Western (later Southern Pacific) Railroad in 1880. Imperial Calcasieu was practically an island in the wilderness before this line was finished. Completion of this line meant the realization of fast, overland travel between Houston and New Orleans and all points in between, and the end of reliance upon stagecoaches, schooners, and slow-moving steamboats. (Courtesy of Imperial Calcasieu Museum.)

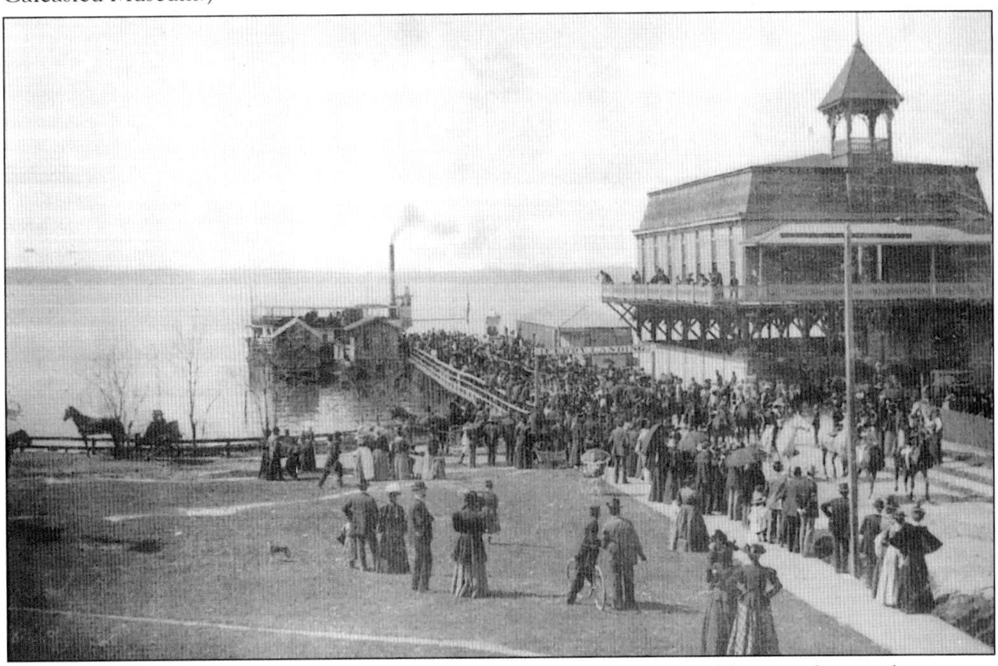

MARDI GRAS AT THE LANDING. Mardi Gras has a long tradition of being a happy, boisterous time in Imperial Calcasieu. In this 1895 photo, Rex and his attendants have just arrived in Lake Charles aboard the *Hazel* at the Pujo Street ferry landing. In the right foreground, masked horsemen are leading the revelers in a parade that will take them through the town's business and residential districts and then back to the landing for the Mardi Gras ball, which would be held above the City Market (the large building on the right). (Courtesy of McNeese Archives.)

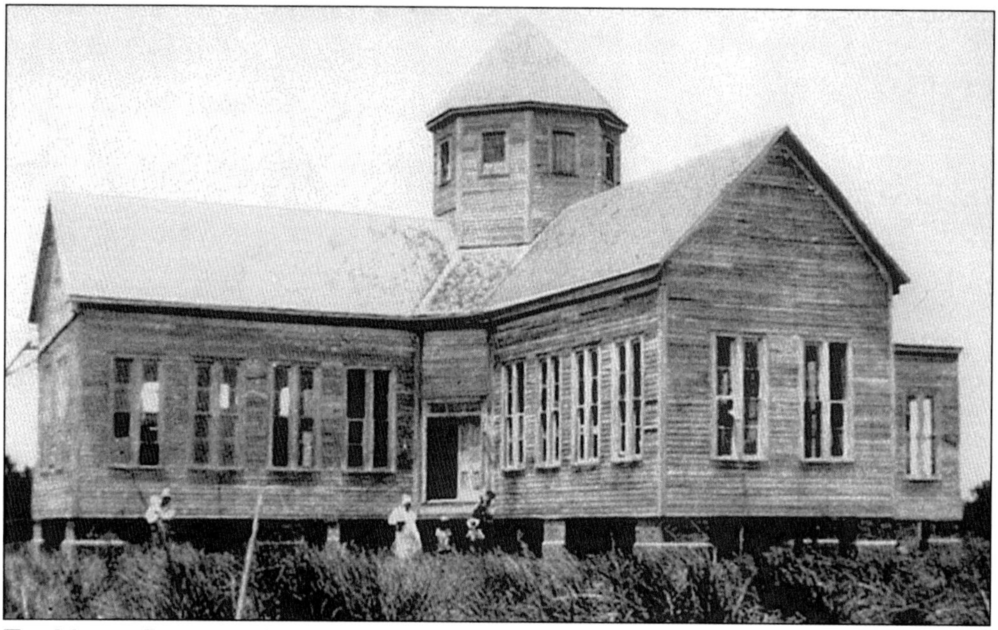

The Marine Research Center. The old laboratory building of the Gulf Biologic Station, the first marine research facility established on the entire Gulf Coast, is the subject of this photo. Located on the east side of Calcasieu Pass, this station was operated by the state of Louisiana and the parishes of Cameron and Calcasieu in cooperation with the federal government and other agencies. The station was operated from 1903 until around 1910 for the purposes of researching and teaching about Louisiana fish, shell fish, and flora. (Courtesy of McNeese Archives.)

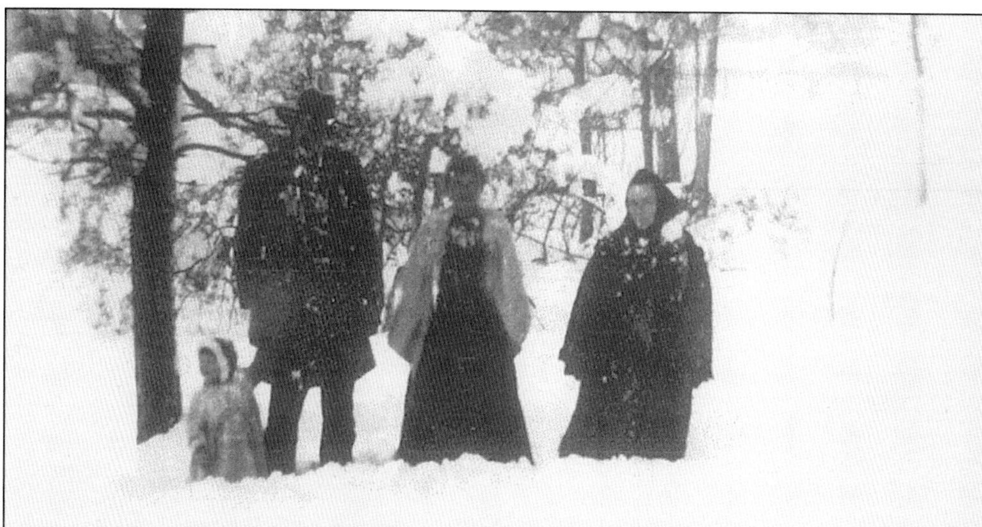

The Big Snow of '95. The "Valentine's Day Snowstorm" of 1895 became a legend in Calcasieu country and for good reason, judging by this photograph taken at Lockport. Reports of this storm say that it continued for two and a half days and resulted in 16 to 24 inches of snowfall. They also say it took two weeks for all of the snow to melt, during which time all of Imperial Calcasieu's commercial and private orange groves were completely wiped out. (Courtesy of McNeese Archives.)

"23 [SKIDOO] FOR BOOZE." The anti-booze movement reached a climax in Calcasieu Parish on June 9, 1908, when the registered voters (men) of the parish were asked to vote for or against the sale of alcoholic beverages. In Lake Charles, to insure the success of their efforts, women and children staged a huge parade down Ryan Street and then demonstrated solemnly at the polls, as seen in this photograph. The "drys" won by a vote of 2,302 to 801. This vote closed 66 saloons in Lake Charles, according to one newspaper reporter. (Courtesy of McNeese Archives.)

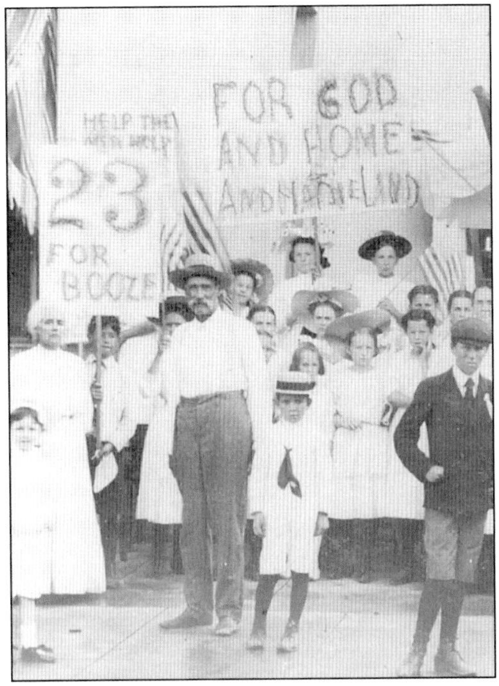

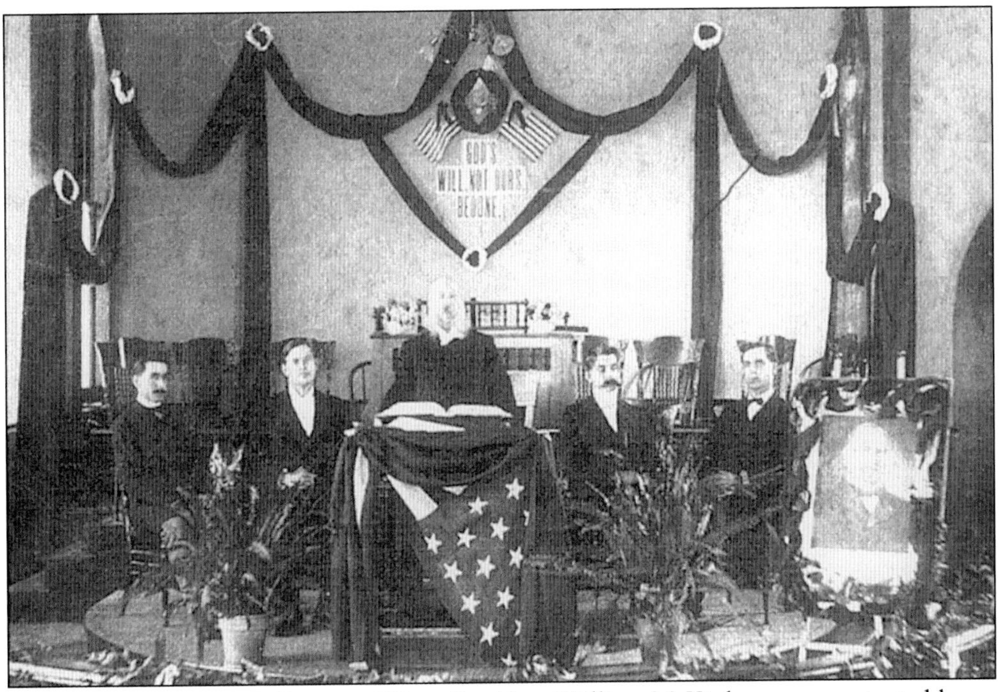

A MCKINLEY MEMORIAL SERVICE. When President William McKinley was assassinated by an anarchist on September 6, 1901, at the Pan-American Exposition in Buffalo, NY, the residents of Imperial Calcasieu entered into a time of mourning along with the rest of the nation. This photo was taken at the First Presbyterian Church in Lake Charles during a memorial service for the fallen leader. A photograph of President McKinley (far right) was displayed during the service. (Courtesy of Imperial Calcasieu Museum.)

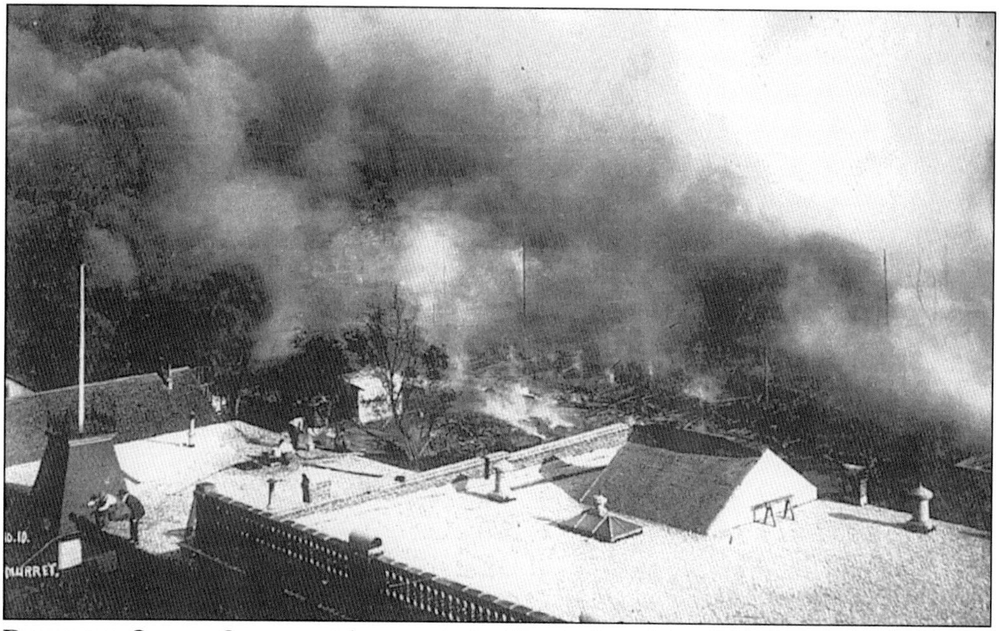

Definitely Out of Control. The great Lake Charles fire of April 23, 1910, raged for three hours, devouring government buildings, businesses, churches, and private residences across a seven-block area. Published reports say it was started accidentally about a half block north of the old courthouse and was pushed southward and eastward by a strong wind. When it was over, 109 buildings had been destroyed. Note the men working to protect the roof of the building in the left foreground. (Courtesy of McNeese Archives.)

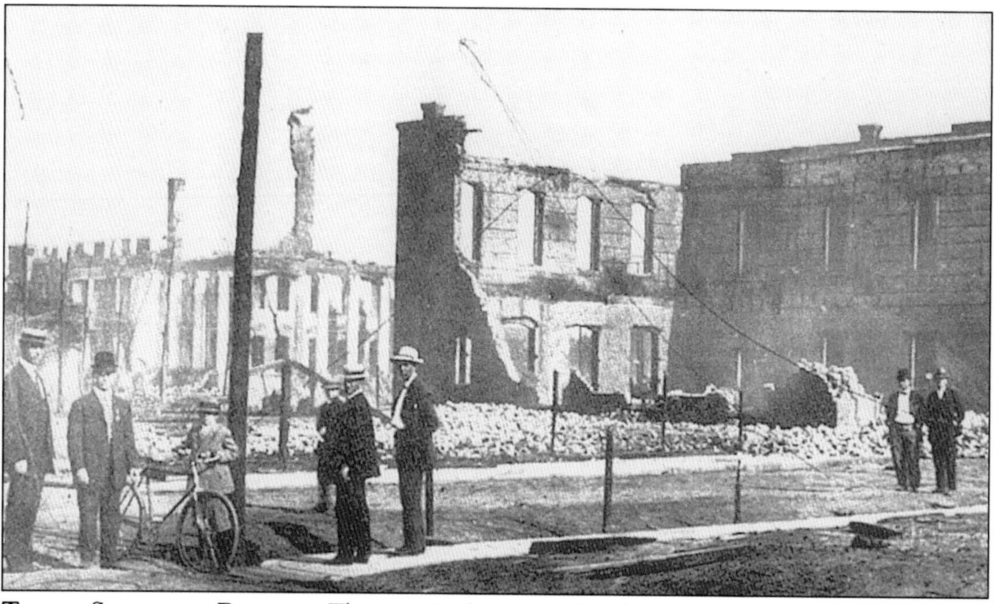

Taking Stock of a Disaster. The men in this photo (could they be insurance adjusters?) are standing in front of the hulks of the old St. Charles Academy (right) and parish courthouse (left). In addition to these buildings, the fire destroyed Gunn's Book Store, the Old Opera House Saloon, Rothkam's Meat Market, the Lake House Hotel, the Bryan Building, and 102 other assorted homes, businesses, churches, etc. (Courtesy of McNeese Archives.)

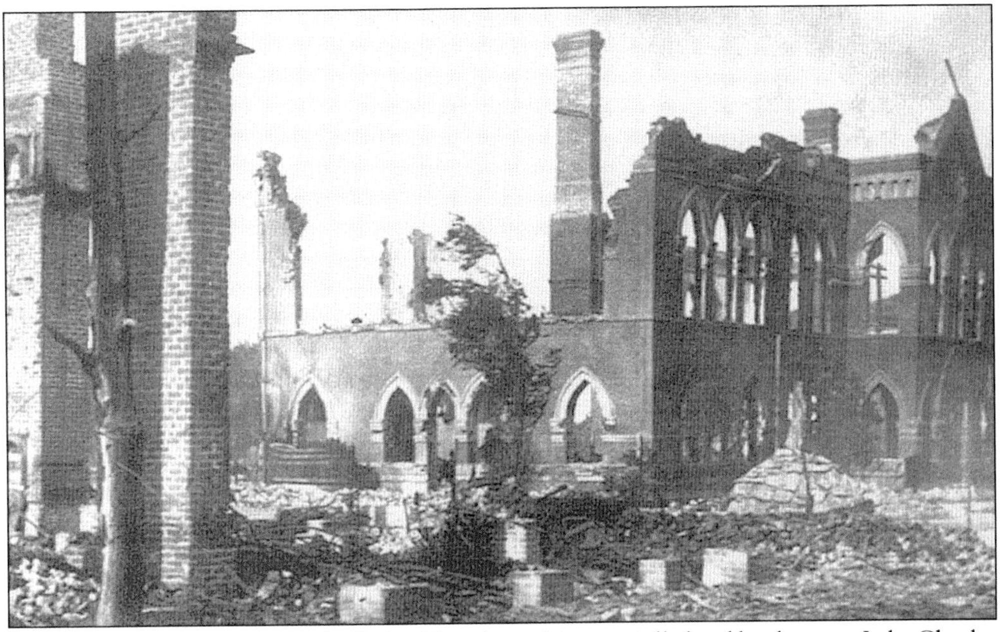

The Convent in Ruins. The Catholic Church was hit especially hard by the great Lake Charles fire of 1910. This photo shows all that remained of the convent of the Sisters Marianites. The Church's other losses included the Church of the Immaculate Conception, the rectory, three school buildings, the girls' school, the boys' school, and the Knights of Columbus hall. The Christian Church was also destroyed, as was the Calcasieu Courthouse and the Lake Charles City Hall, with nearly all of their records. (Courtesy of McNeese Archives.)

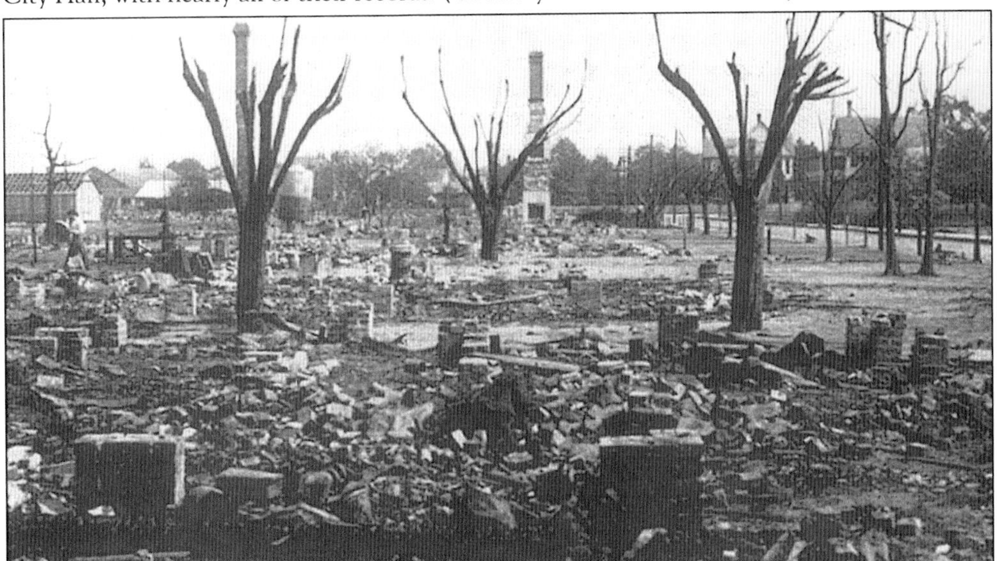

Wrong Side of the Street. The flames of one residence touched off the next as the Lake Charles fire of 1910 moved along Commercial Street. During the first part of the three-hour fire, the city's fire alarm sounded a coded signal telling volunteers where to go to stop the progress of the moving inferno, but the trolleys stopped working and few people had automobiles. This meant that most volunteers had to walk or run to the forward edge of the fire, which eventually ended up about a mile from its point of origin. (Courtesy of McNeese Archives.)

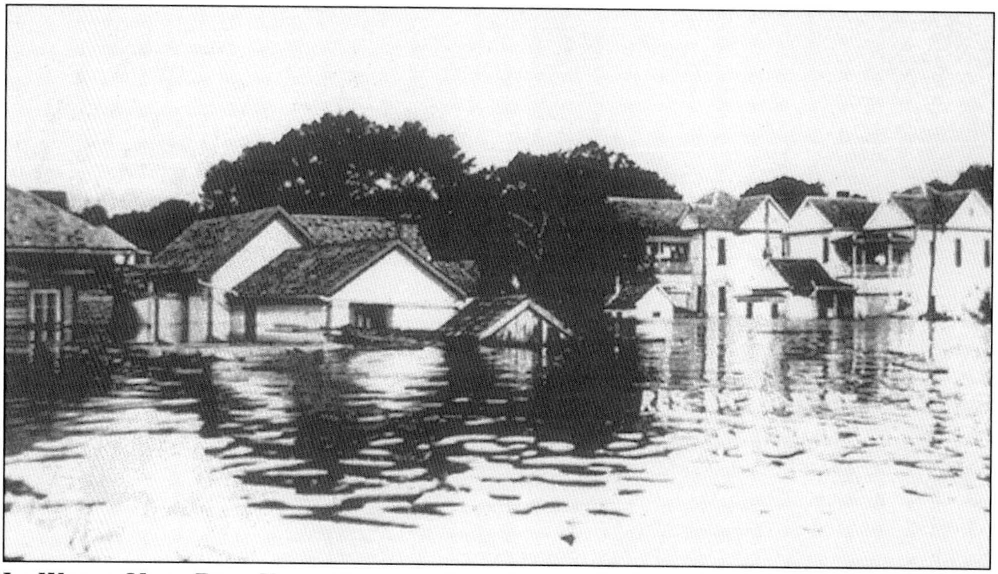

IT WAS A VERY DEEP YEAR. Towns and residences all along the Calcasieu River and its tributaries were subject to occasional severe flooding during the early years of the parish, but 1913 was the worst. This photograph taken in the vicinity of Ethel Street in Lake Charles shows the water to be 6 to 7 feet deep. During that flood, waters also invaded Ryan Street in the Clarence Street area, South Ryan out to St. Patrick Sanitarium, and Broad Street all the way past Orange Grove Cemetery. (Courtesy of McNeese Archives.)

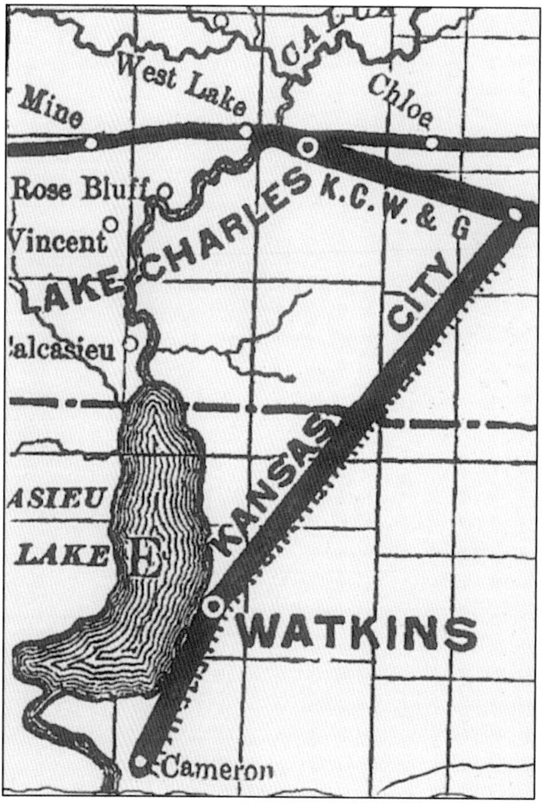

THE RAILROAD TO WATKINS. Jabez B. Watkins—the entrepreneur who built the first bank in Calcasieu Parish, the railroad from Lake Charles to Alexandria, and the Watkins "Dummy" railroad leading east from Lake Charles—also planned but did not succeed in building a railroad to Cameron and a deep-water-port city named after himself on the eastern shore of Calcasieu Lake, as shown on this widely circulated map. These things were part of his plan for the 1.2 million acres of Southwest Louisiana land he purchased from the state in 1883. (Courtesy of McNeese Archives.)

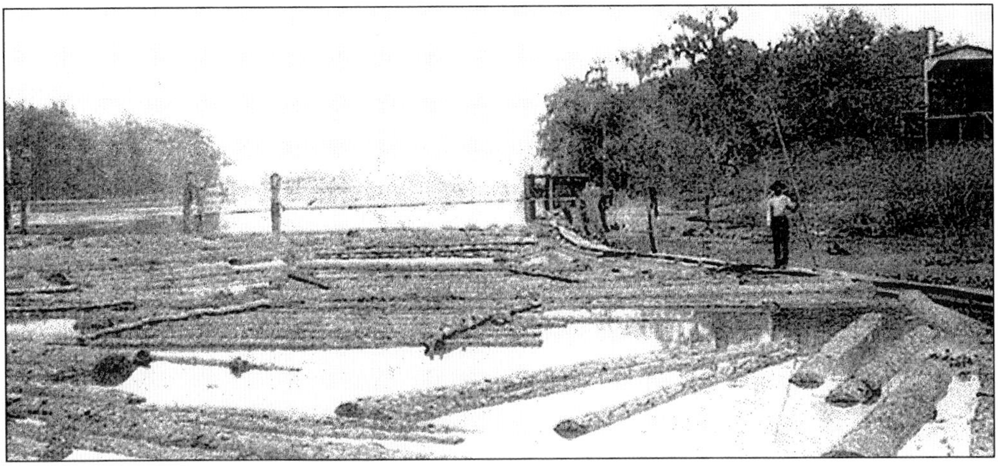

The Calcasieu Log War. The lack of activity in this photo is reminiscent of events on the river during the notorious "Calcasieu Log War" of 1877–1878. In that dispute a federal deputy marshal seized 95,000 "illegally cut" logs in the river. Calcasieu lumbermen protested vigorously, and the federal government sent in troops. The dispute was argued in the courts and in Congress, and the logs were eventually auctioned off on the Calcasieu courthouse steps. The U.S. Senate voted not to prosecute the alleged "lumber thieves." (Courtesy of Imperial Calcasieu Museum.)

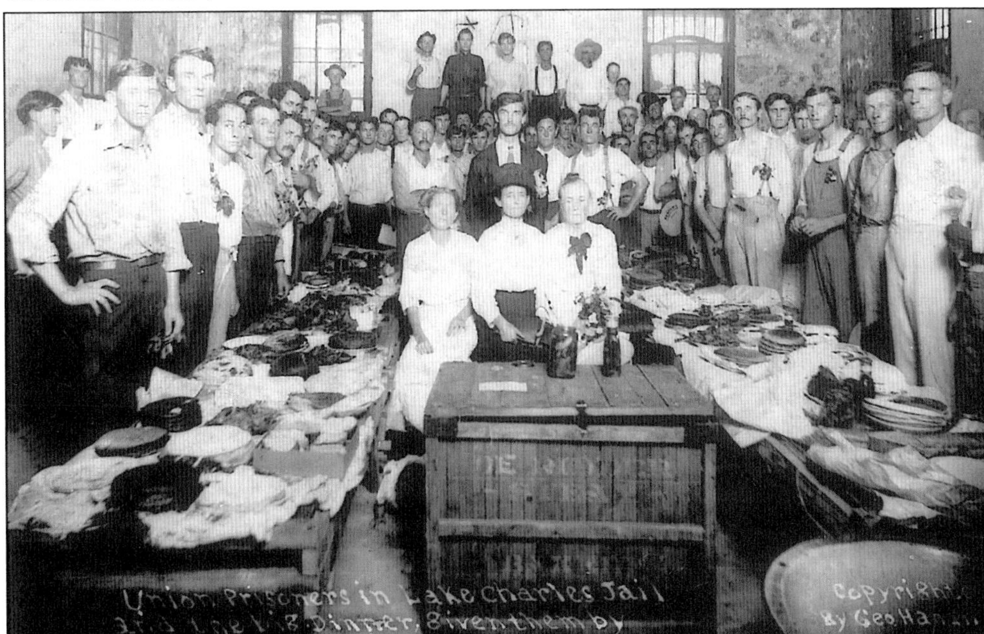

The Grabow Shootout. The 58 men in this photo, taken on July 28, 1912, in the Calcasieu Parish Jail, were awaiting trial on charges of conspiracy to commit murder following a gun battle three weeks earlier at the Grabow sawmill near DeRidder. These prisoners, who were sympathetic to establishing a union at the mill, had been involved in a shootout with mill managers during which three men were killed and 37 were wounded. The women in the foreground brought the prisoners the food laid out on the tables. Four months after the battle all of the prisoners were released. (Courtesy of McNeese Archives.)

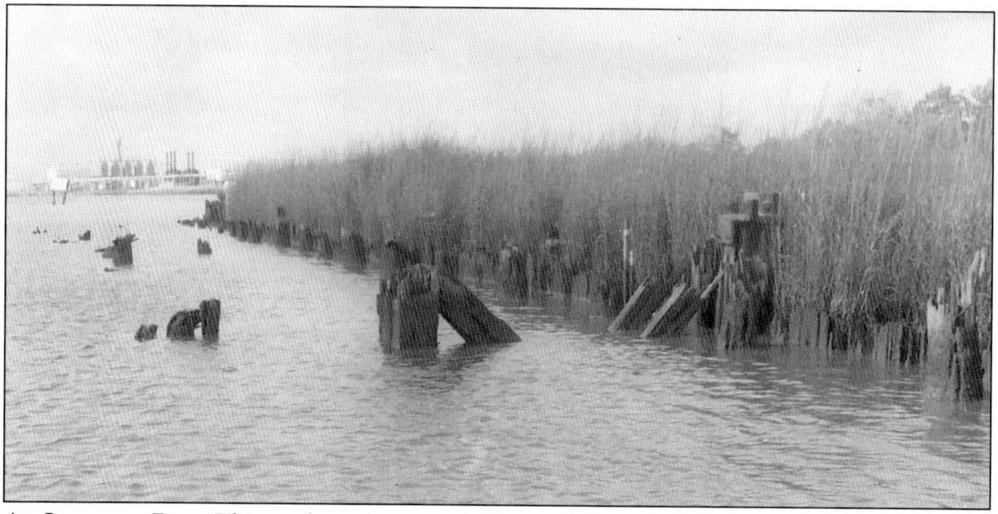

An Ill-fated Dam. This modern photograph shows all that is left 94 years after the destruction of the Mermentau River Dam at Grand Chenier in Cameron Parish. In spite of opposition from the residents of Grand Chernier, rice growers in the upper Mermentau River built the 440-foot-long wooden structure in 1904 to stop serious salt water intrusion. On October 3, 1905, someone dynamited a hole in the dam. The hole was repaired, but a year later the dam was completely wrecked by a second dynamite attack. These pilings on the north side of the river were part of the boat lock around the dam.

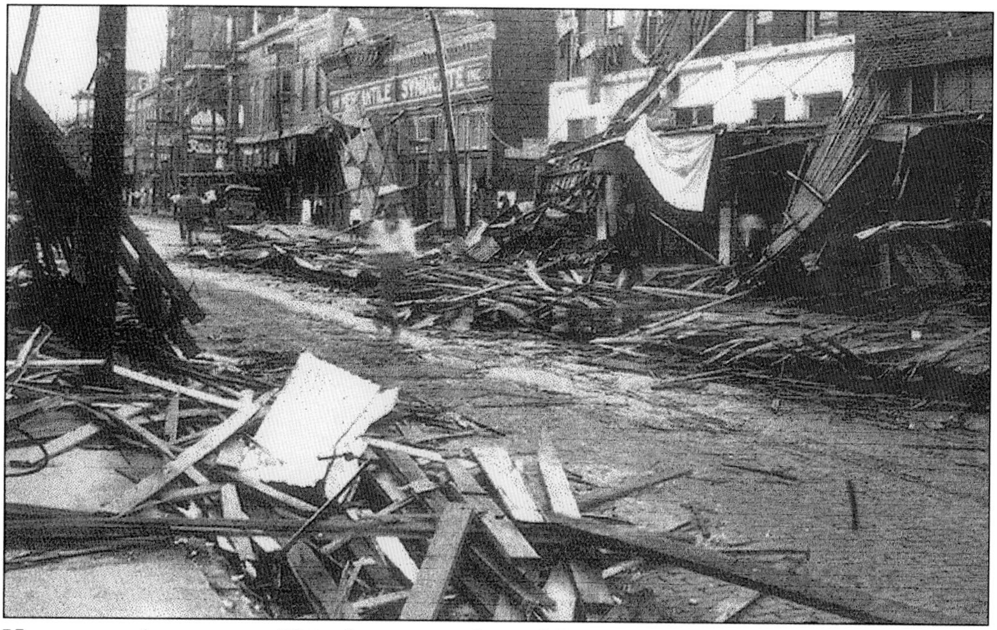

Hurricane Aftermath. This photo was taken of Ryan Street in downtown Lake Charles immediately after the August 6, 1918 hurricane raged for three hours through Imperial Calcasieu. The storm's 120-mile-per-hour winds tore a 10-mile-wide path of destruction from the Gulf of Mexico through Oak Grove-Cameron, Gerstner Field-Big Lake, Lake Charles-Sulphur, and on up through DeQuincy, leaving at least 26 people dead, about 100 injured, and nearly all the buildings in its path either heavily damaged or completely destroyed. (Courtesy of McNeese Archives.)

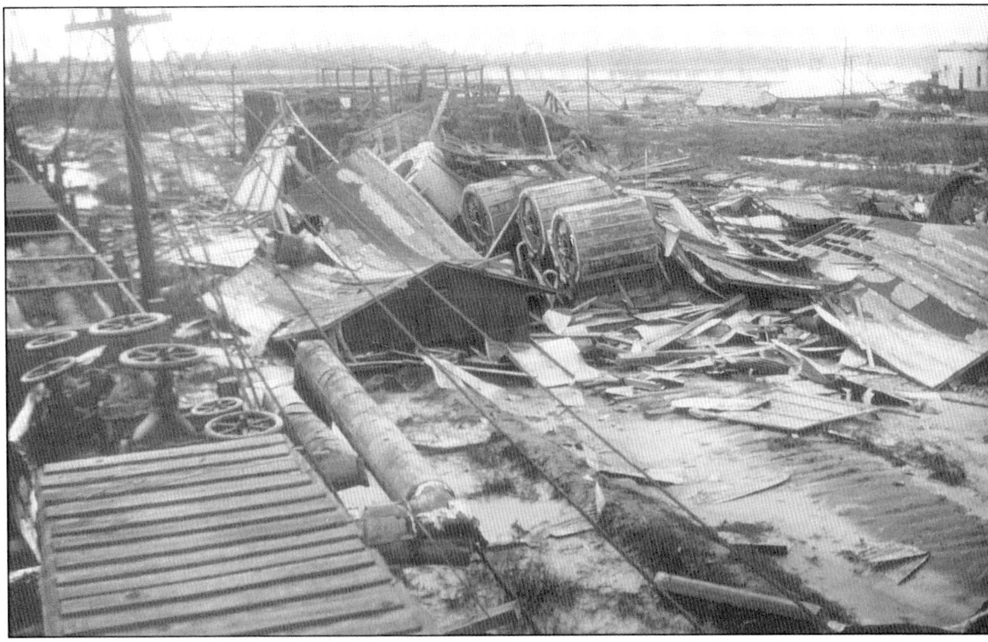

DISASTER IN WEST CALCASIEU. This photo showing the mangled machinery of the Union Sulphur Company demonstrates the damage done to that company and the people in that part of Calcasieu Parish by "the 1918 storm." In addition to the damage done to sulphur retrieval equipment such as this, all of Union Sulphur's many derricks were blown down, most of its new houses for employees were destroyed, and considerable damage was done all around when an embankment gave way, releasing 900 acres of storage salt water. (Courtesy of Imperial Calcasieu Museum.)

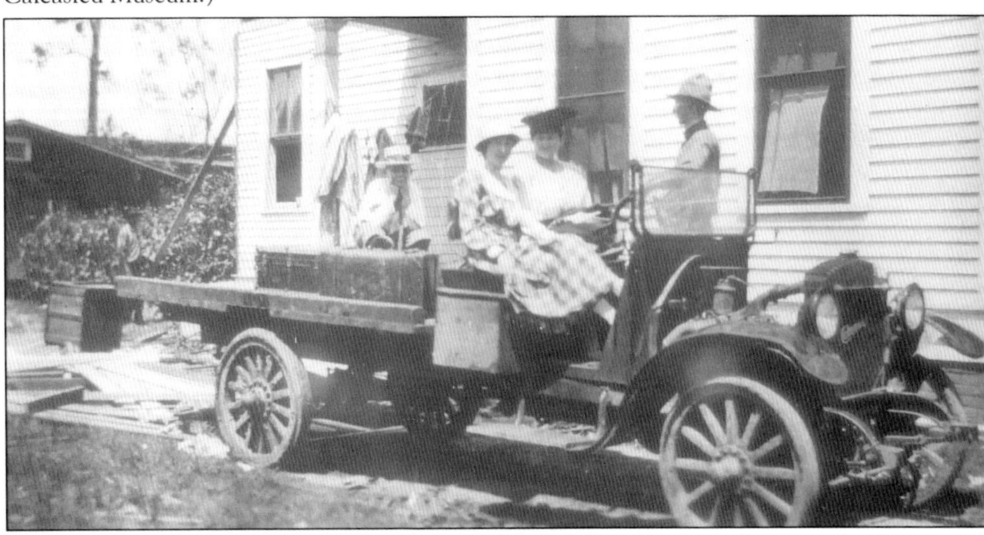

ROOFLESS AND MOVING OUT. This Lake Charles family was prepared to spend a few days or weeks somewhere else while the roof of their house was being repaired or replaced. If their biggest loss was their roof, they were lucky. One unlucky Lake Charles person was killed by a flying brick and another was crushed by a falling building. At Prien Lake, the hurricane sank the steamboat *Borealis Rex*, and at Lockport, the Locke-Moore sawmill caught fire and burned to the ground. (Courtesy Imperial of Calcasieu Museum.)

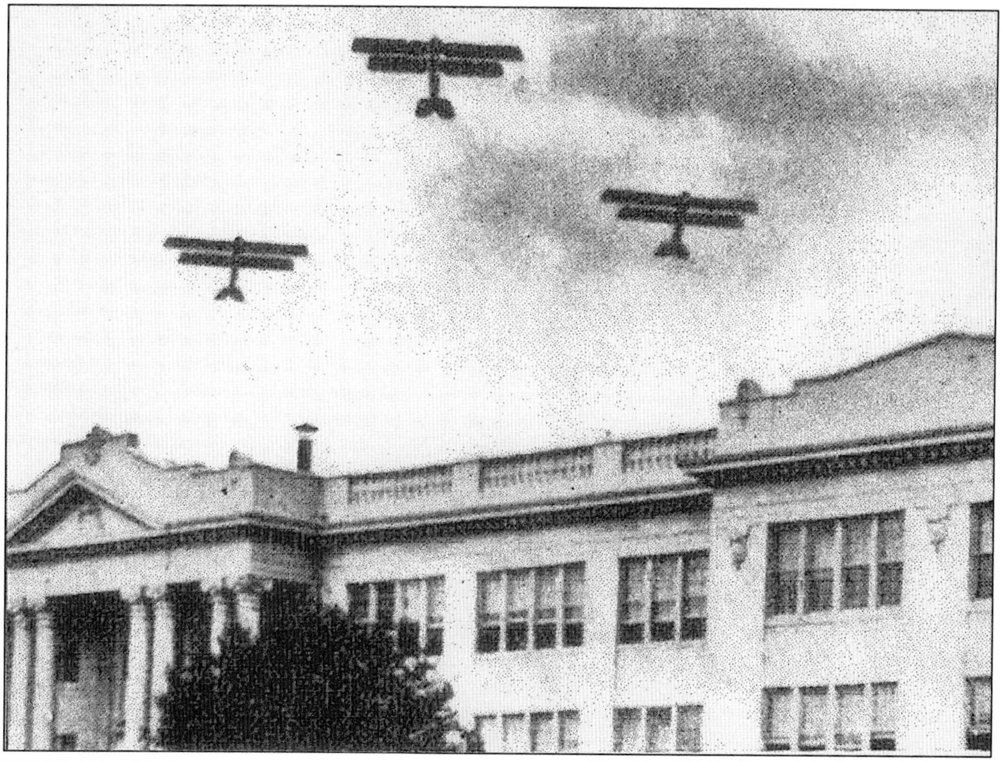

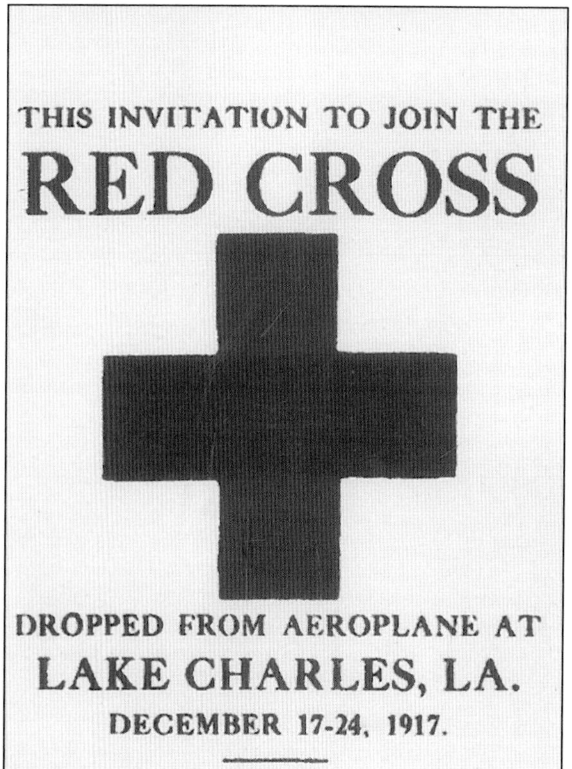
THIS INVITATION TO JOIN THE
RED CROSS
DROPPED FROM AEROPLANE AT
LAKE CHARLES, LA.
DECEMBER 17-24, 1917.

JENNIES OVER LAKE CHARLES HIGH. The thrill of aviation arrived in Southwest Louisiana in a big way in December 1917, when Gerstner Field, a training field for fighter pilots, was opened near Holmwood, about 15 miles southeast of Lake Charles. This World War I aviation training camp was the first military aviation facility to be built in Louisiana. The silhouettes of its Curtiss JN-4 (Jenny) trainers soon became familiar sights over all of Southwest Louisiana. (Courtesy of McNeese Archives.)

LEAFLETS FROM THE SKY. Gerstner Field aviators made a hit with Lake Charles residents when they put in a plug for the Red Cross by dropping leaflets like the one shown here over various Lake Charles neighborhoods. This image is a copy of the leaflet picked up by the mother of Maude Reid and saved by Miss Reid in one of her scrapbooks. (Courtesy of McNeese Archives.)

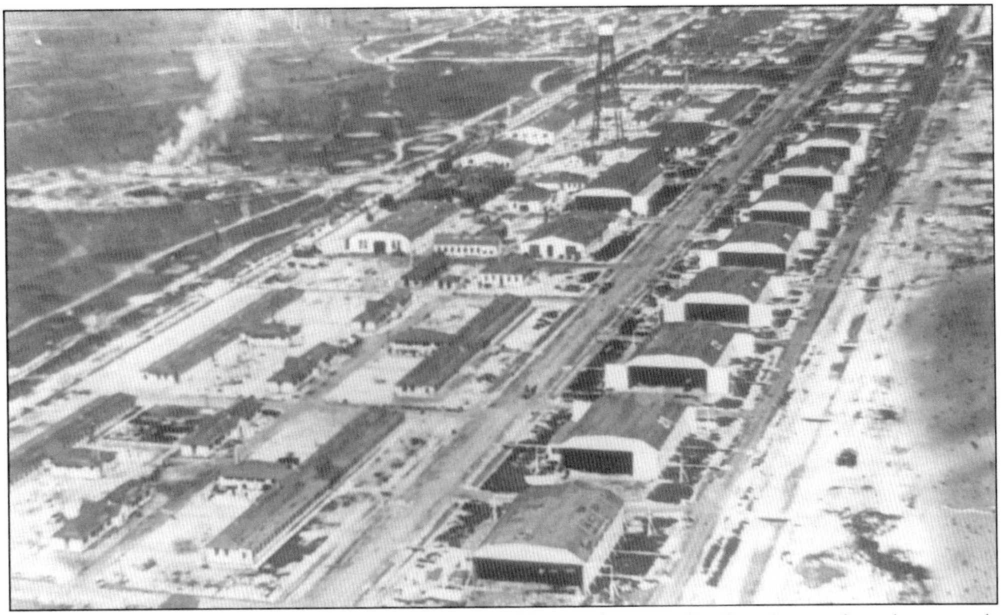

A Huge World War I Airfield. Gerstner Field stretches out for 2 miles in this photograph showing the field from its west end. Camp Road, the field's main thoroughfare, runs from the lower left foreground to the upper right corner of this picture. On the left side of Camp Road were the field's headquarters, barracks, officers quarters, and shops. On the right were its 24 airplane hangars, some of which are missing because of the 1918 hurricane. (Courtesy of National Archives.)

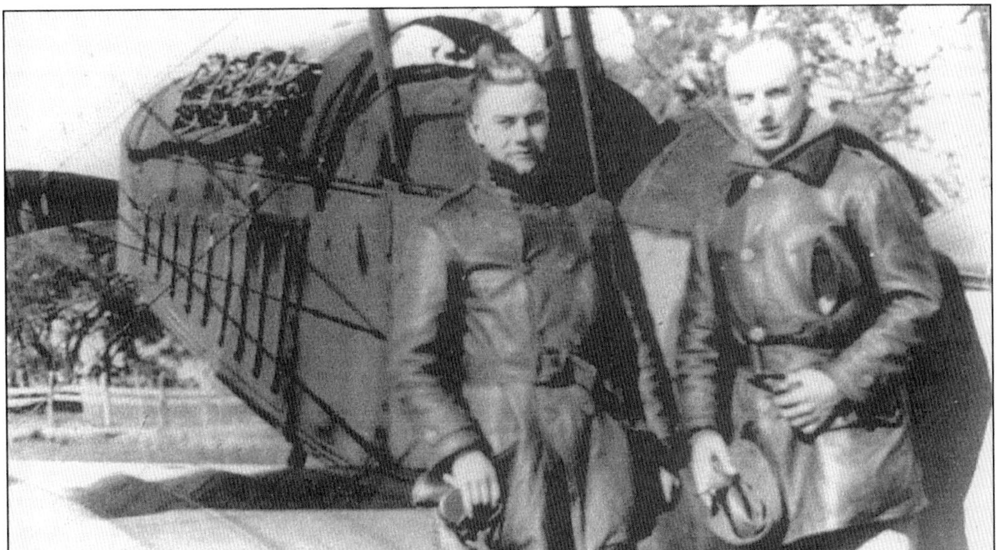

They Loved Cajun Food. Two unidentified Gerstner Field fliers stand beside their Curtiss JN-4 (Jenny) trainer during a visit to a Southwest Louisiana farm. Note the live oak trees and wooden fence in the background. Fliers occasionally made visits such as this to nearby farms where they were treated to home-cooked Cajun meals. They also visited towns like Vinton, Jennings, Welsh, Oakdale, Kinder, and Lake Charles, where citizens cleared landing sites for them.

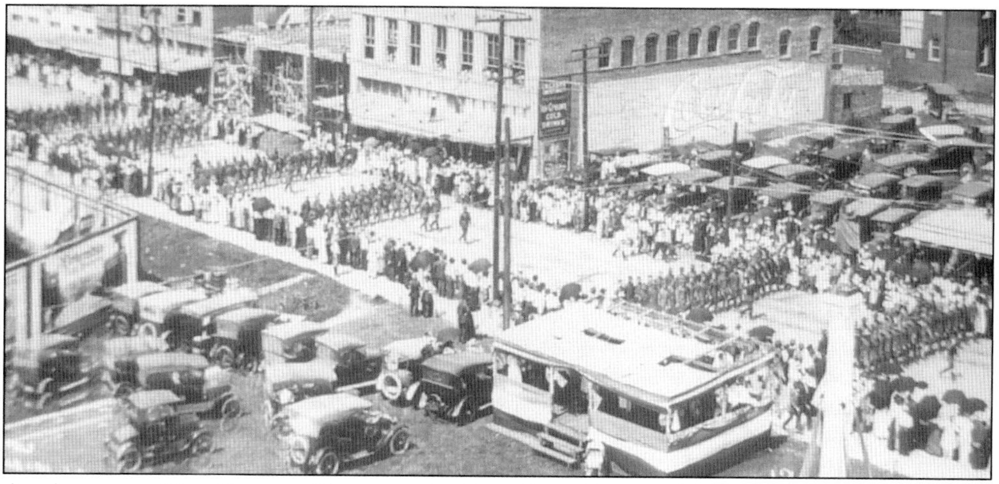

AN ARMISTICE DAY PARADE. Platoons of soldiers from Gerstner Field, the Royal Italian Band, and long columns of cars and trucks filled with happy, shouting people paraded down Ryan Street in Lake Charles on November 11, 1918, in celebration of the end of World War I. Shortly before this photo was taken, several formations of airplanes zoomed back and forth over the parade, and one plane separated from the others and gave a breathtaking exhibition of aerobatics. (Courtesy of Imperial Calcasieu Museum.)

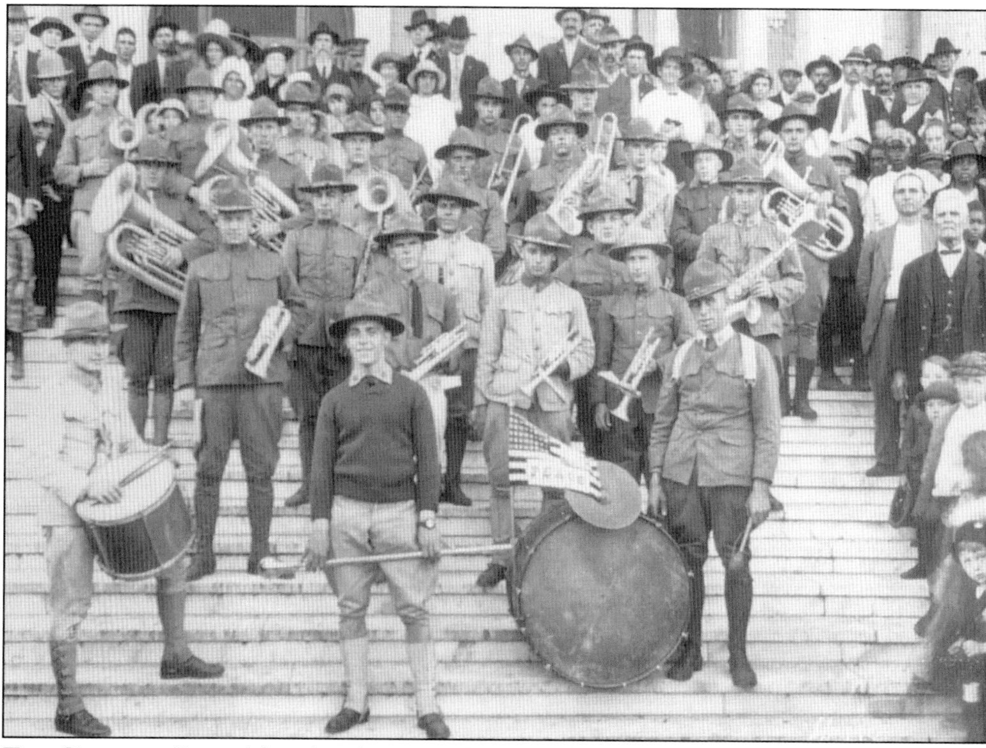

THE GREATEST DAY. After the Armistice Day Parade in Lake Charles hundreds of people assembled in front of the Calcasieu Parish Courthouse where the Gerstner Field Band, shown here, and the Royal Italian Band of Lake Charles took turns playing songs that brought "thunderous cheers" from the crowd. The reporter who wrote about the day's events said it had been "the greatest day in the history of the world." (Courtesy of McNeese Archives.)

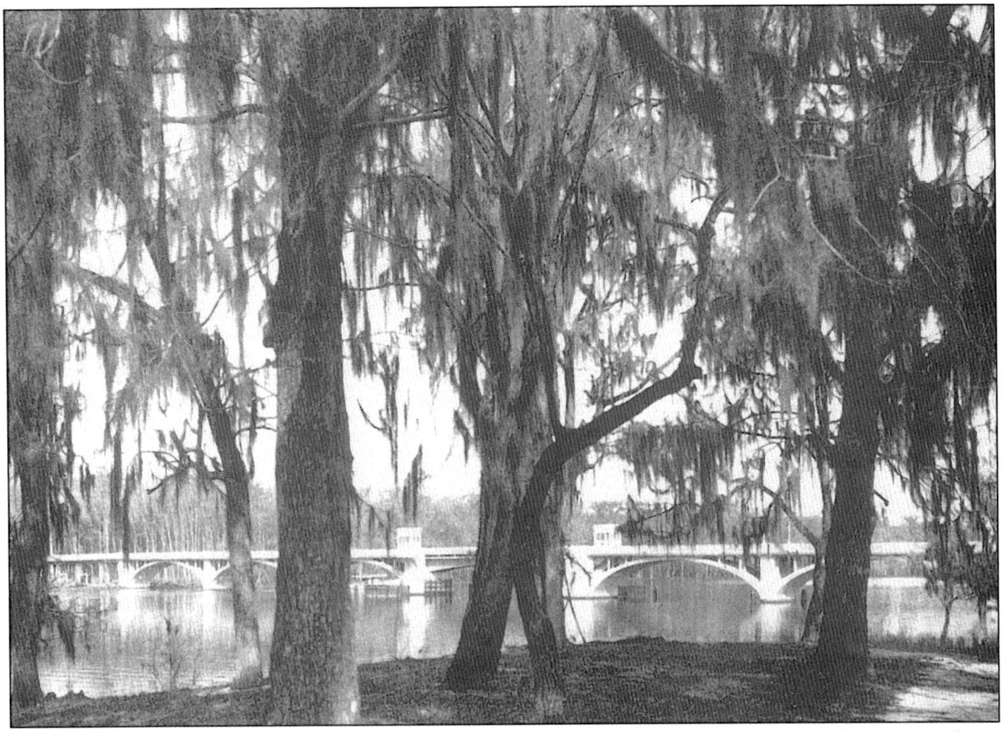

THE CALCASIEU RIVER BRIDGE. The old Calcasieu River Bridge at Lake Charles is seen here through the trees at Walnut Grove (the present site of the Port of Lake Charles). The building of this bridge was started in 1915, and it opened in 1917. Two spans in the middle could be raised to allow for the passage of large boats. Old U.S. Highway 90, the southernmost east-west highway in the country, used this bridge for many years. (Courtesy of McNeese Archives.)

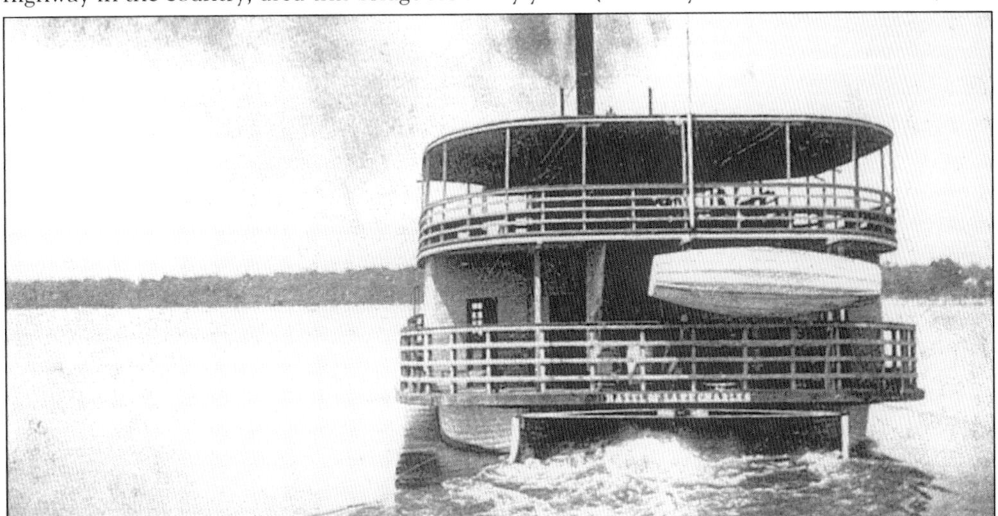

GOODBYE, *HAZEL*. The opening of the Calcasieu River Bridge in 1917 ended the usefulness of the old steam ferry *Hazel*, which then was moved to the Mississippi River for a few more years of service. In the departure of the *Hazel* from the waters of Lake Charles and the Calcasieu River, some area residents may have also noted, symbolically, the passing of the era of old Imperial Calcasieu. (Courtesy of Imperial Calcasieu Museum.)

ACKNOWLEDGMENTS

It is unfortunate that I could not find the names of many of the photographers whose pictures appear in this book. Of the few whose names I could find, I acknowledge indebtedness to E.K. and D.P. Sturdevant of Lake Charles, producers of the 1893 "Sturdevant's Views" series and other photographs; I.R. Murrey of Lake Charles, who was on hand to shoot disasters, schoolchildren, and many other subjects for many years; Charles Davies of Lake Charles, whose photos of prairie farm life were collected by his sister, Helen Davies Kendall, my grandmother, and passed along to her daughter, Helen Kendall Cooke, who generously allowed me to use them here; and these photographers about whom I only know their names: W.A. Davis, Peske, Trost, the Barnett Brothers, and the Southern Art Company.

Almost as important as the actual snapping of the shutter is the preservation of the photographs. The collector and preserver I must acknowledge first in this respect is the late Miss Maude Reid. Her huge scrapbooks about the early years of Lake Charles and Calcasieu Parish were a precious gift to all of us. I used a number of her photos and many points of information about them and other things in this book.

Miss Reid's scrapbooks are archived in the Frazar Library, which is directed most capably by Nancy Khoury at McNeese State University. The Archives Department in this library is headed by Kathie Bordelon. Kathie's unbounded enthusiasm for collecting and preserving area history is matched only by her desire to assist researchers and to produce results—even on the most obscure subjects. In addition to her work in the McNeese Archives, Kathie also recently conducted photo fairs in cooperation with the Southwest Louisiana Historical Association. She contributed to this book in many ways, including vetting the manuscript and providing wise counsel to the author. Patrick Webb, her assistant, and Polly Pousson, also on her staff, were also extremely helpful.

My thanks go to the Imperial Calcasieu Museum, its board of directors, and directors Jennifer Drez and Angela Austin, who permitted the copying of their extensive collection of photos, many of which appear on these pages, and to docents Virginia Nicholson and Gerry Langley.

Thanks also to all of the folk who helped make the photo fairs a success: Paige Hanchey, director of the Calcasieu Parish Library; Pat Heurtin, library publicist; Shirley Burwell, director of the Southwest Louisiana Genealogical Library; Patrick Webb and Truman Stacey; Gingham Ladies Elaine Cameron, Elly Sherwood, Kitty Walker, and May Mancuso; Lauretta Fluitt, director of the DeQuincy Railroad Museum; and to everyone who took old photos to the Photo Fairs to be copied.

I must also acknowledge the special research of Diane McCarthy and the wonderful support of the other members of the Southwest Louisiana Historical Association and their officers: Nell Hayes and Adelaide Cole, first vice presidents; Truman Stacey, second vice president; Kathie Bordelon, secretary; Ann Vestal, treasurer; and Adley Cormier, past president. The Historical Association paid for the photos used in the preparation of this book.

I most sincerely appreciated the quality film processing and printing done by Raymond Stewart and his courteous staff at Photo Express in Lake Charles.

Finally, I wish to thank my mother, Charlsie Kendall Benoit, for digging out old family photos, and George Ann, my wife, for eagle-eyed copy reading and unwavering support and assistance in countless other ways during the preparation of this book.

— R.B.